INTERNET TV WITH CU-SEEME

INTERNET TV WITH CU-SEEME

Michael Sattler

201 West 103rd Street
Indianapolis, IN 46290

Dedicated with love to Kathryn, for everything.

Copyright © 1995 by Sams.net Publishing
FIRST EDITION

All rights reserved. No part of this book shall be reproduced, stored in a retrieval system, or transmitted by any means, electronic, mechanical, photocopying, recording, or otherwise, without written permission from the publisher. No patent liability is assumed with respect to the use of the information contained herein. Although every precaution has been taken in the preparation of this book, the publisher and author assume no responsibility for errors or omissions. Neither is any liability assumed for damages resulting from the use of the information contained herein. For information, address Sams.net Publishing, 201 W. 103rd St., Indianapolis, IN 46290.

International Standard Book Number: 1-57521-006-1

Library of Congress Catalog Card Number: 95-70178

98 97 96 95   4 3 2 1

Interpretation of the printing code: the rightmost double-digit number is the year of the book's printing; the rightmost single-digit, the number of the book's printing. For example, a printing code of 95-1 shows that the first printing of the book occurred in 1995.

Composed in Palatino and MCPdigital by Macmillan Computer Publishing

Printed in the United States of America

Trademarks

All terms mentioned in this book that are known to be trademarks or service marks have been appropriately capitalized. Sams Publishing cannot attest to the accuracy of this information. Use of a term in this book should not be regarded as affecting the validity of any trademark or service mark.

President, Sams Publishing	*Richard K. Swadley*
Publisher, Sams.net Publishing	*George Bond*
Acquisitions Manager	*Greg Weigand*
Development Manager	*Dean Miller*
Managing Editor	*Cindy Morrow*
Marketing Manager	*John Pierce*

Acquisitions Editor
Mark Taber

Development Editor
Dean Miller

Production Editor
Fran Hatton

Editor
Greg Horman

Editorial Coordinator
Bill Whitmer

Editorial Assistant
Carol Ackerman

Technical Reviewer
Brad Pillow

Cover Designer
Tim Amrhein

Book Designer
Gary Adair

**Director of Production
and Manufacturing**
Jeff Valler

Production Manager
Kelly Dobbs

Production Supervisor
Brad Chinn

Production
*Mary Ann Abramson
Carol Bowers, Georgiana Briggs
Mona Brown, Michael Brumitt
Louisa Klucznik, Ayanna Lacey
Kevin Laseau
Brian-Kent Proffitt
Susan Van Ness, Mark Walchle*

Indexer
*Cheryl Dietsch
Jeanne Clark*

OVERVIEW

1	Introduction to Internet Videoconferencing and CU-SeeMe	1
2	Typical CU-SeeMe Usage	13
3	The Internet	27
4	Hardware	47
5	Software	65
6	CU-SeeMe User's Guide	93
7	Reflector Operator's Guide	123
8	History, Culture, and Usage	161
9	Other Videoconferencing Technologies	201
10	What the Future Holds in Store	227

Appendixes

A	Troubleshooting Q&A	235
B	Reflectors Around the World	251
C	Glossary	271
D	Bibliography	279
	Index	287

CONTENTS

1 Introduction to Internet Videoconferencing and CU-SeeMe   1
   What Is Internet Videoconferencing? 1
   What Is CU-SeeMe? 4
   Why CU-SeeMe? 8
      What You Need to Use This Book Effectively 10
      How to Get CU-SeeMe 10

2 Typical CU-SeeMe Usage   13
   Point-to-Point Sessions 14
   One-to-Many (Reflector) Sessions 16
   One-Way (Broadcast) Sessions 17
   Summary 26

3 The Internet   27
   Networks 27
      Local Area Networks 28
      Wide Area Networks 28
      Internets 28
      Internet with a Capital *I* 28
      You Say Tomato... 29
   The Internet of Yesterday 29
      Sneakernet 30
      Always Up 30
      The ARPANET 30
      NSFNET 34
      Usenet 34
      BITNET 36
   The Internet of Today 37
      National Research and Education Network 37
      Commercial Internet Exchange 38
   The Internet of Tomorrow 38
      Technological Problems 39
      Societal Problems 40
   Connecting to the Internet 41
      Giving Your Computer a Unique Identity 42
      Giving Your Network a Unique Identity 43
      Using Names Instead of Numbers 45
      Putting It All Together 46

4	**Hardware**	**47**
	Connectivity Hardware 49	
	Modems 49	
	ISDN 49	
	What Is ISDN? 50	
	Your ISDN Hookup 53	
	Connectivity Options 55	
	One State's Plans for ISDN 56	
	Video Hardware 57	
	Dedicated Cameras 58	
	General-Purpose Videocameras 59	
	Audio Hardware 62	
	Windows 63	
5	**Software**	**65**
	Macintosh 68	
	Using InterSLIP 80	
	Installing TCP/IP for Your Windows System 85	
	Configuring TCP/IP 86	
	Creating a Dial-Up Networking Connection for the Internet 87	
	Installing and Configuring SLIP 88	
	Troubleshooting Your Internet Configuration 90	
	Configuring Windows 3.1 for the Internet 91	
6	**CU-SeeMe User's Guide**	**93**
	Quick Start 93	
	Installing CU-SeeMe on Your System 94	
	Macintosh 94	
	Windows 95	
	Starting CU-SeeMe 96	
	Preferences 96	
	Connecting 98	
	Manual Addressing 98	
	Nicknames 100	
	Other Users' Windows 102	
	Audio Window 103	
	CU-SeeMe's Controls 104	
	The Local Video Window 105	
	CU-SeeMe's Menus 108	
	File Menu 108	
	Edit Menu 109	

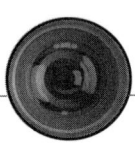

Internet TV with CU-SeeMe

	Conference Menu	111
	Participants Menu	112
	Auxiliary Data Function Modules	113
	AD Trace Menu	113
	Talk Menu	114
	Slide Window	115
	CU-SeeMe Resources on the Internet	117
	Mailing Lists	118
	World Wide Web Pages	120
7	**Reflector Operator's Guide**	**123**
	So You Want To Run a Reflector in a Hurry	124
	What's a CU-SeeMe Reflector?	125
	Why Is a CU-SeeMe Reflector Needed?	125
	Why UNIX?	125
	What Can the CU-SeeMe Reflector Do?	126
	Many-to-Many	126
	One-to-Many	126
	Multicast-to-Unicast	126
	Unicast-to-Multicast	127
	MBone: the Multicast Backbone	127
	Audio-only conferences	127
	Requirements for Running the CU-SeeMe Reflector	128
	A Fast Network Connection	130
	The Reflector Software	132
	Running the Reflector	133
	Configuring the CU-SeeMe Reflector	134
	Advanced Reflector Usage: Linking	154
8	**History, Culture, and Usage**	**161**
	A History of CU-SeeMe	161
	The National Science Foundation Steps In	163
	Friends of the Global SchoolHouse	164
	Back to the People	169
	University of Song	170
	CU-See in Use	170
	Satellite CU-SeeMe?	170
	Drums and Didjerideu	172
	CU-SeeMe in the College Classroom	172
	Ph.D. Defense Over CU-SeeMe	175
	Come Fly With Me	175
	Web Belly: Belly Dancing on the Web	176

"Peace for Sarajevo" Worldwide Video Conference 176
Adam Curry's SparrowCam 177
Journey to Mars 177
Model Lunar Rover 177
Singapore National Day Parade (NDP) '95 Internet Broadcast ... 178
Daughters at Work Day 179
Simulated Shuttle Mission 179
Dan Goldin, NASA Administrator 180
Cancer Update for Physicians 181
Meeks, Stone, and Yoshide 181
Cornerstone Album Release Concert on Internet Video 182
NYSERNet BirdCam 182
Local Telementor at K-12 School 183
Foreign Language Materials via CU-SeeMe 183
Save 25 Cents 184
Timed Video Grabber 184
Sixth Joint European Networking Conference 184
NHK Show About AIDS 185
Party Girl 187
Voices for Diversity 187
The Virtual Human Body: Performance Art 188
Flyvision and Spyder World Wide Web 189
Simulcast Interview of Daniel Fortune 190
Project BillVision 191
The Lobster Lives 191
Japan-Stanford Videobridge 192
CNN via CU-SeeMe at the Aerospace Corporation 193
The Oklahoma City Bombing 194
Machine room Surveillance 194
Giving Consumers a Choice: The New World of
   Telecommunications 195
The Buckman School 195
Earth Day 1995 196
Beijing Spectrometer Experiment 200

9 Other Videoconferencing Technologies   201

Overview of Other Technologies 201
   Avistar 202
   Being There 202
   Bitfield Video Communication System (BVCS) 203
   C-Phone 203
   Cameo Personal Video System 204
   Communicator III 204

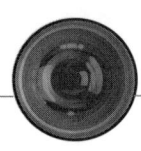

Communique!	205
Connect 918	206
DECspin (DEC Sound Picture Information Network)	206
Eris Personal Video Communications System	206
Face 2 Face	207
ICU Video Services	207
InPerson	208
Interact	208
INTERVu	209
InVision	209
INRIA Videoconferencing System (IVS)	210
Mediafone/Fonewatch	210
Meet-Me	211
MINX	211
Ntv	212
nv (Network Video)	212
Person to Person	213
Personal Viewpoint	213
PICFON	214
PictureTel Live PCS 100	214
PictureTel Live PCS 50	214
PictureTel LiveLAN	215
PictureWindow	215
ProShare Video System 150	216
ProShare Video System 200	216
Paradise Software Video Conferencing (PSVC)	217
ShareVision Mac 3000	217
ShareVision PC	218
ShowMe	218
TelePro with VisionTime	219
TeleView 1000C	220
VC8000	220
VicPhone	220
VidCall	221
VideoVu	221
VISIT	222
Vistium 1200	223
Vistium 1300	223
Vivo 320	224
VS1000	224
Add-On Software that Adds Functionality	225
Cambot	225
ShutterBug	226

Contents

10	**What the Future Holds in Store**	**227**
	The Technological Path	228
	Networking	228
	Video and Audio Technology	231
	The Cultural Path	231
	Last Words	233
A	**Troubleshooting Q&A**	**235**
	Questions About CU-SeeMe in General	235
	Video in Particular	238
	Audio	239
	Macintosh	240
	Video	240
	Audio	242
	Third-Party Hardware	242
	Connectix QuickCam	243
	Windows	246
	Configuration	246
	Video Cards	248
	Networking	249
B	**Reflectors Around the World**	**251**
	USA Reflectors	251
	ASU Geology Department	251
	Atlanta	252
	Classroom Connect	252
	CMU ARPA Speech	252
	CNIDR	252
	Cornell University	253
	Cream City	253
	CyberStudios	253
	Digital Jungle	253
	Eden	254
	Educational Computing Network	254
	GTE-Albion	254
	GTE-Skyhawk	254
	IITAP	254
	Intelecom Data Systems	255
	Indiana State University	255
	Kent State University	255
	KJHK Radio	255
	KVR-InterneTV	256
	LappDoggware	256

laUNChpad EBBS 256
Miami University (Ohio) 256
NASA TV at CMU GSIA 256
NASA TV at IITAP 257
NASA TV at Kent State 257
NASA Johnson Space Center 257
NASA Lewis Research Center 257
NASA Marshall Space Flight Center 258
Network Solutions 258
North Carolina State University 258
NYSERNet 258
Ohio State University 259
Pacific Rim 259
Penn State 259
Radio HK 259
Seattle Pacific University 259
Sprintlink 260
Stanford University Medical Center 260
ThePoint 260
University of Hawaii 260
University of Kansas 260
University of Maine 261
University of Maryland 261
University of Pennsylvania 261
University of Texas 261
Virginia Commonwealth University 261
White Pine Software 262
International Reflectors 262
Adelaide (Australia) 262
Geko (Australia) 262
Murdoch University (Australia) 262
Psy (Australia) 262
RMIT (Australia) 263
University of Melbourne (Australia) 263
University of Queensland (Australia) 263
Vrije Univ AI-Lab (Belgium) 263
PUC-Rio (Brazil) 263
University of Sao Paulo (Brazil) 264
Dalhousie University (Canada) 264
University of Manitoba (Canada) 264
University of Vaasa (Finland) 264
Telecomm Grande Ecole (France) 264
Nijmegen University (Holland) 265

Rotterdam Management (Holland) 265
University of Ulster (Ireland) 265
Weizmann Instistute (Israel) 265
Eurocube (Italy) 265
University of Calabria (Italy) 266
University of Pisa (Italy) 266
Eccosys (Japan) 266
Future Pirates (Japan) 266
Okazaki NRI (Japan) 267
University of Tokyo (Japan) 267
Ostfold/Fenris (Norway) 267
Ostfold/Kark (Norway) 267
University of Trondheim (Norway) 267
University of Lisbon (Portugal) 268
University of Singapore (Singapore) 268
Foeredrag i Lund/Fast (Sweden) 268
Foeredrag i Lund/Slow (Sweden) 268
NASA TV at Lund University (Sweden) 269
Geneva University (Switzerland) 269
Swiss Telecom R&D (Switzerland) 269
Open University Computing Department (UK) 269
Plymouth University (UK) 269
Hallam (UK) 270

C Glossary of Terms   **271**

D Bibliography   **279**

   Index   **287**

ABOUT THE AUTHORS

Michael Sattler has been involved with computers since 1979, when he started using a Korean War surplus teletype (with paper tape and acoustic coupler) to dial up the local timeshare system. He attended Boston University, and has since been working as a computer consultant on both coasts. He lives in San Francisco with his cats, Ptolemy and Copernicus.

John Lauer, a Computer Engineering major at the University of Michigan, has been involved with CU-SeeMe ever since it was released onto the Internet. Some of his numerous contributions to video conferencing software are Go CU-SeeMe; Go, a Web-launching utility for the Windows version of CU-SeeMe, the Event Guide, a public web site for scheduling CU-SeeMe events; and The People Pages, a phone book for CU-SeeMe users. His web site is located at `http://www.umich.edu/~johnlaue` and contains links to all the work he has done for the CU-SeeMe community.

Acknowledgements

No book is the work of one person alone. While my name appears on the cover, I've been fortunate to share the CU-SeeMe experience with literally a cast of thousands. Thanks to all of you.

The CU-SeeMe Development Team. Thanks for CU-SeeMe, thanks for answering all my questions, and thanks for keeping yourselves accessible to the CU-SeeMe User Community. None of this would have been possible without the gracious assistance of Dick Cogger, Tim Dorcey, Larry Chace, and the rest of the wonderful crew in Ithaca, New York.

The CU-SeeMe User Community. Thank you to the many people I've met on the public CU-SeeMe reflectors world-wide and through the CU-SeeMe Discussion List. The way you help newcomers (and old-timers) by sharing information and experiences has made being a part of the CU-SeeMe User Community (and writing this book) a pleasure. Being able to interact directly with an on-line video community that spans from Japan to Norway, from Australia to San Francisco, and from UK to the Antarctic has made all the difference. There are far too many of you to name individually, but I'd like to give special thanks to Yvonne Marie Andres, Judson Elliott, Daniel Fortune, Jher, Eduardo Kac, Halvor Kise, Reneé Krupp, John D. Lauer, Børre Ludvigsen, Timothy Mulkey, Jean Armour Polly, Leigh Anne Rettinger, Stephen A. Stiner, and Liz Thomson.

The Financial District San Francisco Team. Abed, Gus, Luis, and everyone else at CompuTown. Ted at Grand Vitesse Systems.

The Haight-Ashbury San Francisco Team. Kathryn, Kaeli, Wendy, and Kevin. The management, staff, and clientele of the People's Café (where I wrote most of this book). Another double decaf latte, please.

The Sant Joan de Labritja Team. Daniel, Schrada, Mayra, and Djamal. The management, staff, and clientele of Fernandito's café (where I wrote the remainder of this book). Another cafe au lait, por favor.

The Sams.net Team. Thank you Mark Taber, Fran Hatton, and Greg Horman. For patience beyond the call of duty, for assistance just when I needed it, for guiding me through the process, and for rescue when things looked bleak (I swear I'll ground everything from now on).

Introduction to Internet Video-conferencing and CU-SeeMe

After you read this chapter, you will know

- What Internet videoconferencing is
- How CU-SeeMe fits into the picture
- How to get the most out of this book
- How to retrieve the free CU-SeeMe software

What Is Internet Videoconferencing?

You're busy doing your work, writing papers, checking e-mail, and juggling numbers in a spreadsheet, when a window pops up on your screen. It's someone you know. You see him, and he sees you. You speak with him, all the while gesticulating wildly to emphasize a point. Ideas are exchanged, a dinner date is made, and the conversation ends. You both hang up and go back to work. Videoconferencing in action.

# Internet TV with CU-SeeMe

Computer-based videoconferencing is startling. It redefines your relationship with your computer and, more importantly, how you communicate electronically with other people around the world on the Internet and on private networks. My first experience with computer-based videoconference was as amazing as using the first Macintosh (the Lisa) was, over a decade earlier. The first time I visited a videoconferencing watering hole on the Internet—a reflector—was through my employer's high-speed network. Eight small flickering moving pictures appeared—people from all over the world gathering at the same virtual spot. The images were grainy collections of eight-pixel-square sections, each one of which was updated as the image changed, resulting in a strobe-light dance floor effect. Six faces peered at me. Two windows contained images of the outdoors: the New York State Thruway and a building being constructed in Manhattan. The following images were taken from CU-SeeMe sessions.

Figures 1.1–1.6. The faces of CU-SeeMe.

My inital nervousness at seeing *faces* was quickly replaced by the excitement of seeing *people*. It's a strange feeling to see people and to try to extract meaning and personality from the choices people make regarding hair and clothing style, office knick-knacks, and the method of scribbling on the inevitable office whiteboards behind the talking heads.

Only a few of us had audio capability. The sound came through my stereo speakers in fits and starts—squacking, barely intelligible speech that was often cut off as the company-wide network became filled with a burst of information from people doing real work. To compensate, we would type notes to one another in our video windows. We could barely push enough information into these conversations to become misunderstood. The novelty of connecting to people on the other side of the planet was sufficient.

Introduction to Internet Videoconferencing and CU-SeeMe

Despite small black and white images, distorted sounds, and misspelled words, it was novel enough—even thrilling—to connect to and communicate with people from all over the planet. I shared the joy of anticipation of the birth of a video acquaintance's first child, expressed in a last-minute conversation before he rushed off to the hospital in Perth, Australia. I saw the inhabitants of a house-on-the-Net live, work, and vacuum the floors. I saw people at work, reaching out to others on the Internet. We communicated.

Videoconferencing over the Internet doesn't have to be simply two-way communication between people. Breathlessly, I watched live video of the Earth turning under the space shuttle while astronauts danced in the opened cargo bay, sending a satellite on its way. Stunned, I watched a huge effigy of a human figure set on fire in the annual Burning Man festival in the Nevada desert (see Figure 1.7).

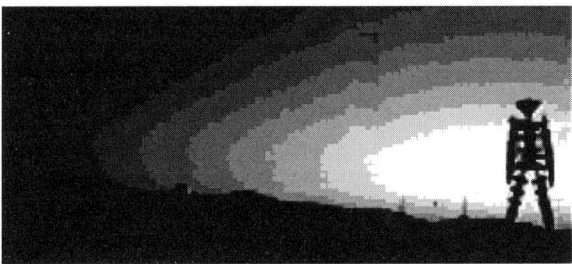

Figure 1.7. The Burning Man.

Bemused, I watched the antics of Britons at a night club, broadcast all over the world for those of us still at the office to enjoy. With a feeling of fragile connectedness, I watched the changing scenes of our planet, one live feed per continent, disseminated to celebrate the twenty-fifth anniversary of Earth Day. With horror, I watched live footage of the aftermath of the bombing of the federal office building in Oklahoma City (see Figure 1.8). With great curiosity, I watched the proceedings of parlimentary deliberations in other countries.

Figure 1.8. Footage from the Oklahoma City bombing.

Internet TV with CU-SeeMe

While authoring some World Wide Web pages in 1993, I wrote that CU-SeeMe has me more excited about being part of the global village than anything that has come before it. The phrase "interactive desktop—laptop?—videoconferencing" doesn't do it justice; it simply describes the basic vehicle being used. More important, however, is the tremendous potential it has for connecting us over the Internet in ways not possible until now: global, interactive, multi-sensory human communication and collaboration by the computer-equipped masses. That's the experience we're heading toward. The ability to see and hear fellow Internauts has made me acutely aware of the other people with whom I share this planet.

Through years of encountering the same people repeatedly in nonvisual media—such as the frequent contributors to the Usenet newsgroups that I read—I had in my mind's eye an image of them. Pleasantly, unlike movies and television, which tend to erode the imagination inspired through earlier media such as books and radio, I find that two-way video adds to the feeling of kinship that I've built up with people who I've never before heard or seen. In this book, I'll show you how to join me and, indeed, all of us in the already large and fast-growing Internet videoconferencing community.

Videoconferencing enables you to communicate by means of typed text, audio, and video across a computer network (such as your company's private IP network) or the world-wide Internet. You decide whether to be a sender, a receiver, or both.

Plenty of people want to broadcast to the world. The offerings have been interesting—and are getting more so every day. The individual and small group possibilities inherent in being able to transmit specialized audio and video promises to be an educational and recreational tool of great impact. Children following the GlobalSchoolNet's *Where in the World is Roger?*—a trek around the world by a man and his truck that is broadcast from various stopping-points via CU-SeeMe—have been transported in an interactive way with their counterparts in Europe and Asia.

What Is CU-SeeMe?

CU-SeeMe—pronounced "See you, See me"—is a videoconferencing system developed at Cornell University—the *CU* in CU-SeeMe. It works on the Internet or any network that uses Internet Protocol (IP). Macintosh and Windows clients are currently available, and CU-SeeMe may be ported to more computers now that the source code is available to interested parties.

CU-SeeMe users can connect directly to one another in a point-to-point manner, or they can connect to a group conference by connecting to a reflector—a UNIX

Introduction to Internet Videoconferencing and CU-SeeMe

computer running software that redistributes the audio and video streams to everyone connected. Basic connection methods are described in Chapter 2, "Typical CU-SeeMe Usage."

The only things required to view incoming video are a video monitor (computer display) capable of providing 16 levels of gray or color and a connection to a network using IP—either a private network or the Internet itself. To transmit video to others requires only a video camera and a digitizer board. Some computers, such as AV Macintoshes, have a video digitizer built in. A camera/digitizer package is available for Macintosh and Windows computers in a combined golf-ball-sized package for under $100. CU-SeeMe video is 16-level (4-bit) grayscale, as shown by the arrow in Figure 1.9. Color CU-SeeMe will appear in the near future.

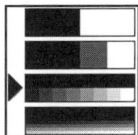

Figure 1.9. 1, 2, 4, and 8-bit grayscales.

Video resolution is available in two choices: high-quality 320 by 240 pixels—which is half the diameter of NTSC television—or low-quality 160 by 120 pixels. The high-quality video is available only for Macintosh-to-Macintosh connections. The Windows version currently supports only low-resolution video.

> **Note:** NTSC (National Television System Committee) is one standard for the transmission of video signals. It is not the only one, however. Depending upon where you live in the world—or how much hardware you collect—you will come across NTSC, PAL, and SECAM. These standards are discussed in depth in Chapter 4.
>
> NTSC was developed in the United States in 1953. It is used throughout North America, in some countries in South America, and in Japan. NTSC uses color images of 525 horizontal lines of resolution at 30 frames per second.
>
> PAL (Phase Alternation by Line) was developed in Germany and adopted in 1967. It is used in much of Europe, Africa, the Middle East, and Far East. PAL uses color images at 625 horizontal lines of resolution—except in Brazil, where PAL-M is used—and supports 30 frames per second with 525 horizontal lines of resolution. PAL is the most widely used and supported color video standard.

Internet TV with CU-SeeMe

> SECAM (Systeme Electronique Couleur avec Memoire) was adopted in 1967. It enjoys scattered use throughout the world, in the former Soviet Union, and in areas of French influence. SECAM uses color images of 625 lines of resolution at 25 frames per second.
>
> These standards become important when you're purchasing hardware to convert images from your video camera to a form that your computer can use and transmit. Some hardware understands only one standard; other hardware can automatically recognize the standard used by the video source and can handle the signal accordingly.
>
> Many countries support more than one standard. HDTV (High-Definition Television), with all its competing standards, hasn't yet become a factor in Internet videoconferencing.

The capability to transmit sound between conferencees is available on both the Macintosh and Windows versions of CU-SeeMe. The quality of the audio is limited by a combination of the computer's basic horsepower (processor, memory, and I/O bus speed), the connection method and speed, and the audio capture capability (the quality of the audio capture board, speakers, and microphone).

The connection method determines the amount of sound and video data that can be sent to and from the computer. Faster connections—that is, greater bandwidths—are preferable to slower ones. The computer's speed determines which sound encoding method can be used. Because everything must be done in real time if the conversation is to be understandable, a faster computer can use a more efficient encoding method and can get more sound into the available bandwidth.

Telephone-quality audio, when encoded with a method available to a system running at the speed of a typical Macintosh or Windows computer, requires about 16K of information per second (kbps) be sent. A 14,400 kbps modem clearly cannot provide the necessary bandwidth for audio—to say nothing of video. A 28,800 kbps modem is just barely enough to carry audio. ISDN, discussed in Chapter 4, can carry audio and video simultaneously. Fiber optic cable, with its megabit bandwidth, will be deployed by U.S. cable television companies to households across the country. This will provide more than enough bandwidth for the current requirements of videoconferencing. By that time, though, we will expect color, stereo sound, and other bandwidth-eating developments.

Another factor in audio transmission quality is whether the audio capture/play hardware supports full-duplex or half-duplex audio. Full-duplex audio enables the simultaneous capture of audio that you are sending and the play of audio that you are receiving, much like a telephone. Half-duplex audio enables only one or

Introduction to Internet Videoconferencing and CU-SeeMe

the other at a time. You can speak—in which case the playback of audio being received from others is blocked—or you can hear the audio being received from others but not transmit.

Half-duplex audio conversations can be compared to the conversation you have over a walkie-talkie, CB radio, or a typical, low-end speaker phone used for audioconferencing over telephone lines. The off-the-shelf audio support built into every Macintosh is full-duplex. Intel-based PCs are dependant on the board used; some boards available for the PC, such as Media Vision's Pro Audio Spectrum, support full-duplex audio. Most low-end boards support only half-duplex audio.

To gain a bit of perspective, consider this. Six months ago, 32 kbps were required to transmit audio. Today, only 16 kbps are required, thanks to better software compression technology. As raw computing power increases, your computer of tomorrow will be able to perform even more complex decompression in real time, lowering yet again the bandwidth requirements for sending audio. As connections get faster and compression gets better, you will be able to get stereo sound and who knows what else.

> **Note:** CU-SeeMe was never intended to operate on low-bandwidth (modem) connections. Its developers were connected with a 10 megabit Ethernet network, and they expected the same of CU-SeeMe users. In spite of this, people have found ingenious ways of making CU-SeeMe usable over 14.4 kbps modems. They've found satisfaction by typing instead of speaking and by configuring CU-SeeMe to use a slower refresh rate.
>
> Even at one frame every 10 to 15 seconds over a 9.6 kbps connection, CU-SeeMe can still prove to be an effective visual communication tool in situations such as a presentation, where the image being received doesn't change frequently. Even in situations where the scene being captured changes frequently, a periodic sampling of the image is often surprisingly adequate.

CU-SeeMe's audio capabilites have been taken from Charlie Kline's program called Maven. Charlie contines to upgrade Maven, and he has recently added even more audio encoding features. CU-SeeMe and Maven can be used in tandem. (Before CU-SeeMe provided audio, this was how CU-SeeMe pioneers spoke to one another.)

Internet TV with CU-SeeMe

CU-SeeMe has a built-in method for extending its capabilites: the Auxilary Data Function Module system, which is described in Chapter 6, "CU-SeeMe User's Guide." Plug-ins currently available include

- The Slide window, which is a bare-bones whiteboard capability that transmits full-size 8-bit grayscale still images and permits remote pointer control.
- The Talk window, which enables the attendees of a conference to coverse by typing in an Internet Relay Chat sort of way. This is useful when some participants are connected via busy networks or modems and don't have the bandwidth to send or receive audio.
- AuxData Trace, which enables plug-in developers to debug their extentions to CU-SeeMe.

Timothy Dorcey wrote: "The main objective in the development of CU-SeeMe was to produce an inexpensive videoconferencing tool that would be useable today. As well as providing direct benefit to its users, we expected that valuable lessons could be learned about how videoconferencing actually works in practice, how the experience should be organized, what features are necessary to support multi-party conferencing, and so on. While others worked to advance the state of the art in video compression, high-speed networking, and other low-level technologies necessary to support high quality videoconferencing, we hoped to facilitate the accumulation of experience that would provide impetus for those efforts and guide their direction."

CU-SeeMe has done this and more. Throughout this book, you will find evidence of the body of understanding that we have learned due to widespread use of CU-SeeMe. Some of the knowledge has to do with responsible use of network bandwidth; other knowledge is much more anecdotal and less quantitative.

Why CU-SeeMe?

There are many videoconferencing options, including hardware and software combinations that cost about $100 for a complete system and others that cost many thousands of dollars per seat/room. Dedicated high-end systems can easily run into the hundreds of thousands of dollars for a virtual conference room system, such as the ones at Hewlett Packard. A handful run over TCP/IP; they include CU-SeeMe, NV, VidCall, and Intel Proshare. Others, such as PictureTel and Creative Labs, use H.320 and proprietary solutions. Each option has advantages and drawbacks.

CU-SeeMe is well known in the Internet community, has been extensively used over the last few years, and can be had for free. Commercial, supported versions

Introduction to Internet Videoconferencing and CU-SeeMe

will shortly be available from White Pine, the master licensee of the CU-SeeMe technology.

One great advantage to using CU-SeeMe is that, because it runs over TCP/IP, you can use it on the same computer system that you use for virtually all your other telecommunications needs—e-mail, reading Usenet newsgroups, and so on. Dedicated systems tie up one of your telephone lines if you're an at-home user of CU-SeeMe and don't enable you to do any other Net-surfing. Other systems don't allow multi-point connections and the ad-hoc assemblage of users.

Timothy Dorcey forwarded to me the final part of an e-mail conversation he had had with an employee of Pacific Bell. It illustrates much of the social ambiance that is generated by the widespread usage of a free videoconferencing tool.

> CU-SeeMe is available to anyone, although it works only on IP networks. It doesn't work very well at modem speeds, though we've been amazed at what particpiants connected via low-bandwith methods seem willing to put up with. Gray-scale video at one frame per second is not very impressive compared to a face-to-face meeting, but pretty exciting compared to telephone or e-mail.
>
> Actually, though, I think videoconferencing is most interesting when not compared to anything at all. It is not the replacement of any existing communication that is most interesting, but rather the generation of new communication. I was talking to a guy at Penn State today. He was saying how unhappy AT&T would be if it knew how much long-distance phone revenue it was losing since he has been using CU-SeeMe to maintain a long-distance romance. Yeah, except that he met her on CU-SeeMe, and there wouldn't have been any communication at all if it hadn't been for CU-SeeMe! He ended up driving nine hours to visit with her in person. So much for the idea that videoconferencing is going to reduce travel—it's going to increase it!
>
> I actually think there is a good lesson in that little story, and it's applicable to business communication as well as social. I hope that the economic and regulatory environment develops in such a way that we simply have a lot more communication going on. Traditional providers will still come out ahead, even if they are getting much less revenue per information exchange. How's that for a speech?

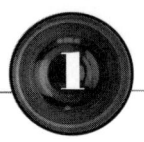

Internet TV with CU-SeeMe

Videoconferencing might not reduce travel for personal use, but it likely will for business. In fact, that is a cornerstone for justifying its cost to management. Every business traveller costs several hundred dollars for the trip and a recurring daily cost for food, car rental, and lodging. One meeting handled through videoconferencing can save all that expense and more than pay for itself. Better yet, it can enable a face-to-face meeting that would not otherwise have occurred at all. For a team dispersed around the world, several multi-thousand dollar trips to Europe each year per team member is understandably frowned upon. The several hundred dollar, one-time, per-seat cost spread over several years' use is much more likely to win approval.

What You Need to Use This Book Effectively

You know how to operate your Macintosh or Windows computer. You won't find any explanations of mice, keyboards, or floppy disks here.

You are already connected to the Internet (or some other TCP/IP network) or you are ready to purchase, install, and configure the necessary software and hardware, which I discuss in Chapter 4.

That's it.

How to Get CU-SeeMe

CU-SeeMe is available for free from Cornell University at `ftp://cu-seeme.cornell.edu/pub/cu-seeme`. What follows is a step-by-step guide to retrieving the latest version of CU-SeeMe, as done with Anarchie, my Macintosh ftp client of choice. The same steps apply to other ftp clients for both Macintosh and Windows systems.

1. Start Anarchie. Enter the Uniform Resource Locator (URL) for CU-SeeMe's location (see Figure 1.10).

Figure 1.10. Entering CU-SeeMe's URL.

Introduction to Internet Videoconferencing and CU-SeeMe

2. A listing of the contents of /pub/cu-seeme appears (see Figure 1.11). Later versions of CU-SeeMe will likely appear as well.

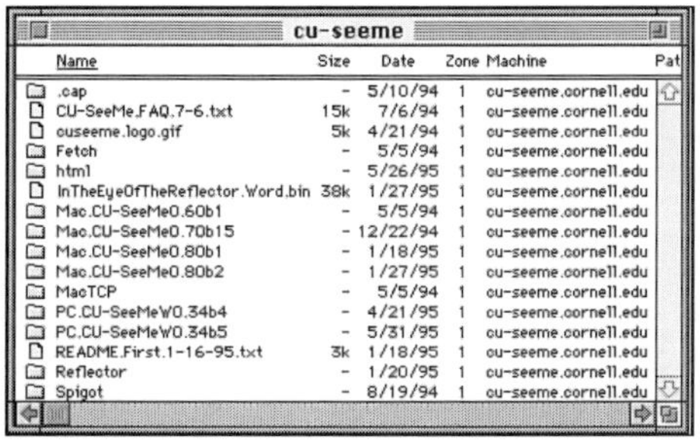

Figure 1.11. Where CU-SeeMe lives.

3. Read the file beginning with README.First. In it, you will find last-minute, up-to-date information about CU-SeeMe, reflectors, and other pertinent issues.

4. CU-SeeMe for Macintosh is found in folders beginning with Mac. Select the highest-numbered folder—for example, Mac.CU-SeeMe0.80b2 in Figure 1.12.

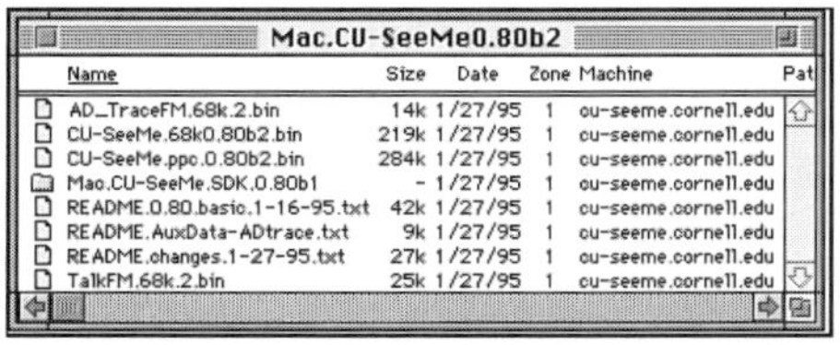

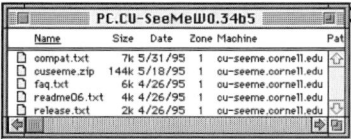

Figure 1.12. CU-SeeMe for Macintosh.

CU-SeeMe for Windows is found in folders beginning with PC. Select the highest-numbered—for example, PC.CU-SeeMeW0.34b5 in Figure 1.13.

Figure 1.13. CU-SeeMe for Windows

5. The CU-SeeMe frequently asked questions are contained in a text file beginning with CU-SeeMe.FAQ. Read this file. It contains answers to the questions that you will have.

Internet TV with CU-SeeMe

Macintosh owners of the discontinued VideoSpigot card can find the necessary drivers in the folder named Spigot (see Figure 1.14).

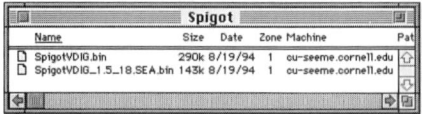

Figure 1.14. VideoSpigot Files

6. If you want to run a CU-SeeMe reflector (discussed in Chapter 7), you will find source code and late-breaking information in the Reflector folder (see Figure 1.15).

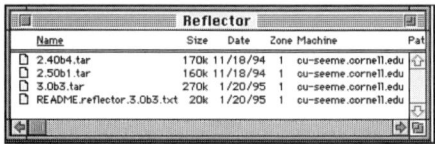

Figure 1.15. Reflector files.

Chapter 2 contains complete information on setting up and using CU-SeeMe.

Chapter 2
Typical CU-SeeMe Usage

There are several variations of basic CU-SeeMe usage, each having to do with the direction of traffic and the number of participants. All use the same "muscles," so you can carry what you learn in one mode over to others.

The most basic variation is a point-to-point connection directly between two computers running CU-SeeMe on a network. This most closely resembles the videophones of science-fiction stories.

The next variation is a one-to-many connection consisting of one computer that runs the reflector software and the other computers connected to it, which run CU-SeeMe. Video and audio sent from any of the connected CU-SeeMe users to the reflector are visible to all others connected to that reflector. This is group videoconferencing.

The third variation is specialized one-way broadcasting. This is where a reflector operator elects to transmit programming that is of general interest to the CU-SeeMe community without offering to receive any video and audio from the participants. Examples of this include NASA TV, a broadcast of live footage of shuttle missions, press conferences, and the like.

 Internet TV with CU-SeeMe

After you read this chapter, you will know

- How a point-to-point session looks and feels
- How a one-to-many session looks and feels
- How a one-way session looks and feels

This chapter is designed to familiarize you with the dynamics of CU-SeeMe usage—and nothing more. A complete CU-SeeMe user's guide appears in Chapter 6, "CU-SeeMe User's Guide."

Point-to-Point Sessions

The first time you run CU-SeeMe, you will see a Preferences window, as shown in Figure 2.1. You can change the values at a future time by selecting the Preferences item on the Edit menu.

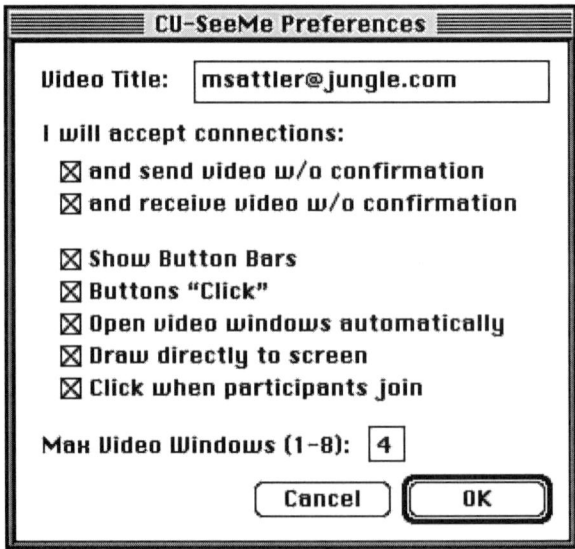

Figure 2.1. CU-SeeMe Preferences.

Consider the following scenario. A Net-connected friend on the other side of the world wants to talk with you. (The videoconferencing community still hasn't come up with a better verb to use than "talk." I've noticed the same thing in people who use e-mail. The utterance "I talked to Ginger today" could equally well refer to the telephone, e-mail, or videoconferencing.)

She has sent you e-mail, asking you to e-mail her when you are awake—it's the middle of my night when she types her note. Your PowerBook has turned itself on before you rise. You respond to her with a short note. Moments later she sends you her IP address. (Whenever she connects via modem to her Internet service provider, she is given an IP address from a pool of addresses; this is called "dynamic" addressing. Because she doesn't have a fixed address, you have to do this dance whenever you want to initiate a CU-SeeMe connection.)

Armed with her IP address, you select **Connect To** from the Conference menu to bring up the Connection Window (fig. 2.2).

```
┌─────────── Connect ───────────┐
│                               │
│ Connect to...                 │
│ IP Address:   [132.236.91.204]│
│ Conference    [0]             │
│ ID:                           │
│                               │
│        ☒ I will send video    │
│        ☒ I will receive video │
│                               │
│         [ Cancel ] [ Connect ]│
└───────────────────────────────┘
```

Figure 2.2. Connection Window.

You type her IP address into the field. CU-SeeMe attempts to connect to the CU-SeeMe program running on her computer. If everything works out, a window will open and you will see what the video camera attached to her computer sees. With luck, she will be sitting at her computer, and you can have a conversation. If things proceed less than optimally—there might be a network failure between the two computers, or her computer might not be running CU-SeeMe when you try to connect—you will get a `no response from <her IP address>` error message.

No such luck. You see Figure 2.3 and realize that you are playing videophone tag. You send her e-mail. Later you have better luck.

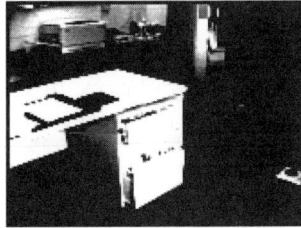

Figure 2.3. An empty office.

One-to-Many (Reflector) Sessions

There is no procedural difference between connecting point-to-point and connecting to a reflector. The IP address you enter is simply that of a computer running a multi-cast reflector rather than that of a computer running CU-SeeMe.

Instead of seeing only one video window, reflector conferences tend to yield several windows, each with a flood of data behind it trying to overwhelm your network connection. With a slow connection method, such as a 28.8 kbps modem, you might see some interesting, yet bizarre, images like the ones shown in Figures 2.4–2.9.

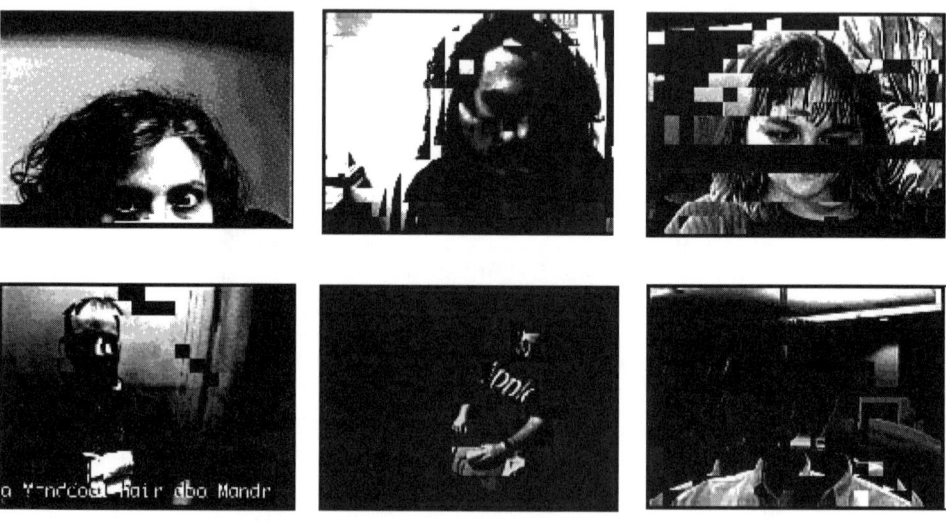

Figure 2.4–2.9. These are examples of the poor-quality images that CU-SeeMe transmits over low-speed connections.

The way CU-SeeMe transmits images in little boxes is discussed in Chapter 4, "Hardware." Even in this unfriendly technical situation, however, it is amazing how much human-to-human communication can occur.

There has been much interest in CU-SeeMe among the deaf community. Being able to transmit signed languages visually between low-cost computers would be quite a coup. Sadly, a modem doesn't provide the necessary bandwidth to do this—yet. With the advent of faster computers that can decompress more quickly and cheaper, faster network connections that can shuffle data around more quickly, we are getting closer.

One-Way (Broadcast) Sessions

CU-SeeMe offers would-be broadcasters a method of reaching the masses, and it has shown us real-time images of places we would otherwise never see if we only had the mainstream media to guide us.

The National Aeronautics and Space Administration makes available a space-related broadcast called NASA TV, which is carried around-the-clock on several CU-SeeMe reflectors around the planet. (You will find more about NASA TV in Chapter 7, "Reflector Operator's Guide.") Through NASA TV, you can see all the facets of on-going operations, often live, including press conferences, activities inside the cockpit (shown in Figure 2.10), launches and landings (shown in Figure 2.11), and mission control during an operation. All these images are provided for one-way consumption.

Figure 2.10. Inside the space shuttle.

Figure 2.11. Outside the space shuttle.

Figure 2.12 shows the space shuttle during an extra-vehicular activity. It is bringing satellites on board for repair; afterwards it sends them on their way.

Figure 2.12. In the space shuttle's cargo bay.

Figure 2.13 shows the Soviet space station *Mir* (*Peace*) from the space shuttle. Figure 2.14 shows the space shuttle from *Mir*.

Figure 2.13. *Mir* as seen from the space shuttle.

Figure 2.14. The space shuttle as seen from *Mir*.

You can also see cultural events, such as the Burning Man extravaganza in the Nevada desert, courtesy of *Monk* magazine. The colorfully painted Monkmobile appears via CU-SeeMe in Figure 2.15. This broadcast was intended to be relayed to the reflector in real time. The negotiations about renting satellite time became the most difficult technical hurdle, so a tape of the event was rushed to San Francisco, where it was sent to the reflector, with only a few hours delay.

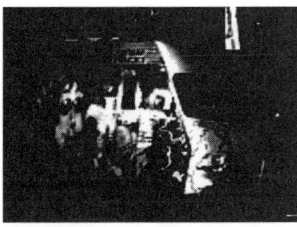

Figure 2.15. The Monkmobile.

You can peer into the home office of Adam Curry (shown in Figure 2.16), as well as Eva and Børre Ludvigsen's Norwegian home-on-the-web (shown in Figures 2.17 and 2.18).

Figure 2.16. Adam Curry's home office.

Figure 2.17 and 2.18. Eva and Børre Ludvigsen's place.

Not only government agencies and video hackers are using CU-SeeMe to share video experiences. Artists and show business entrepeneurs are providing content, too. Movies, music shows, and newsworthy events are sent digitally around the world.

The film *Plan 10 from Outer Space* premiered on the Internet before it was seen in any other venue or on any other medium. The film's creators took questions from CU-SeeMe users all over the world during their accompanying interactive press conference. Only after the citizens of the Net enjoyed the show did the film have a traditional premier at the Sundance Film Festival. (The Sundance Film Festival opening night gala was also broadcast via CU-SeeMe by these folks.) Figure 2.19 shows one of the aliens just before the Sundance opening night gala.

Figure 2.19. *Plan 10 from Outer Space.*

John Carey (one of the film's creators), Karen Black (one of its stars), Walter Hart (the producer), and Thomas Barron (the owner of Image G, a special-effects firm in Hollywood famous for doing all of the special effects motion control work for Star Trek), added to their CU-SeeMe firsts the broadcast of three-dimensional images using CU-SeeMe. They created a three-dimensional rig (shown in Figure 2.20) and a viewer to help users fuse the images. "Unfortunately," John said to me, "we made only two viewers, so there were not a lot of folks who were able to take advantage of this part of the event, but it was fun to be first."

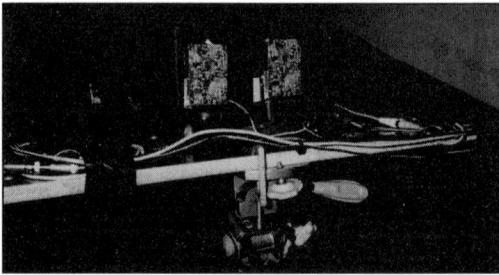

Figure 2.20. The three-dimensional CU-SeeMe rig.

Others have paid tribute to the *Mystery Science Theater 3000* television show by superimposing the shadow mask of the show's three stars (shown in Figure 2.21) onto whatever they are transmitting.

Figure 2.21. *Mystery Science Theater 3000.*

Musicans have always featured prominently in CU-SeeMe broadcasting. Carl Stone (shown in Figure 2.22), a musician known for his combinations of natural sounds, acoustic instruments, and electronically reproduced fragments of familiar musical pieces; Otomo Yoshide (shown in Figure 2.23), a "turntable artist" and guitarist; and vocalist Min Xiao-Fen performed for a CU-SeeMe audience from Beanbenders in Berkeley, California.

Figure 2.22. Carl Stone.

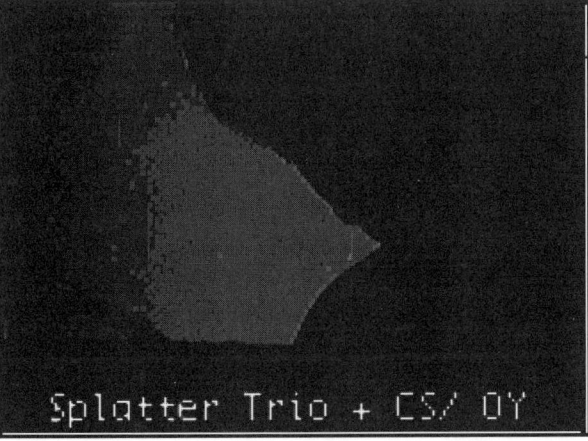

Figure 2.23. Otomo Yoshide.

 **Internet TV with CU-SeeMe**

InterneTV, in Austin, Texas, whose logo appears in Figure 2.24, has been broadcasting live shows, including those of Bruce Springsteen (shown Figure 2.25) and Toad the Wet Sprocket (shown in Figures 2.26 through 2.28).

Figure 2.24. InterneTV.

Figure 2.25. Bruce Springsteen.

Figures 2.26–2.28. Toad the Wet Sprocket.

The awarding of the Nobel Prize for Peace to P.L.O. leader Yasir Arafat (shown in Figure 2.29) and Israeli Prime Minister Ytizhak Rabin (shown in Figure 2.30) on December 10, 1994, was broadcast around the world from the ceremony in Oslo, Norway.

Figures 2.29 and 2.30. Yasir Arafat and Ytizhak Rabin, respectively, receiving the Nobel Prize for Peace.

CU-SeeMe also enables you to share in historic events, such as the view over the Kent State University campus (shown in Figure 2.31) 25 years after the fatal confrontation between student protesters and the National Guard, a watershed event in America's perception of the Vietnam War.

Figure 2.31. Kent State University.

Figure 2.32 shows the Gay Pride Parade in New York City.

Figure 2.32. The Gay Pride Parade in New York City.

Although being on the Net is no substitute for going outside for a walk, breathing the fresh air, listening to the wind rustle through the leaves, and hearing the birds chirp, it sometimes can take you to places you would probably not see in a given afternoon. Earth Day 1995 is a case in point.

Internet TV with CU-SeeMe

To celebrate the 25th anniversary of Earth Day, video cameras were set up on each of the seven continents. For a full day, images were sent out via a linked network of reflectors. It was easy to feel that we, the videoconferencing community, had brought together the far points of our planet as we watched—live—the terminator sweep across Earth, changing night into day, awakening the cities as their citizens filled the streets.

Figures 2.33 through 2.36 show four stills from Earth Day 1995: MacMurdo Station in Antarctica, marsupials in Australia; Cape Town, South Africa; and Salzburg, Austria. Other stills from Earth Day 1995 appear throughout this book.

Figure 2.33. MacMurdo Station in Antarctica.

Figure 2.34. Marsupials in Australia.

Figure 2.35. Cape Town, South Africa.

Figure 2.36. Salzburg, Austria.

CU-SeeMe has been used to educate. You can hear the viewpoints of former U.S. Surgeon General C. Everett Koop (shown in Figure 2.37) and computer entrepreneur Mitch Kapor (shown in Figure 2.38).

Figure 2.37. C. Everett Koop.

Figure 2.38. Mitch Kapor.

The children in Figure 2.39 participated in the Global School Net. They were able to share Take Your Daughter to Work Day with the daughters of the employees of the National Science Foundation, who appear in Figure 2.40.

Figure 2.39. Children participating in the Global School Net on Take Your Daughter to Work Day.

Figure 2.40. The National Science Foundation on Take Your Daughter to Work Day.

Many events are worth sharing, and everyone has experiences that can be shared via CU-SeeMe. Using a two-way videoconferencing tool has worked out well as a one-way broadcasting tool. It is already working on computers. You don't need to allocate disk space or waste precious time getting a second system up and running. This single consideration alone is justification enough to use CU-SeeMe as a tool for disseminating information in-house.

Summary

You have seen the basic ways in which you can use CU-SeeMe. The remainder of this book is devoted to helping you install, configure, and use CU-SeeMe to share in the experiences of others and to bring others along to an event of yours, be it a poetry reading, the immolation of a four-story human figure of wood, or any educational experience.

The Internet

After you read this chapter, you will know

- What a network is
- How the Internet evolved
- What the IAB, IETF, IRTF, and ISOC are
- How to use technology to deal with information overload
- How Canter & Siegel spammed the Internet
- What IP addresses and subnet masks are
- What subnetting and supernetting mean
- How the Domain Name System makes your life easier

Networks

In the beginning, there were computers. Well, not that early on, but some time thereafter. Some people thought that computers were good things, and they did cool things with them. Then they did really cool things. Next they decided that the whole would be greater than the sum of the parts—I should have access to your data and you to mine. Networking was born.

Today, almost every personal computer comes ready-to-network, right out of the box. Every Macintosh, since day one, in 1984, is sold with AppleTalk installed and LocalTalk hardware. The latest version of Windows has networking in its standard configuration. This has turned out to be a good thing, as it happens.

 **Internet TV with CU-SeeMe**

Local Area Networks

There are several different kinds of networks. The most basic network occurs when two or more computers in the same physical location are physically connected with short bits of wire. This, basically, is a local area network, or LAN.

Wide Area Networks

When several buildings are networked together with a bit of extra hardware, perhaps in a campus or business park, a wide area network, or WAN, is created. In most cases, this is a distinction of interest only to the system and network administrators. Users of the network usually cannot tell whether they are on a LAN or a WAN.

Internets

Sometimes it becomes useful to connect two different networks together. Perhaps the Engineering and Accounting departments started out with two different networks—after all, Engineering was using screaming workstations and Accounting was using little Macintoshes. In this age of just-in-time manufacturing, however, organizations want to marry, or *internetwork*, the two. An internet is the conglomeration of two or more networks.

Instead of forcing one group to abandon its machines and adopt the hardware of the other group, connecting the two networks with specialized hardware and software enables everyone to work as before, but now they have access to more computers. The equipment required to internetwork depends on the specific type of networks to be connected, the networking languages—that is, networking protocols—they speak, and the type of hardware used to connect computers on the networks.

Internet with a Capital *I*

The Internet, with an uppercase *I*, refers to the worldwide conglomeration of internets. The Internet is growing in leaps and bounds. Any numbers that I might give would be hopelessly out of date a few months from now. It doesn't really matter, though. The Internet is big—really big. The actual total number of computers and people connected to the Internet is useful only at boring—or very technical—parties. Suffice it to say that over a thousand computers are being connected to the Internet each day, and that many millions of people in almost every country on the planet have access to the Internet.

The Internet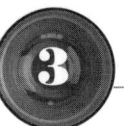

*And so these men of Indostan
disputed long and loud
each in his own opinion
exceeding stiff and strong
though each was partly right
and all were in the wrong!*

——John Godfrey Saxe

The story of the blind men and the elephant is a telling one. There are many facets of the Internet, and people think of the ones they know when they describe the Internet to others. Few people have a good working understanding of the breadth and depth of the information available on the Internet. They know about some of the different kinds of programs that they use to access the different kinds of information available on the Internet. They use one kind of program for reading and writing e-mail, another for retrieving files from other computers, a third for meeting people and chatting with them, and yet another to play Go, chess, or role-playing games. Of course, they use CU-SeeMe to exchange audio and video with others.

The word *Internet* refers simultaneously to the physical hardware that makes up the Net, the information on the individual computers that populate the Net, the software used to get at the different kinds of information, and the vast multitudes of people who give the Net its feel.

You Say Tomato...

CU-SeeMe works over networks that use the Transmission Control Protocol/Internet Protocol (TCP/IP) method of moving information from one place to another. Many private networks use TCP/IP because it is a method guaranteed to deliver data intact to the intended recipient. Not surprisingly, the largest network that "speaks" Internet Protocol is the Internet itself. For this reason, you as a user of CU-SeeMe are interested in the Internet.

The Internet of Yesterday

The Internet, much like humans, appears to be far too complicated to have arisen from an evolutionary set of changes. It is most likely true of humans, and definitely true of the Internet. The Internet started out as a small military project designed to increase the survivability of the United States' defense capability. It has since metamorphosed into a venue for academic institutions to share research results and into a mixed environment of personal, academic, and commercial uses.

Today it is used to explore audio and video, electronic anonymous cash, and the feasability of distributed information storage—the World Wide Web. Tomorrow's uses should be quite interesting.

Sneakernet

From the first days of modern computers in World War II to the early 1970s, computer networking was nonexistent at worst to primitive at best. The only way of communication between two computers was the manual transfer of information by humans via punched paper tape, punch cards, and magnetic tape. Sneakernet, the tongue-in-cheek name given to people walking between the computers, served early computer users well, as long as the computers involved accepted the same physical media. If you did only tapes and I did only cards, we had a problem.

Always Up

The next step in computer networking was to wire computers—in those days only "big iron" mainframe computers existed—together so that they could communicate. One requirement of early networking was that each computer be up and running when any computers on the network were communicating. If one went down—whether for maintenance or because something caused it to crash—the entire network went down. This made networking unreliable and annoying.

The ARPANET

After World War II, the United States found itself in the escalating Cold War. Tensions were high, and enemies were everywhere. Joe Rinaldi, a regular at the cafe where I wrote this book, recalls, "Russia was the enemy. Gen. Douglas MacArthur was a hero to my family; he wanted to cross the 38th parallel and use atom bombs to make a 50-mile wide swath of radioactive cobalt so that the North Koreans could never come down the peninsula again. Gen. George Patton was a folk hero; he had asked President Eisenhower at the end of World War II to sanction an invasion of Moscow to clean up the Communists once and for all. Sen. Joseph McCarthy was a patriot to my family. I was only a seven-year-old and didn't have much of my own mind then. He was hunting for Communists, and to be a Communist was a very bad thing indeed."

School-kids were taught that a nuclear attack was a conceivable event, and that it could be survived by using the school's hallways as a shelter and doing a "duck and cover" when a nuclear flash was seen. Towns had Civil Defense volunteers, and Emergency Fallout Shelter signs appeared on many public buildings. Supplies were stocked in the public shelters and the private ones being built in the backyards of many families. For many, the 1950s were a process of "learning to love the bomb."

The Russians launched Sputnik, and attack from the skies was added to our worries. The United States was humiliated. In perhaps his best-remembered response, President John F. Kennedy announced that the United States would join—and win—the space race by landing a man on the Moon by the end of the decade. Offensive capability had to be augmented by defensive stratagies. The interstate highways were built as a transportation mechanism for tanks and troop carries for when the American heartland was invaded by the Reds. It isn't surprising that computers, used by the military since World War II, and the recently-created networks, would be "hardened" to survive the inevitable enemy onslaught.

By the early and middle 1960s, the U.S. Department of Defense was a great consumer of computer technology. Because the (relatively) high-speed data processing was such an advance over the manually-calculated bombing tables of a few years earlier, computers represented a critically important resource to the Armed Forces. Networks that could be disabled by the malfunction of a single computer were clearly a major vulnerability—something clearly inferior to a network that would survive if some or most of the computers on the network didn't—an eventuality that was considered by military planners as a distinct possibility.

In 1963, the Advanced Research Projects Agency (ARPA), the branch of the DoD responsible for handing out grant monies, funded the Information Processing Technologies Office. At that time, ARPA-funded research didn't need to be directly related to military applications, which enabled ARPA to support basic research in novel areas. By 1969, Congress had second thoughts about allowing basic research to be supported by the defense budget, and required that ARPA show that its programs could be directly applied to the problems of military science. (Sen. Edward Kennedy was one of the legislators responsible for the new requirement.) In response, ARPA became DARPA, short for Defense ARPA. Also in 1969, goals for a reliable network that could be used to link DoD, military research contractors, and the universities that were doing military-funded research was published by DARPA. Those goals included

- The network would continue to work even if many computers or the connections between them had failed.
- Many different types of computers would have to be accomodated, so a standard method of exchanging information smoothly would have to be designed and adhered to.
- The network would have to reroute information automatically around nonfunctioning parts, such as a disruption caused by enemy attack. Such routing would have to occur dynamically, and be transparent to users of the network. The Internet has rarely been subject to enemy attack, but an errant backhoe or construction crew cutting a network link (which

recently happened in downtown San Francisco) is just as much of a threat to robust communication.

- The network would have to be a network of networks, so that if only one computer on a network was on the ARPANET, all computers on that network could exchange information through that one connection with other computers on the ARPANET.

These goals were implemented in the early 1970s as the ARPANET. They have been inherited by us, the users of its descendant—namely, the Internet.

The ARPANET, connecting several computers in California and one in Utah, was born. The inclusion of military contractors and universities allowed Bolt, Beranek, and Newman (BBN), the maintainers of the ARPANET, to learn from the problems that the expanding network was having. New computers and more users changed the load on the ARPANET and stressed it in unexpected ways. Maintaining the speed of traffic on the network turned out to be far less troublesome than keeping the constituent computers speaking the early Packet Switch Node (PSN) language of the ARPANET.

Stewart Brand, better known as the founder of the Whole Earth Catalog, wrote in his book *II Cybernetic Frontiers*:

> At present, some twenty major computer centers are linked on the two-year-old ARPA Net. Traffic on the net has been very slow, due to delays and difficulties of translation between different computers and divergent projects. Use has recently begun to increase as researchers travel from center to center and want to keep in touch with home base, and as more tantalizing sharable resources come available. How net usage will evolve is uncertain.

Increased use and a first-attempt programming solution was at the root of the growing pains the ARPANET was having in the late 1970s. PSN was a technology insufficient to support such a rapidly growing network. Engineers call this a scaling problem—what works in a small system might not work when the size of the system is scaled by 10, 100, or 1000. Deficiencies in PSN prompted research that resulted in the creation and adoption of TCP/IP as the lingua franca of the ARPANET. TCP/IP had the advantage over PSN in that it allowed for almost unlimited growth. We are only today feeling the pinch of the original TCP/IP implementation. All computers on the ARPANET were required to switch to TCP/IP by 1983.

A feature of IP is its guaranteed delivery. On an IP network, each computer can determine the quickest route to a destination computer. This routing is done dynamically, and portions of a network that have been bombed back into the Stone Age, cut by a backhoe, or inadvertently disconnected by a telephone technician are taken into account and routed around. This makes for a flexible and robust network.

The Internet

Stewart Brand also said,

> There's a curious mix of theoretical fascination and operation resistance around the scheme. The resistance may have something to do with reluctance about equipping a future Big Brother and his Central Computer. The fascination resides in the thorough rightness of computers as communications instruments, which implies some revolutions.

Computing and networking technologies are a double-edged sword. Our rights to privacy may be irretrievably lost if care isn't taken, but IP has been a help in a strange way. It has been noted that the Internet routes around censorship in the same way in which it routes around physical damage. The efficacy of the original design goals and their subsequent implementation has been proved again and again.

> **Can the Internet survive an enemy attack?**
> During the Gulf War, the U.S. military targeted the Iraqi command, control, communication, and information networks—often abbreviated C^3I. Because the Iraqis used commercially-available network routers that employed standard TCP/IP routing and recovery protocols, which worked well under the extreme stress of war, their network was able to withstand the punishment inflected by the U.S. and coalition forces.

In the middle and late 1980s, companies such as Sun Microsystems made popular the engineering workstation. These powerful desktop computers, usually with a large monitor, made it possible for scientists to model complex systems at will, without needing to schedule time on a large mainframe. Most of these workstations ran a version of UNIX, an inexpensive and popular operating system in academic and scientific environments. UNIX was created at Bell Labs and enhanced at the University of California at Berkeley. Although Bell Labs was the home of telephonic networking, it took the folks at Berkeley to provide comprehensive networking capabilities for UNIX.

Two situations were coming to a head. Engineering workstations were being attached to networks not designed for great loads, and each workstation, because of its speed, could generate more network traffic by itself than could the entire ARPANET population of a decade earlier. The sagging ARPANET couldn't survive this onslaught of popularity.

 **Internet TV with CU-SeeMe**

NSFNET

In 1986, the National Science Foundation (NSF) made a decision that was to shape the future look and feel of the Internet. NSF wanted to purchase a few expensive supercomputers, set them up into computing centers dedicated to research use, and provide them to researchers across the United States, who would submit programs and data across the network and quickly get back the results. The prohibitive cost of these supercomputers limited the plan to five machines at as many sites.

Their original plan to use the ARPANET as the connecting medium having fallen through, the NSF created small regional networks to connect researchers in the same geographic area and its own network to connect the regional networks to the computing centers. NSFNET was born.

The ARPANET had been used as a practical model for NSFNET. Because many of the companies and academic institutions that were on NSFNET were also on the ARPANET and because they both used TCP/IP as a communications standard, the two networks began a synergetic growth. The network managers began to cooperate in technology advances. Most notably, NSF pushed forward the research into higher-speed links. In many ways, the NSF mirrored the sheparding of network technologies that ARPA had done years earlier. DARPA was eclipsed by NSF in its commitment to the advancement of the network.

At the request of the NSF, universities encouraged both staff and students to have access to the NSFNET, resulting in a much larger user population. This, in turn, resulted in increased network traffic. Coupled with the faster network links, the NSFNET was a great success, and in 1990 absorbed the ARPANET. MILNET, however, continues to this day.

The cornerstone of the original NSFNET plan—sharing supercomputers—never lived up to its expectations. They were too expensive to purchase and maintain, and they were difficult to use. With the rapid evolution of the engineering workstation, they became not as attractive as they once had been. Luckily, the network itself was enough to keep the NSF involved in the project, and things survived without the computing centers. Most of what you know as the Internet is the NSFNET of recent years.

Usenet

Despite its name, the Usenet—the User's Network—is not a network in its own right in the same way in which the ARPANET or the Internet are. It is a method of exchanging information, based on the bathroom graffiti model that is available via other networks, including the Internet. The brainchild of two Duke University graduate students, Usenet was born in 1979 when a third student implemented their ideas and connected Duke and the University of North Carolina. The basic features of Usenet are the ability to read news, post news, and transfer news between computers.

Areas of interest are broken into newsgroups, which are known in other systems as *forums*. Newsgroups operate with the same conversational dynamic as bathroom graffiti. Someone scribbles a message, called a *post*. Later someone responds, with another post. At yet a later time, someone rebuts or confirms the previous contribution, with yet another post. Follow-up posts create a thread. When someone scribbles a new topic of discussion elsewhere on the wall, a new thread is said to have started—although, of course, the first response really makes the thread. This conversation happens in a linear order, without any real-time interaction. Minutes or months may pass between postings, although most systems expire postings after a while to save disk space.

Depending on their administrative setup, Usenet newsgroups can be propagated around the planet. Some newsgroups, such as `ba.singles` (events for single people in the San Francisco Bay Area), are available, but usually not read, outside the Bay Area. Other newsgroups, such as `comp.sys.mac.apps` (applications that run on Macintosh computer systems) are available and read all over the world. Although English is the lingua franca of most newsgroups, there are hierarchies in German, Finnish, and other languages.

There is no central administrative authority for Usenet, a by-product of its growth. Each site administrator selects the newsgroups to be provided at that site—or lets them all pass—but he cannot select the newsgroups that are available elsewhere on the Internet. If enough site administrators don't approve of an action, such as the creation or deletion of a particular newsgroup, it doesn't happen. Of course, most site administrators have better things to do with their time than micromanage Usenet. Major events on Usenet require support of a significant part of the community.

Early on, you got a Usenet feed—the entirety of the Usenet message traffic—for free, provided that you were willing to pass the feed on to others for free. This engendered a feeling of cooperation, community, and sharing. Not everything is sweetness and light, though. Usenet is one heck of a noisy bunch of people. Even so, the signal-to-noise ratio is just enough to make the entire process worthwhile.

Just as some organizations steer the Internet, the Usenet has its own bodies. The Usenet group moderator spearheads the process. The Usenet group mentors provide an advisory body to assist in evaluating the feasability of a particular newsgroup proposal and in drafting requests for discussion (RFDs) and calls for votes (CFVs). (Newsgroups are created for the population at large, even though some of them are quite technical. Proposed newsgroups with undetermined interest levels are usually run as mailing lists to gauge interest and participation.) The Usenet volunteer votetakers provide an independent body to run the votes.

Usenet is often mistakenly lumped in with the ARPANET, NSFNET, and the Internet. The Usenet newsgroups are actually just some of the many resources available to users of the Internet. Moreover, the existence of Usenet today is a direct result of the growth of IP networks.

The telephone charges incurred by using modems to connect the Usenet machines for the transfer of news were substantial, especially in the case of long-distance connections. Bean-counters, with their pens poised to slash any frivolous expenses from their budgets, were a real threat to the continued survival of the Usenet. The Network News Transfer Protocol (NNTP), released in 1986, implemented news transmission, posting, and reading using TCP/IP connections instead of using the traditional UNIX-to-UNIX Copy (UUCP), which enabled the news to travel over network connections that were already in place as result of the growth of the ARPANET, NSFNET, and the Internet. The switch from modem-based to network-based transfer cut costs and ensured the survival of Usenet. Two additional software enhancements to Usenet, InterNetNews and News Overview (NOV), increased the efficiency of maintaining and serving news to the user community, which further helped USENET's survival chances.

BITNET

About two years after Usenet started its journey, a similar project began several hundred miles to the north. People at Yale University and the City University of New York started networking their IBM mainframes and exchanging information. The BITNET (Because It's Time NETwork) was born.

Aside from a bit of playing around on the ARPANET during visits to BBN and the Massachusetts Institute of Technology Artifical Intelligence Labs, BITNET was the first network that I had solid experience on. During my time as an undergraduate student at Boston University, I was able to send e-mail and participate in mailing lists over BITNET.

Unlike USENET's model of decentralized, cooperative anarchy, BITNET has a hierarchical organization, run by an executive committee. This gives BITNET a feel and size different from that of Usenet. IBM provided much of the money, expertise, and technical support to BITNET. In 1984, IBM provided funds for centralizing network services, something inconceivable in the Usenet world. BITNET became a not-for-profit endeavor in 1987. Two years later, it merged its bureaucracy with that of the Computer+Science Network (CSNET) and changed its name to the Corporation for Research and Educational Networking, or CREN.

BITNET has become increasingly irrelevant in a world where Usenet is spreading in leaps and bounds, due in large part to its use of the TCP/IP communication standard. BITNET still uses an outdated IBM networking standard and is available to end-users through less compelling means than the graphic clients that Macintosh, Windows, and UNIX users can use to read Usenet newsgroups via NNTP over TCP/IP.

BITNET and FidoNet, yet another network, were unaffiliated with the ARPANET and NSFNET. As all these networks grew, their users wanted to share information, so gateways—computers that straddled two or more networks—were put online. My early years of being on the Internet at Boston University resulted from being able to pass messages from the BITNET, which the IBM mainframe was on, to the Internet through ucbvax, a DEC VAX computer at the University of California at Berkeley.

The Internet of Today

The tasks of management and upgrading the NSFNET was contracted out in 1987 to a group that included MCI Telecommunications, IBM, and Merit Networks. Merit is known for its development of MacPPP and its management of educational networking in the state of Michigan. MCI and IBM need no introduction. This contract is important to us because the experience these companies developed in running the NSFNET became the bedrock of the Commercial Internet Exchange, or CIX, described shortly.

National Research and Education Network

The High Performance Computing Act of 1991, sponsored by then-Senator Al Gore, was born of his conviction that America, to remain competitive in the world market, must have better and faster computing and network resources available to all citizens, especially school-children. NSFNET benefitted "higher education" in the USA, leaving others out in the cold. The act mandated extending the "information superhighway," combining kindergarten, elementary, primary, and high schools, two-year colleges, community colleges, schools, public libraries, academic institutions, researchers, and governmental agencies into one very fast network called the National Research and Education Network, or NREN (pronounced "ehn rehn").

NREN will allow teachers to collaborate on courses of learning and special projects, it will allow students to share the learning experiences, and it will allow businesses to assist in the process. We don't have to wait for NREN to do any of this, though. Organizations like the Global School Net (discussed in Chapter 8, "Usage, History, and Culture") have been bringing innovative and entertaining educational programs from all over the world to school-children in participating schools. The current expansion of the Internet to the poorer and more remote parts of the

American school system (by special grants and cooperation between business and schools and entities such as GSN) is generating a lot of excitement. I'll provide some pointers to World Wide Web pages that contain articles by "Internet ambassadors," school-children who are involved in the on-going connectivity of the educational system.

The Internet is, de facto, the NREN until the political, commercial, and engineering struggles are resolved and the new network can be built (or more likely, evolved with the help of grant money).

President Bill Clinton's National Information Infrastructure (NII) proposal for expanding the Internet within the USA will provide both resources for the establishment of a far-reaching NREN tomorrow and a faster and more robust Internet today.

Commercial Internet Exchange

The NSF's Acceptable Use Policies forbid commercial activities on the NSFNET. These policies were vague and confusing to individuals—can I let you know I'm trying to sell my stereo via e-mail?—and businesses that were on the Internet—can employees in far-flung offices discuss business via e-mail? These policies also made it difficult for those without any connection with DoD-related research to gain access to the Internet at all. For many years people would maintain a presence in an institute of higher learning to keep access to the network, others would go through even stranger machinations. Many of these people were the hackers who torture-tested the network technologies, making things safer and more reliable for everyone else. When the existence of these folks was finally acknowledged by the NSF, an avenue for granting them access couldn't be far behind.

It wasn't. Several private companies banded together to provide a for-profit alternative connection between the regional networks (in parallel with the NSFNET). The Commercial Internet Exchange, or CIX, is comprised of well-known names such as IBM and Sprint and some lesser-known names (to the public) such as Performance Systems International and Alternet. CIX has been such a success that the NSFNET was put out to pasture in the middle of 1995, its traffic completely taken over by the CIX.

The Internet of Tomorrow

The Internet exists today as a symbiotic relationship among many self-preserving organisms. All must strike a gentle balance between exerting their will and killing their host. Several volunteer groups help regulate the wheels of Internet progress, thereby increasing its survival chances.

The Internet Engineering Task Force (IETF) is a public forum dedicated to discussing and handling the technical problems facing the Internet. The IETF is committed to doing its business in a manner accessable to all; some of its meetings have been held via Internet videoconferencing. Problems deemed worthy of effort result in the creation of working groups—assemblages of computer scientists who craft recommendations for solving the problem and report back to the IETF. The system works because people who are interested in a problem and are willing to contribute time and effort to solving it volunteer to do the work.

A good example of an IETF solution to an Internet-at-large problem deals with the inherent limits of the current IP addressing scheme. The explosion of machines connecting to the Internet was rapidly exhausting all the possible addresses—clearly a catastrophe. Several ideas were evaluated by the working group. Ipng, short for IP: The Next Generation, was the result. IP addresses will be made longer, and more systems can be added.

The Internet Architecture Board (IAB) sets the communication standards for the many different software and hardware systems that populate the Internet. An important facet of the survival of the Internet today and tomorrow, the IAB is not open to the public at large but has invitation-only attendance. This hasn't proved to be a problem.

The Internet Research Task Force (IRTF) handles long-term issues, such as those that will affect the Internet in the next decade.

Technological Problems

As the Internet grows in leaps and bounds, information overload becomes a real problem. If you subscribe to several mailing lists, you could get over a hundred e-mail messages daily. If you use e-mail to stay in touch with friends and coworkers, the amount of e-mail that you must contend with can become problematic. A mail reader that sorts incoming e-mail by user or content helps with part of the problem, but what do you do when you need to find something from the past?

Similarly, as more and more information is tossed onto the World Wide Web, it becomes more difficult to find sources of information to satisfy your research needs. Cypberpunks speak of "security by obscurity," an unflattering description of keeping things secret by hiding the method of encrypting the information; this method rarely works. There is a very real "security by obscurity" situation in an area in which you don't want security—being flooded by an ever-increasing number of Web sites, mailing lists, and e-mail is the defining problem facing the Intenet today.

Hundreds of years ago, librarians at the great library at Alexandria faced the same issues of cataloging and indexing information that we face today. Now, however, machines permit you some measure of mastery over the information flow. Search engines, such as those found at Yahoo and Lycos, help you plow through piles of data on the Web. Well written mailers, such as Eudora, help you search through the e-mail that you receive and have saved. Tomorrow, "intelligent agents" might do your work for you, learning from your past work habits and interests.

Societal Problems

Were it only that technical problems faced us. Consider the infamous Green Card Debacle of 1994. The now-reviled law firm of Canter & Siegel, a husband and wife team, posted a blatantly commercial advertisement about a U.S. resident alien—or green—card lottery and related immigration services. Annoying in its own right, this advertisement was posted to all the Usenet newsgroups then in existence—over 5000—regardless of topic. Such an act is called spamming, because the act mimics the physical behavior of the famous luncheon meat when it is dropped onto rapidly-turning fan blades.

Canter & Siegel's spam interrupted on-going discussions in newsgroups devoted to Macintosh system software, the Simpsons television show, and the Andrew Beal fan club (where I came across it). People in the United States and around the planet, who heretofore had never even given a thought to the green card lottery, saw the spam derail the marketplace of ideas, at least for a short time. Outraged, thousands of people sent flame mail to Canter & Siegel and to Internet Direct, the postmaster of the Internet service provider from which Canter & Siegel posted—megabytes of infuriated responses, copies of the spam, miscellaneous large files designed to wreak havoc on the miscreant's e-mail system, and presumably some requests for more information.

The most common response was to swear off any future business with Canter & Siegel—voting with your money is always a worthwhile response. Some people used software expressly designed to deliver mail bombs—not the explosive kind—that repeatedly sent the offending message back to the offender, usually from nonexistent return addresses. Others wrote software to track down and cancel the spam posting and any others originating at the same e-mail address. Discussion raged across the Internet community—questions about how to spot and cancel spams, how to differentiate between appropriate, but wide-spread postings, and spams and about how to deal with spammers. In a more humorous vein, a few people set themselves up as the judges of the Internet. (In cyberspace, as in real space, we have all kinds.)

As the case progressed, users of the Internet learned valuable information about how such a reprehensible act happened and that Canter & Siegel had done it before. Internet Direct cancelled Canter & Siegel's account, and sued them for violating their stated acceptable use policy—a document that Canter & Siegel evidently never signed—and for the consequental impact on Internet Direct's business. The thousands of people who spammed Canter & Siegel back caused Internet Direct's mail server to crash, depriving Internet Direct's customers of e-mail. It is especially true in frontier justice on the Internet that the good of the many outweigh the needs of the few. The innocents on Internet Direct's mail server were mourned as being in the wrong place at the wrong time, victims of the vagaries of life.

Nobody was surprised when Canter & Siegel counter-sued, claiming a large percentage of return mail was requests for information about their services. Verifiable data has never been provided. Information about Canter & Siegel's past transgressions surfaced. It had been booted from other Internet service providers for similar spams and was suspended in 1987 from the Florida Bar for conduct deemed contrary to honest by the Florida Supreme Court.

And yes, before you ask, Canter & Siegel did spam the Net again, after the Green Card Debacle.

Paradoxically, given the disruption of the Internet, Canter & Siegel revelled in the bad press, even going so far as writing a book and giving newspaper and radio interviews, suggesting that the Internet was too much an anarchy and could use protection from disrupting forces. Will the irony ever end?

What can you learn from all this? Several things, not all of them good. Some people are interested in furthering their own ends, regardless of the harm it causes others. It is difficult to police the Internet, and transgressions often result in a response that does collateral damage to innocents who happen to be sharing the same machine. Peer pressure, boycotts, bad press, and technology in the form of *cancelbots* and *spambots*—pseudo-intelligent robotic entities that monitor postings to Usenet—might help deal with the worst offenders.

The Internet of tomorrow must survive an onslaught of new users and a corresponding percentage of disruptive actions. It looks as though it has a running chance at survival.

Connecting to the Internet

Now it is time to sketch out what you need to do to be a part of the Internet. By the end of this section, you will know enough to handle Chapter 4, "Hardware," and Chapter 5, "Software."

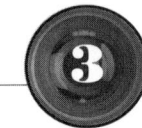# Internet TV with CU-SeeMe

Giving Your Computer a Unique Identity

Every computer connected to the Internet, from the slowest Intel 286 box to the fastest Connection Machine, has a unique address. This isn't a surprising concept—it is like your telephone number. Everyone on the world-wide telephone system has a unique address. Telephone addresses are of the form

```
+ (country code) . (area code) . (exchange) . (unit)
```

This is the standard promulgated by CCITT. For example, the number of the pay telephone closest to the corner of Haight and Ashbury streets in San Francisco is +1 415 252 7869. (Before you bother, it is for out-going calls only.)

> **Note:** The CCITT, the International Telephone and Telegraph Consultive Committee, is one of the better known standards-setting bodies. You will encounter it in the next chapter, when ISDN is described. The CCITT was recently renamed the Telecommunications Standards Bureau of the International Telecommunications Union. Its new—unwieldy—acronym is CCITT/ITU-TSB.

What does the telephone number mean? The country code for the United States is 1. The area code for the San Francisco peninsula and part of Marin County is 415. The telephone exchange is 252, and the unit is 7869. If you are calling a phone from outside the country that it is in, you must supply the digits that specify an international call. For example, if I wanted to call Germany—country code 33—I would begin with 011 33.

Why the digression? Your computer, once it is connected to the Internet, has its own number—its address. In the current networking scheme, it is a 32-bit number, such as

```
10001100101011101110010100000111
```

That is not easy for anyone to remember, and it is difficult even to write down. Because bytes (the smallest commonly-accessed unit of computer memory) are eight bits (the smallest actual unit of computer memory) long, you could write the address as

```
10001100.10101110.11100101.00000111
```

which is a bit easier to deal with. It's not the best you can do, though. Suppose that you use the decimal (base 10) system instead of the binary (base 2) system. In that case, you would see something like

```
140.174.229.7
```

That is almost human-friendly. If you can remember your phone number, social security number, and your shoe size, remembering an IP address is possible, too. You rarely need to memorize an IP address, but you will write down some special ones in Chapter 5 when you are getting ready to configure your connection.

Giving Your Network a Unique Identity

Just as your computer has an IP address, so does the network to which it is connected. (Remember that the Internet is simply a huge collection of interconnected networks.) Network numbers are composed of two parts: the network and the machine. Here is where the telephone explanation comes in. When you look at a telephone number in the United States, you can figure out the area code, the exchange, and the unit. That is because fixed-length fields are used. It also has the advantage of being easy to read. What happens when you run out of exchanges for a particular area code, as just happened in the San Francisco Bay Area? Lots of people have to switch to a new area code.

Now consider a different scheme for telephone numbers.

Remember that pay telephone with the number +1 415 252 7869? How else might you use those eleven digits to specify a particular telephone? Could you come up with a scheme that makes more sense than the one currently used? I think so.

Compare San Francisco and Escalon. San Francisco is a big city, consisting of three quarters of a million residents plus about a quarter-million daytime visitors, workers, and so on. It is known for its free-wheeling lifestyle, tolerant inhabitants, sourdough bread, and earthquakes. Escalon is a small town. It is best known as "the place you turn right at the stop light" on the way to Yosemite National Park, but its rapidly-dwindling orchards and speed traps are memorable as well.

What would happen if you assigned the following?

```
+1.3XXXXXXXXX - San Francisco, the third-largest city
+1.10000YYYYY - Escalon, the ten-thousandth largest city
```

San Francisco would have nine digits to use to specify telephones—one hundred times the number of telephones than the current scheme allows. Escalon would have five digits to specify telephones—a maximum of 99,999 phones for that town, which is more than enough for the foreseeable future.

Consider each city as a network of telephones. San Francisco has a network number of 3 and has nine digits to specify particular network members (telephones). Escalon has a network number of 10000 and has five digits to specify particular network members. Not bad, except how can you distinguish the network part from the other part? You must make a network mask—something that masks off parts of the number. For example,

Internet TV with CU-SeeMe

```
+1.3XXXXXXXXX - San Francisco, the third-largest city
+9.8777777777 - San Francisco's network mask

+1.10000YYYYY - Escalon, the ten-thousandth largest city
+9.8888877777 - Escalon's network mask
```

Each position with a 9 is a country code. An 8 signifies a city code. A 7 signifies a unit code. It is easy to see that both San Francisco and Escalon have one digit devoted to a country code—not surprising, since they are in the same country—and different numbers of digits devoted to city and unit codes. Armed with a telephone address and a network mask, you can identify the parts of this telephone addressing system.

Well, real network addressing works the same way. Each address has a network part (signified by *N*) and a computer part (signified by *C*). Networks come in three sizes: large, medium, and small—known in techo-geek-speak as class *A*, *B*, and *C*. Table 3.1 shows what they look like.

Table 3.1. Network numbers.

Class	Format	First Number	Maximum Computers
A	N.C.C.C.	1–126	16,387,064
B	N.N.C.C.	128–191	64,516
C	N.N.N.C.	192–254	254

Note: There are gaps in the first number. The numbers 0 and 255 are missing; they have special meanings in IP addresses and should never be used. Additionally, 127 might have a special meaning; you should avoid using it in the first number.

Because IP addresses use fixed-width fields, you don't need a mask to figure out how many digits describe the network part and the computer part. Just look at the first number; it tells you. I wouldn't have gone through the trouble of showing a mask in the hypothetical telephone scheme, however, if it didn't benefit you in some way.

When a network administrator wants to divide the maximum number of computers in her class of addresses into smaller chunks—a process called *subnetting*—she uses a subnet mask.

Consider the IP address 140.174.229.7. The first number, 140, tells you that this is a class B address. Therefore, the mask would be NNN.NNN.CCC.CCC. What if the network administrator wants to make two smaller networks, perhaps one for Engineering and another for Administration? She would use part of the computer part as part of the network part—for example, NNN.NNN.CCC.CCC. How does this help her? She gets two completely separate networks—traffic from one won't swamp the other—but she loses the addressing capacity of the original big network. The subnet mask for the 140.174.229.7 IP address is 255.255.255.0. Remember that 255 is a special number. Therefore, you know to interpret the IP address as a class C address with 254 possible siblings on the same network.

Why all this blather about network masks? Isn't it just like calculus—vaguely interesting to geeks but never used by mortals? No. Knowing your subnet mask is vital to communicating on the Internet. You don't have to know what it means, but it will put you one up on those poor folks who don't understand a thing about the magic going on. Your Internet service provider can tell you the appropriate subnet mask for your connection.

> **Note:** There is absolutely no reason that you or your network administrator needs to follow the standards described throughout this book. As long as things are consistent across your site, everything will work well. If you ever want to connect to the Internet, however, woe be to you. Following standards frees you up to worry about things that really matter.

A minor note to satisfy the gods of pedantry: Some site administrators have the reverse problem. Instead of breaking down a large address into subnets, they have more machines than can fit in the address space that they have been allocated. These days, because of the demand for network addresses, it is practically impossible to get anything bigger than a class C address. When this happens, the administrator gets an adjacent block of network numbers and supernets them together. I have never seen it, but I have heard of it.

Using Names Instead of Numbers

Right now you are probably thinking, "The Internet has been around in one form or another since the Sixties and Seventies. Is this the best these people can do?" The answer is no. (The minutes you have spent reading the last section will, however, put you in good stead.) Most computers on the Internet use names instead of numbers.

The machine that I have been using as an example (140.174.229.7) is known as terra. This is the style of name used in the early days of the ARPANET—a single-part name. There was a master list of computers on the net—a solution that worked

with only a few computers. Imagine the difficulties in trying to create unique names for millions of computers, not to mention maintaining and delivering the list to all those machines.

The solution was to use multiple-part names. This scheme called the Domain Name System, or DNS. Under this system, terra is known as terra.sirius.com. terra belongs to my Internet service provider, Sirius Communications. What does com mean? Table 3.2 gives the answer.

Table 3.2. Rightmost name elements in the United States.

Name	Example	Meaning
com	jungle.com	Commercial ventures and businesses
edu	mit.edu	Educational institutions of all levels
gov	jpl.nasa.gov	Governmental organizations and departments
int	undp.int	International organizations
mil	dockmaster.mil	U.S. military
net	clark.net	Network-related organizations
org	acm.org	Anything else, including nonprofit organizations and professional societies

Elsewhere in the world, for the most part, the rightmost name element is the country code.

Even though DNS started in the era of uppercase letters, during the heydey of FORTRAN and COBOL, lowercase can be used for computer names. Because the case is irrelevant, you often see some strange combinations. For example, Sirius' mail server once decided that it wanted to be sirius.COM.

Putting It All Together

You understand how computers have a unique identity in their community—be it a small two-machine network or the global Internet. Now it is time to tie it all together. How do *you* get on the Internet?

You must provide your computer with a way of physically connecting to the Internet. Most commonly, this is a modem from home and a wired network at the office. These are discussed in Chapter 4, "Hardware." Then you have to get your computer speaking TCP/IP, which is covered in Chapter 5, "Software." After you have done that, dial your modem if you are using one.

Hardware

This chapter is about the hardware that you can use to connect your computer to the Internet, to capture and send video and audio, and to listen to audio that others are sending to you.

After you read this chapter, you will know

- What hardware you can use to connect your computer to the Internet
- How to capture and send video and audio
- How to listen to audio that others are sending to you

Because of the rapidly-changing nature of the computer industry, I deal mostly with concepts and explanatory examples in this chapter. Trying to present the entire state of the art today would be both strenuous and futile; by the time you read this, less expensive, smaller, and niftier devices will be available. Speak to the people on the e-mail lists and surf the web sites for up-to-the-minute information. There are, however, some sources for additional continually updated information on the Internet.

ISDN

- Yahoo's directory at http://www.yahoo.com/Computers_and_Internet/Networking_and_Communications/ISDN/
- news:comp.dcom.isdn

 **Internet TV with CU-SeeMe**

- FAQ at http://www.cis.ohio-state.edu/hypertext/faq/usenet/isdn-faq/faq.html
- ISDN User's Guide by Pacific Bell at http://www.pacbell.com/isdn/book/

Regional Bells

- Ameritech http:://www.ameritech.com/
- Bell Atlantic http://www.bell-atl.com/
- Bellcore - Bell Communications Research http://www.bellcore.com/
- BellSouth http://www.bst.bls.com/
- NYNEX http://www.nynex.com/
- Pacific Bell http://www.pacbell.com/
- Southwestern Bell http://www.sbc.com/
- US West http://www.uswest.com/

Modems

- Yahoo's directory at http://www.yahoo.com/Computers_and_Internet/Hardware/Peripherals/Modems/
- news:comp.dcom.modems
- Tutorial at http://www.racal.com/dcom/modem.tutorial.html
- High Speed Modem Page at http://www.teleport.com/~curt/modems.html

Sound Cards

- Yahoo's directory at http://www.yahoo.com/Computers_and_Internet/Hardware/Peripherals/Sound_Cards/
- GFX News at http://www.rpi.edu/~hsiaoe/soundsite/soundsite.html
- news:comp.sys.ibm.pc.soundcard.advocacy

Video

- Quickcam at http://www.connectix.com/
- Macintosh AV FAQ at http://www.csua.berkeley.edu/~jwang/AV/AV_Video.html
- news:comp.multimedia
- news:comp.compression
- news:comp.dsp
- news:rec.video
- news:ucb.digital-video

Connectivity Hardware

There are basically two methods of connecting your computer to the Internet: a direct connection to a network (such as the Ethernet you might have in your office) and a dial-up connection (via a modem or an Integrated Services Digital Network device). Only dial-up devices are discussed here; direct connections would be handled by your site administrator.

Modems

Most people have a passing acquaintance with modems. The word *modem* comes from its function: modulator-demodulator. Digital data, which is what your computer uses, is converted—modulated—into analog audio data, is sent over the wires of the telephone system, and is converted back—demodulated—into digital data for another computer to enjoy. Modems are connected to your computer's serial port—the Printer port or Modem port of a Macintosh or the COM port of a PC.

The price of modems has plummeted from the $700 that I paid a few years ago for a 9,600 baud unit to about $150 for the top-of-the-line 28,800 baud unit that I just acquired.

Keep the following points in mind if you are purchasing a modem. Modern modems transfer data at a base rate of 28,800 bits per second. They may be able to achieve higher rates, depending on the data being transferred and the type of compression negotiated with the other modem during the dial-up phase. You want a modem that supports communications in the 14.4–28.8 kbps range, V.42 error correction, and V.42bis data compression. Look on the box to make sure the modem uses the V.32terbo/V.32bis, V.34, and V.32 standards.

ISDN

Integrated Services Digital Network, or ISDN, is a hot property these days. Who wouldn't want an affordable higher-speed connection to the Internet? Anyone who is using Internet videoconferencing certainly covets more bandwidth through which to pump multiple audio/video streams. Unfortunately, many people don't understand what ISDN can do and how much it can cost. These misunderstandings, often unwittingly promoted by ISDN providers themselves, have led to a collection of myths surrounding this exciting technology. This section will clear up some of these misconceptions.

Internet TV with CU-SeeMe

What Does ISDN Mean to Me?

At the most basic level, ISDN means you have a faster connection to the Internet. You can transmit more information per second— because there is greater bandwidth. This "bigger pipe" to the Internet is the up side.

The down side is the added costs. You have to spend money on extra connection hardware—what is commonly referred to as an ISDN modem—and you have to spend some time configuring your system to use the new technology. You also must pay more per month in access and usage fees.

For example, in San Francisco, I can get unlimited 28.8 kbps modem access through my Internet service provider for $15 per month. ISDN access consists of a $30 per month basic service fee through Pac Bell, a one-cent per minute charge for the connection during the business day, and a fee from my Internet service provider that is based upon the type of service. On-demand access is charged by the minute; dedicated around-the-clock access costs about $200 per month.

What Is ISDN?

As its name implies, ISDN is a digital network that you can extend into your home or office with a minimum of added equipment. The primary advantage of ISDN is its capability to carry far more data than the fastest modems can. ISDN gives you the same kind of flexibility and connectivity that you have in a wired office, but you don't have to change out of your pajamas.

The brute-force aspect of ISDN—the higher speed of data transmission—alone is enough to spur advances in and acceptance of technologies and strategies such as telecommuting (I love working wireless to an ISDN connection from a cafe), videoconferencing (CU-SeeMe sings over my ISDN connection), teleteaching and remote broadcasting (something that CU-SeeMe users have seen for years but is now available to everyone), interactive network games (finally, to play Marathon with the people stationed in Antarctica), and a variety of medical applications.

Because of its design, users of ISDN can have two voice or data conversations and one packet-switched conversation (such as a stock-market ticker tape, a credit card approval, or a connection to the Internet) going at the same time over one basic ISDN connection. Depending on the capabilities of your telephone provider's central office switch, it is also possible to run eight devices—computers, fax machines, telephones, and so on—with up to 64 separate phone numbers over that same basic ISDN connection. This is great news for small businesses that don't want to be playing around in their telephone closet all day long and would rather concentrate on doing business.

Because the world's digital and analog telephone systems are already interconnected by the telephone companies, your phone-over-ISDN can make and receive calls from ordinary analog telephones all over the world. What I am talking about here is a switched digital system that enables you to initiate high-speed communications with telephones and computer networks anywhere.

ISDN costs differ greatly based on your provider (Ameritech, Pacific Bell, etc), your location (extra surcharges), and your ISP. So beware that ISDN might not be a cost-effective choice. It's a great advance in communication technology but potentially out of reach for the average consumer.

For further information on ISDN hardware visit:

- ISDN*tek at http://isdntek.com/i
- Motorola at http://www.mot.com/MIMS/ISG/
- SCii Telecom at http://www.scii.co.uk/scii/
- US Robotics at http://www.usr.com/isdnrel.html
- ZyXEL at http://www.zyxel.com/html/elitei.html
- Index of other hardware vendors at http://alumni.caltech.edu/~dank/isdn/isdn_hw.html

Contact numbers for the major providers of ISDN

- Ameritech 1-800-TEAMDATA
- Bell Atlantic 1-800-570-ISDN
- Bellcore - Bell Communications Research 1-800-521-CORE
- BellSouth 1-800-858-9413
- NYNEX
- Pacific Bell 1-800-4PB-ISDN
- Southwestern Bell 1-800-SWB-ISDN
- US West 1-800-898-9675

What Hardware Do I Need for ISDN?

The twisted pair of copper wires coming into your house—the same wire that has been used since the days of switchboard operators ("Murray Hill 5-9000, please")—is sufficient for an ISDN connection. Some really antiquated homes and buildings might need rewiring, but most places in the United States are ISDN-ready.

Out of your control—and a requirement for ISDN connectivity—is a suitably equipped digital switching system in your telephone provider's central office. If it has AT&T 5ESS or Northern Telecom DMS-100 digital systems, you are probably in luck. (In San Francisco, ISDN is a victim of its own success. Digital switches are available, but the demand for ISDN is saturating the central offices' ability to provide for everyone, which leads to a delay of several months in getting service.)

Internet TV with CU-SeeMe

On your side of the telephone jack, you need one of each of the following:

- A Network Termination Device—known in the the trade as an NT1. It is the interface between the telephone company's connection to your home or office and your ISDN segment.
- A power supply for your local ISDN segment.
- A Terminal Adapter, to which you attach your computer, fax machine, videocamera, and so on.

The most common solution for Internet tinkerers is to purchase an all-in-one box.

Important Features of ISDN

As with most things in the networking world, ISDN is a collection of standard protocols that providers around the world have adopted for the sake of interoperability. ISDN is a standard promulgated by the CCITT (the International Telephone and Telegraph Consultative Committee), a body that was recently renamed the Telecommunications Standards Bureau of the International Telecommunications Union. You will see the acronym CCITT/ITU-TSB on ISDN documentation.

> **Standards Are Not**
>
> Of course, what follows all proclamations of standard protocols is the disclaimer. There are variations in the ISDN service provided by AT&T, the regional Bell operating companies, and other countries. Efforts are underway—driven by Bell Laboratories Research Company (Bellcore)—to bring all providers in compliance with a national standard and, sometime thereafter, into compliance with the CCITT/ITU-TSB standard. Ask your potential ISDN provider for the gory details in your area.

Now examine the characteristics of ISDN. Its distinguishing features set it markedly apart from the modem access that you are used to.

- ISDN handles many devices on a single line.

    Up to eight ISDN-savvy computers, fax machines, or telephones can be connected to a single ISDN line. They can be assigned up to 64 different telephone numbers—what your telephone company salesman terms *call appearances*. In fact, one of the choices that you will face is whether to keep your non-ISDN telephone connection once your house is ISDN-connected.

- ISDN is built from modular—and extendible—transmission channels.

  All ISDN implementations are built on a modular design that combines a number of Bearer channels and a supporting Data channel. The Bearer, or B, channels are high-speed conduits for things such as the human voice and computer data, including CU-SeeMe audio and video streams. Each ISDN connection has one Data, or D, channel to carry call setup, coordination, synchronization, signalling data, and so on—things that users never see.

  ISDN carrying capacity is based on the number of Bearer channels the connection is configured to use. This configuration can change dynamically, depending on the load on the system.

- ISDN supports multiple simultaneous conversations.

  ISDN allows one voice or data conversation per Bearer channel and one data-only conversation on the Data channel. This gives you the same kind of capacity that previously would have required multiple drops from the telephone company, with a monthly charge for each one.

- ISDN can vary its carrying capacity.

  Bearer channels can be combined to carry more data—something that your telephone company salesman calls *inverse multiplexing* or *bonding*. You can combine Bearer channels for a specific heavy load—for example, for a multiple audio and video stream event like a rock concert—and later break them down into their normal configuration, assuming that you have lots of Bearer channels. Your ISDN provider also provides you with even more carrying capacity, if your normal setup is one or two Bearer channels, for a fee.

- ISDN uses switched digital connections.

  In the old days, you had two choices for communications connectivity: flexible inexpensive arrangements using comparatively low-speed modems or inflexible expensive high-speed connections via dedicated leased lines. ISDN gives you the best of both worlds: dialed digital access to the world-wide telecommunications network.

Your ISDN Hookup

ISDN is a combination of a number of Bearer channels and one coordinating Data channel. Each Bearer channel carries 64 kbps that you can use for dialed voice and data transfer. The capacity of the Data channel varies; it must be wide enough to carry all the coordinating information required by the Bearer channels. It's typically 16 kbps. The D channel is known as a *packet-switched call set-up and signalling connection*.

Internet TV with CU-SeeMe

> **Standards Are Not**
>
> The most common deviation from the CCITT/ITU-TSB ISDN protocol standard is where the D channel call-signalling information is transmitted. The standard calls for that information to be sent out of band, through a separate telephone network specifically designed for worldwide transmission of call-signalling information. This out-of-band network is known to your ISDN provider as Signaling System 7, or SS7.
>
> Instead, many ISDN providers transmit this information in band, through the Bearer channels. This results in a 64 kbps Bearer channel having a working capacity of 56 kbps. PacBell currently suffers from this configuration. It claims that SS7 is functional throughout California. Call-signalling information will soon be moved out of band to the Data channel, and Bearer channels will be able to carry a full 64 kbps each.

Basic Rate Interface

Basic Rate Interface, or BRI, is the basic home ISDN connection. Defined as two 64 kbps Bearer channels and one coordinating 16 kbps Data channel, BRI is also known as a 2B+D connection.

The two Bearer channels can be inverse multiplexed—that is, combined—to carry data at 112 kbps or 128 kbps, depending on whether the Data channel call-signalling information is carried in band or out of band.

Primary Rate Interface

Primary Rate Interface, or PRI, is more common in larger organizations because of its greater capacity and cost. PRI configuration varies geographically. In the United States, a PRI connection is defined as twenty-three 64 kbps Bearer channels and one coordinating 64 kbps Data channel. PRI is also known as a 23B+D connection. With a total carrying capacity of 1.544 mbps, a PRI is transmitted through a standard North American T-1 line, which might physically be nothing more than one pair of twisted copper wires.

In Europe and the Pacific Rim countries, a PRI connection is defined as thirty or thirty-one 64 kbps Bearer channels and one 64 kbps Data channel—in other words, 30B+D or 31B+D. It is delivered through a standard 2.048 E-1 line.

Even though regional, national, and international variations in ISDN configurations and service exist, interoperability among variations is available to customers.

Connectivity Options

You have several options for your ISDN service. Your decision will be based on a combination of the bandwidth capacity that you want delivered over ISDN and the carrying capacity of your pocketbook. (It is important to factor in the cost savings derived from using ISDN in a business setting.)

- A single BRI from the central-office switch.

    The so-called "home ISDN" is typically a single BRI connection delivered from the telephone company's ISDN-ready central office switch. The 2B+D line connects to the Network Termination Device in your house, beyond which you create and maintain a local network of one or more devices.

    You should check with your Internet service provider for the terms of service. The charge for one to four computers generating some traffic is usually different from the charge for an entire campus' or division's population of 400 computers. The number of individual addressable devices varies among all-in-one ISDN boxes. Your provider can help you purchase the equipment that best suits your needs.

- Multiple BRIs from the central office switch.

    A business or household that requires greater bandwidth can obtain multiple BRIs from the telephone company's ISDN-ready central office switch. These 2B+D lines can connect directly with ISDN-savvy equipment, a Network Termination Device, or with a Public Branch Exchange (PBX) system. A PBX system has the advantage of allowing in-house devices, such as ISDN-based telephones, to communicate with one another without having to initiate an outside call to the central office switch. Of course, multiple computers can be inexpensively networked together in house through an Ethernet.

- BRIs through ISDN Centrex service at the central office.

    The telephone company's ISDN-ready central office switch can also have Centrex capability. This has the advantage of connecting all your users without necessitating the purchase or lease of an on-site PBX system. Additionally, your provider might be able to link together physically separate locations with Centrex service—as long as all the locations are near to the same central office—which further reduces your costs.

- A PRI from the central office switch.

    You can also get a 23B+D PRI connection from the telephone company's ISDN-ready central office switch. By connecting through a PBX or other control device, such a setup provides Bearer channels as needed throughout your organization. The control device can be a combination of gateways, routers, multiplexers, or ISDN controllers—in a configuration designed to distribute the load evenly across your network and to reduce congestion at the point of connection.

Internet TV with CU-SeeMe

One State's Plans for ISDN

Pacific Bell, my telephone provider, has announced a $16 billion plan to expand its in-state digital network. The program, named California First, calls for the laying of high-speed fiber optic network cable throughout the state and the replacement of the copper telephone lines that serve California's millions of businesses and residences before the end of this century.

Even before then, PacBell's Education First program will bring four ISDN lines to each of California's public and private K-12 schools, public libraries, and community colleges by the end of 1996. One of these lines can be used for telecomputing and the rest for interactive telelearning.

To make sure all parties that are connected as a result of this expansion have something to do, Pacific Bell created the California Research and Education Network (CalREN) in 1993 to fund and stimulate the development of new applications for high-speed data communications services. PacBell's ISDN user's guide reads,

> Through a competitive selection process, CalREN funds collaborative projects whose applications revolutionize the ways organizations communicate and share information. CalREN application development work will establish a foundation for broadband services including state-of-the-art telemedicine research, diagnosis, and treatment; online schools with no geography, distance, or resource constraints; electronic democracy in the form of online, real-time interaction between government and citizens; and new business partnerships and ventures made possible by vast information storage, retrieval, and sharing capabilities.

What is most interesting to me about PacBell's plans is that the ISDN to your house and mine is just the "fast" lane on the information superhighway. "Faster" and "fastest" lanes are already paved.

> "Fast" is Integrated Services Digital Network (ISDN) and Switched Digital Service-56 (SDS-56). This lane operates at speeds up to 144 kilobits per second and is suited to a wide range of uses. These include access to the Internet, images, and stored video; certain types of medical imaging and remote diagnosis; electronic democracy; desktop videoconferencing; and telecommuting. "Faster" is Switched Multimegabit Data Service (SMDS) and Frame Relay. This lane operates at speeds up to 1.544 million bits per second. It is best used for applications such as computer-assisted design and manufacturing, and animation. "Fastest" is Asynchronous Transfer Mode or ATM Cell Relay. This portion of the superhighway is able to transmit data, voice, and video at up to 155 million bits per second today. This service will evolve to the gigabit or billion bits per second range. It is designed for applications that use data, audio, image, and

video within the same network. Possible uses include remote medical diagnostics, interactive scientific and industrial design, high-definition imaging, and virtual reality.

Video Hardware

CU-SeeMe, as an Internet videoconferencing tool, benefits greatly from the use of a videocamera—or, more commonly, simply *camera*—by the participants, although a camera isn't required. To date, most computing systems don't come packaged with a camera installed and ready for use. With the prices of both cameras and 28.8 kbps modems plummeting, look for that to change. The evolving development of consumer-based cameras is resulting in an ease of use that rivals modems for their plug-and-play simplicity. Soon there will be no excuse for being without a camera.

There are two basic types of cameras:

- Dedicated digital cameras that you buy at a computer and plug directly into your computer
- General-purpose analog cameras, such as the ones that you use to make home videotapes to show to friends and relatives

The difference to you is money. This will become clearer as I walk you through how a camera interacts with your computer. Consider how you see. A scene, illuminated by a light source—such as the sun or the fluoescent tubes in your office—scatters light, some of which falls on the outer lens of your eye. That light is focused on your retina, an array of sensitive biological devices that converts the light energy into pulses that travel through the optic nerve to your brain, where scene-processing takes place.

Compare that to a dedicated digital camera. A scene, illuminated by a light source—such as the sun or the fluorescent tubes in your office—scatters light, some of which falls on the outer lens of your camera. That light is focused on a charge-coupled device, an array of sensitive hardware devices that converts the light energy into pulses that travel through a wire to your computer, where scene-processing takes place.

The general-purpose analog camera adds one more step. It uses a digital-to-analog (D/A) converter to convert the digital signals generated by the CCD into analog pulses for use by a television or video-cassette recorder. If you are using a general-purpose analog camera for videoconferencing use, you must reverse this last step with a analog-to-digital (A/D) converter.

 **Internet TV with CU-SeeMe**

If you already own a general-purpose camera, it might be more cost-effective to purchase a video capture card for your computer. If you own no cameras at all, it will be much cheaper to purchase a dedicated camera, which today costs less than $100 for a grayscale camera.

Dedicated Cameras

The best-known dedicated camera is QuickCam, by Connectix. Currently available for Macintosh and now for Windows machines, QuickCam is an all-in-one camera about the size of a golf ball. It is inexpensive and simple to connect and operate. It works with software that uses QuickTime or Video for Windows and connects to your Macintosh via a serial cable to your Printer or Modem port, or your PC via the parallel port.

Technically, QuickCam

- Provides images up to 320 by 240 pixels in 4-bit gray—that is, 16 shades of gray.
- Operates at up to 15 frames per second, depending on the horsepower of your Macintosh.
- Draws power from your Macintosh's serial port or your PC's parallel port.
- Has an on-board microphone. Using it, however, makes the audio bits compete with the video bits for the serial cable bandwidth. Use your Macintosh's built-in or add-on microphone or your sound card's Microphone input.
- Has a field of view of about 65 degrees, or the equivalent of a 38mm lens of your 35mm camera.
- Is a fixed-focus—that is, 18 inches to infinity—camera with a maximum lens speed of f1.9.

A color version is reputed to be in the works.

QuickCam works with any Macintosh that has at least a Motorola 68020 processor, one available serial port on the motherboard, 4M of RAM, hard disk space available for the supporting software and the pictures and movies that result. Likewise, the operating system must be at least System 7.0. Therefore, QuickCam doesn't work with

>The Portable
>The Macintosh 128 and 512
>The Mac Plus and SE
>The original Mac Classic

QuickCam doesn't work with Apple Unix (A/UX).

> **What Goes Around Comes Around**
>
> QuickCam is manufactured by a manufacturing subcontractor of Connectix in Fremont, California, in the building that housed Apple Computer's old factory, where many Macintosh innovations first saw the light of day. A fitting place to be making cameras.

QuickCam's supporting software includes

- Audio and video drivers—known as *extentions* to Macintosh users
- QuickPICT, an application for creating still pictures
- QuickMovie, an application for creating and editing QuickTime movies
- QuickSaver, an After Dark-compatible screen saver module.

QuickCam is distributed worldwide by distributors affiliated with Connectix. It is currently approved for export to NAFTA signatories, members of the European Common Council (and those countries that allow CE-approved devices), and Japan.

In Chapter 1, I covered the basic differences between video transmission standards such as NTSC, PAL, and SECAM. QuickCam works on Macintoshes running an internationalized version of its operating system because it uses direct digital video. It also works on all QuickTime-compatible Macintoshes. Because it draws its power from the computer, you do not need special power adapters. The higher-level software that you use, such as a particular videoconferencing tool, might have limitations with regard to which video transmission standards are supported.

You will see QuickCam again in Chapter 8, "Usage." Several people have set up World Wide Web pages to display scenes in their homes and offices. You can find more information about QuickCam and CU-SeeMe in Appendix A, "Troubleshooting."

General-Purpose Videocameras

Using a general-purpose videocamera, which outputs analog signals, results in an extra conversion step. Buying a video capture card for your computer might be the most economical way of leveraging an existing investment in a videocamera.

Macintosh users have few choices in video capture boards. The discontinued VideoSpigot continues to be a favorite, even though Radius has left those customers without support as it pushes a much more expensive video solution.

Windows users have more choices. Albert Foo, of the Missouri Research and Education Network at the University of Missouri at Columbia, maintains a list of video capture boards and how they work with CU-SeeMe for Windows. The list

Internet TV with CU-SeeMe

sometimes changes, so you might want to check out my Web site for updated information. Contact information for the board manufacturers is available at the Web site.

The Cornell CU-SeeMe site also includes Albert's latest list at the URL http://cu-seeme.cornell.edu/supportedwin.html. The online list also contains pricing information.

Table 4.1 lists video capture boards that work with CU-SeeMe.

Table 4.1. Video capture boards that work with CU-SeeMe.

Board	*Manufacturer*	*Remarks*
Video Spigot	Radius	Discontinued
Video Blaster FS200	Creative Labs	
Video Blaster SE100	Creative Labs	
ComputerEyes RT	Digital Vision	
ComputerEyes 1024	Digital Vision	
Screen Machine Classic	(unknown)	
miroVideo DC1 TV	miro Computer Products	
Reveal tv300	Reveal	
Orchid Vidiola Pro/D	Orchid Technology	
Win/TV	Hauppauge Computer Works	
Cinema/TV	Hauppauge Computer Works	
Celebrity/TV	Hauppauge Computer Works	
HighQ	Hauppauge Computer Works	
Targa Plus 16, 32, and 64	TrueVision	
Movie Blaster	(unknown)	
MediaPro+	Rombo	
Captivator	VideoLogic	
WatchIT! Pro	New Media Graphics	

Table 4.2 lists video capture boards that don't work with CU-SeeMe.

Table 4.2. Video capture boards that don't work with CU-SeeMe.

Board	Manufacturer
Intel Smart Video Recorder Pro	Intel
Intel Smart Video Recorder PCVD1000	Intel
Video Blaster RT300	Creative Labs
SNAPplus VL	Cardinal Technologies
Pro Movie Studio, Pro Movie Spectrum	MediaVision

Table 4.3 lists popular video capture boards that have not been tested yet.

Table 4.3. Popular video capture boards that have not been tested yet.

Board	Manufacturer
Reveal VC500	Reveal
Video Blaster MP400	Creative Labs
WaveWatcher TV-II	Aztech International
Megamotion	Alpha Systems Lab
Video Basic	ATI Technologies
Video-It!	ATI Technologies
Video Galaxy Gamma	Aztech Labs
VideoStar Pro	Diamond Multimedia Systems
ComputerEyes/VLB	Digital Vision
Movie Machine Pro	Fast Electronic U.S.
Picture Perfect Pro	In-Motion
MovieMan	Logitech
Marvel II	Matrox
Marvel	Matrox
Vidiola	Orchid Technology
Maxmedia VR	UMAX Technologies
Maxmedia MR Pro	UMAX Technologies
VideoPacker Plus	VIC Hi-Tech Corp
MovieWave Studio	MultiWave Technology

Audio Hardware

CU-SeeMe for Macintosh currently supports audio input only if you are using a Macintosh with a built-in audio input facility. You must be able to plug your microphone directly into the back of your Macintosh. Audio input will not work on a Mac IIci or earlier Macintosh that doesn't have a built-in microphone jack, or with the MacRecorder or QuickCam's built-in audio. People are working on getting non-built-in audio input working for the Macintosh versions of CU-SeeMe.

Macintosh users have several choices of input devices:

- The external microphone or the PlainTalk microphone that is appropriate to your machine.

  David Reider, a music education specialist at Bolt Beranek & Newman, says, "I'm implementing music education curricula over the Net, through MIDI transfer, and in workshops and lessons with CU-SeeMe. I have weekly conferences with a student in Seoul, Korea—I'm in Cambridge, Massachusetts—and the PlainTalk microphone (on a Mac 840AV) works perfectly—no problems. I even sing and play musical keyboard examples to him."

- The built-in microphone.

  My PowerBook 520c has a microphone built into the flip-up video panel.

- Third-party microphones, such as Jabra's EarPhone Streamline.

  John Vittal, the manager of the Adaptive Systems department of GTE Laboratories, says, "It's gotten to the point that the only device that I use on my Mac is the Jabra unless I'm just listening/lurking. Then I *might* switch to some external speakers—mostly it's a volume issue, since the speakers have an internal amp built in so that I can really jack up the gain if needed. The Jabra is better than a phone—because it's hands-free—but it's not stereo. Depending on the situation, this may be a problem."

  Howard Upchurch notes, "Radio Shack Nova 42 headphones do a fine job."

  Another contributor says, "I have one of those fancy AudioVision monitors here at work on a PowerPC Macintosh 6100/60AV, and its built-in microphone works with CU-SeeMe."

- Your general-purpose videocamera's microphone.

  Børre Ludvigsen, whose home on the Net is littered with videocameras says, "I use the built-in microphone on my camcorder that has both video-out and audio-out RCA plugs. The video goes into my Video Spigot board. The audio goes onto one of those Mac audio yokes with 2 RCA female plugs on the yoke and a short wire with a small male phono-style plug to be plugged into the Macintosh."

Hardware

Jan Engvald of the Lund University Computing Center, says, "We are using a PowerPC Macintosh 7100/80AV connected to a videocasette recorder (VCR) for sending taped lectures and the like. I've found that to avoid hearing that unpleasant *tch* sound when there is that *sss* sound in the input source material, I need a low-pass filter between the VCR and the Mac. I'm using a 11 kHz 12 dB/octav LC-filter, but it should probably need even more attenuation for best result."

One CU-SeeMe discussion list contributor was having uncommonly good luck. "We have plugged in VCLs, the TV signal from our Public Broadcasting System TV station, both Macintosh microphones, and an audio synthesiser. I've been able to get to work anything that I can plug into my Macintosh 840AV and get sound out.

Steve Meloan, a freelance journalist who writes about CU-SeeMe, notes that you can send audio even without a camera. Chapter 6, "CU-SeeMe User's Guide," shows the proper settings for sending audio.

Windows

CU-SeeMe for Windows recently had audio support added. Many people have had great success with the audio support. Fortunately for Windows users, any sound input device that has a Windows driver will work. You don't have to worry about whether your computer has a built-in microphone or not (most PC's don't come with built-in audio anyway). So if you can get sound into your computer with another Windows application, 99% of the time it will work with CU-SeeMe.

The only issue with your soundcard is whether it supports full-duplex audio in and out. Unlike the Macintosh side of things, where all built-in audio is full-duplex, the majority of sound cards for Windows are half-duplex. What this means is your sound card can't input and output audio at the same time. A walkie-talkie or CB radio is a good example of a half-duplex device. You can't speak while the other person is speaking. The telephone on the other hand is full-duplex. You can speak at the same time as the other person. There are full-duplex audio cards available for the PC. Unfortunately, one of the most common sound cards for the PC, the SoundBlaster, is only half-duplex. So if you are one of the many people who has this card, you are out of luck. It will work, but you'll have to watch cutting each other off. It's actually quite difficult to figure out whether your sound card is full or half duplex because most vendors don't put it in their product specifications. So you will have to either talk directly to technical support or try it firsthand with CU-SeeMe. Here is a list of a few sound cards that information was available for that are full-duplex or half-duplex.

Full-duplex

- MediaVision Pro Audio Spectrum 16
- Half-duplex
- SoundBlaster 8
- SoundBlaster 16
- SoundBlaster AWE32

The audio encoding method used seems to require more bandwidth than is available from a 14.4 kbps modem—not to mention the infeasability of simultaneously transmitting audio and video. Cross-platform audioconferencing software that uses more aggressive compression algorithms are one way by which you can speak with others across the Internet. Chapter 9, "Other Videoconferencing Technologies," has pointers to software that may help you.

Matthew Sanderson says that over a 14.4 kbps modem connection, using compressed SLIP, the audio-capable CU-SeeMe for Windows version that he is testing "has produced exactly one intelligble word of English speech in about three months of use." The CU-SeeMe development team is working on improving audio in both the Macintosh and Windows versions, as are third-party software developers. Audio transmission will improve only as better algorithms that use the limited bandwidth available from slow modem connections are widely adopted and as 28.8 kbps modems become more common.

Software

CHAPTER 5

In order to use any Internet videoconferencing audio or video software, you'll need to be connected to an IP network. The most common ways you'll be connected are directly (a wire attaches your computer to the network), via modem (you dial up and connect to an Internet service provider), or via ISDN (described in Chapter 4, "Hardware"). Less common methods include packet radio (enjoyed by amateur "ham" radio operators). A number of common issues face the Macintosh or Windows user who wants to connect to an IP network, so I'll cover the common ground first, and attack the platform-specific areas later.

Regardless of your connection method, you'll need to configure your TCP/IP software after you install it. Table 5.1 shows the information you'll need to get. I suggest you photocopy these pages, call your site administrator or Internet service provider, and fill in the blanks. Doing this ahead of time will make installing and configuring your network connection much less frustrating.

 Internet TV with CU-SeeMe

Table 5.1. TCP/IP connection information.

Item	Example
Connection method	Direct, modem, ISDN
Addressing method	Manual (aka "Static" or "Fixed") Server, Dynamic
IP address (if Manual)	X.X.X.X
Gateway address	X.X.X.X
Network class	A, B, or C
Subnet mask	255.255.255.0
Primary Nameserver	X.X.X.X
Secondary Nameserver	X.X.X.X
Your domain	jungle.com
NNTP news server	nntp.jungle.com
SMTP mail machine	smtp.jungle.com
POP account	cu-seeme-book@jungle.com
Email address	cu-seeme-book@jungle.com

Those of you using modems to connect to an IP network (typically via SLIP or PPP) will need the information shown in Table 5.2. Since you'll be getting this information from the same people, you might as well get it all at once.

Table 5.2. Modem connection information.

Item	Example	Your settings
Provider's phone number	555-1212	Who do you dial to get connected to the Net?
SLIP or PPP?	SLIP	What connection protocol will you be using? SLIP is also known as RFC 1066; PPP is also known as RFC 1661.

Item	Example	Your settings
Compressed headers?		Can you eke a bit more bandwidth by using compressed headers? This is also known as RFC 1144 TCP Header Compression, CSLIP, VJ SLIP, and Van Jacobsen SLIP. PPP communicates compressed header information during session negotiation; there's no such thing as CPPP (nor for that matter, CCCP).
Login (or Username)	Susername	How will your provider identify you? It's common to have a leading capital S or P to denote SLIP or PPP, respectively.
Password	cat7green	How will you "authenticate" yourself? The minute money or reputation is concerned (and your net connection has both) this becomes important.
MTU, MRU		What's the maximum transmit (or receive) unit size? Typical numbers for MTU are 1006 (SLIP) and 296 (CSLIP); for MRU expect to see 1500 for PPP.
Login procedure?		PPP typically requires no script; its negotiation procedure is "automagic." SLIP typically requires a script to understand what your provider's site is doing. A well-commented SLIP script (that I've used for years with my Internet service provider) may be found at (PUT URL HERE).

Whew! Time to take a rest. Hopefully you were able to get all the necessary information. Now we divide the Macintosh and Windows users.

 **Internet TV with CU-SeeMe**

Macintosh

TCP/IP has come a long way on Macintosh since the first release of MacTCP. MacTCP 2.0.6, the current, and probably last release of MacTCP, offers rather robust TCP/IP connectivity with a few eccentricities. (Some might say "bizarre quirks.") In autumn 1995, Apple will phase out the existing, separate, packages for AppleTalk and MacTCP delivery. In their place will come *Open Transport for Macintosh*, delivering multiprotocol support in one package. This will be for both 68K Macintosh and Power Macintosh. Minimum system requirements will be

- System 7.0 or greater
- 68020 processor or more powerful
- 4MB RAM or greater

Open Transport will move into the MacOS mainstream, too.

- First as a component of the system software that ships with future Power Macintosh computers that include PCI bus. Open Transport v1.0 provides networking for these machines.
- Version 2 of Open Transport will become a part of the operating system for all supported Macintosh models, with the "Copland" OS reference release.

Open Transport may be obtained in many ways: it's part of many Macintosh system software releases (beginning with MacOS 7.5.2), it's a stand-alone software package, and it'll be licensed and available from many of your Internet service providers. But since MacTCP won't be going away just yet, I cover its use here as well.

These are the steps you'll take to get your Macintosh speaking TCP/IP:

1. Install the TCP/IP layer software—Open Transport or MacTCP
2. Install the modem layer software—one of several SLIP or PPP packages
3. Restart your Macintosh
4. Configure what you've just installed
5. If you've installed MacTCP, restart (so that it can build its MacTCP DNR document)

Installing Open Transport

Open Transport is a snap to install; it comes with its own installer. An Easy Install will result in two new control panels, AppleTalk and TCP/IP, and a variety of support files being placed into your System folder. If you're upgrading from MacTCP to Open Transport, be warned that the installation process will delete the MacTCP control panel. Please, before you install Open Transport, open up MacTCP and jot down the settings information.) After installation, you'll be prompted to restart your Macintosh.

Once you're back up and running, open the TCP/IP Control Panel (shown in Figure 5.1).

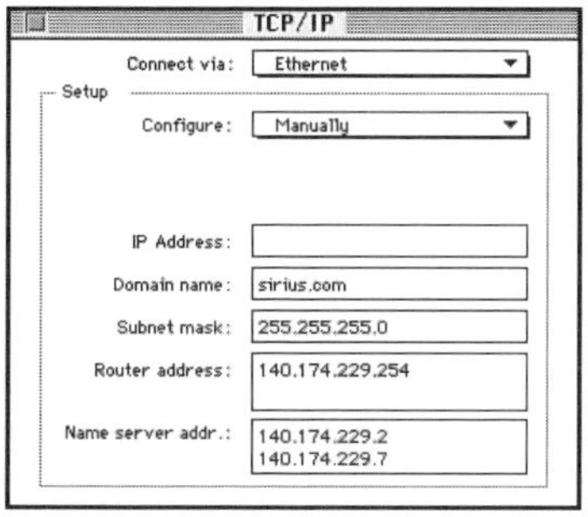

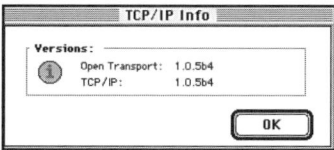

Figure 5.1. TCP/IP Control Panel.

This is the way you'll control your Macintosh's ability to speak TCP/IP to the outside world.

To start things, select Get Info from the File Menu. The version information window will appear. Note that I'm using Open Transport 1.0.5b4, the latest version available to beta-testers to date. By the time you read this, a release will be available. I don't expect the user interface to change, but if what you see on your screen doesn't match what you see here at least you'll know why. (An informed reader is a happy reader.)

Figure 5.2. TCP/IP Get Info window.

Open Transport is easy to configure, provided you have the requisite information. Starting from the top, I'll show you how I set up my TCP/IP Control Panel.

The Connect via pop-up menu displays the current connection paths that TCP/IP knows of. Depending upon your hardware and software configuration, you'll see options different from what appears here.

 **Internet TV with CU-SeeMe**

The Configure pop-up menu displays ways TCP/IP has of finding configuration information.

- The most common option is Manual—you enter configuration information directly into the TCP/IP Control Panel.

    Since I use server-based addressing (also known as "dynamic IP" addressing), my Macintosh receives its IP address when I connect. So I keep this box blank. All other configuration options will result in the IP Address text field looking like Figure 5.3.

    IP Address: < supplied by server >

Figure 5.3. One IP address configuration.

- If your site uses the Dynamic Host Configuration Protocol (DHCP), then your Macintosh requires the address of a DHCP server, from which it will get the configuration information it needs over the network.
- The Boot Protocol (BOOTP) is a predecessor to DHCP. BOOTP is sufficient to get the configuration information required. If your site is considering moving to a server-based configuration scheme like BOOTP and DHCP, the latter is preferred. DHCP is more powerful, more flexible, and can provide you with much more information about network resources than can BOOTP.
- Reverse Addressing Protocol Type (RARP) requires you type your provider's domain name into the Domain name text field.

    The subnet mask describes how addresses on a network are interpreted. (See Chapter 4 for an in-depth example.) Open Transport relies on being able to communicate with the network device that is the gateway between your local network and the outside world. This device is known to Open Transport as "the router." Type the subnet mask of your provider's gateway router into the Subnet mask text field.

- Type the IP address of your provider's gateway router into the Router address text field.

Lastly, Open Transport needs to know where it can find Domain Name Services to translate text machine names (like gildenstern.jungle.com) into numeric IP addresses (like 555.55.55.5.555).

When you're finished entering this information, close the TCP/IP Control Panel. You'll be asked whether you wish to save this configuration. Say yes. Uncharacteristically for a Macintosh application, you won't be prompted for a configuration name; Open Transport will name this configuration Default.

If your Macintosh speaks TCP/IP over several different networks, you'll have several different TCP/IP configurations. Choose Configurations from the File menu; the Configurations window will appear (see Figure 5.4).

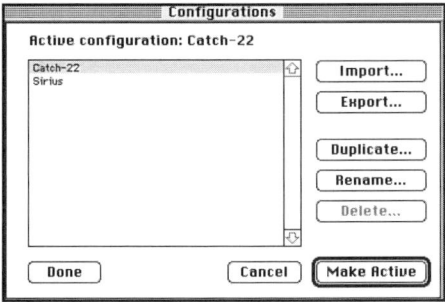

Figure 5.4. TCP/IP Configuration window.

I renamed Default to Sirius, and then created a new configuration named Catch-22, to reflect the settings I need to use in order to use another Internet service provider that I use in San Francisco. When you want to switch TCP/IP between different configurations (because you've moved from one network to another), you'll use the Configuration window to pick the current one. And you won't have to reboot your Macintosh for the new choice to become active. That's right, you can switch between radically different configurations "on the fly," without rebooting. (Thank you Open Transport development team.)

To finish up Open Transport, here are a few odds and ends.

Select User Mode from the Edit menu. You'll be presented with the User Mode selection window (see Figure 5.5).

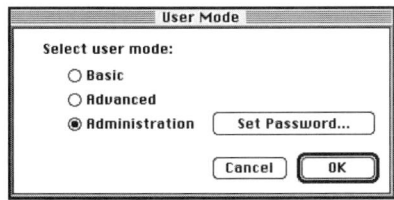

Figure 5.5. TCP/IP User Mode selection window.

- Basic mode is what almost everyone will use—the commonly tweaked items are within your grasp. It's all that I use in real life.
- Advanced mode provides you with more things to set. It's unlikely that you'll need them, but they're there.

 Internet TV with CU-SeeMe

- Administration mode allows you to use a password to lock down a TCP/IP configuration, perhaps for distribution to others in your organization. (Especially to those people who would fiddle around, change the settings, and then tell you that their computer is broken). Figure 5.6 shows the TCP/IP Administration configuration window. The padlock icons prevent that item from being changed.

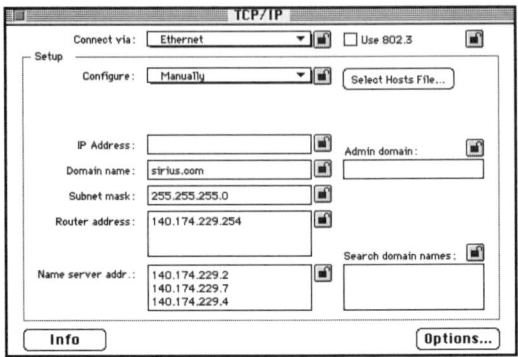

Figure 5.6. TCP/IP Administration configuration window.

Because you don't need to reboot after changing your TCP/IP configuration, you'll need to know when connectivity options are available to you. When you're using or configuring TCP/IP you'll be told things like AppleTalk is not available to you because it's inactive (see Figure 5.7), when it's not available to you because it's busy (see Figure 5.8), and when it finally becomes available to you (see Figure 5.9).

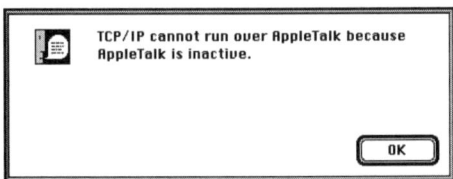

Figure 5.7. AppleTalk not active.

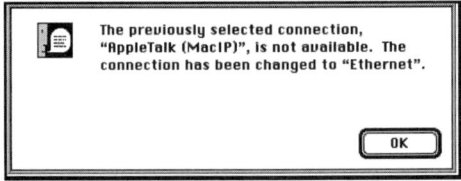

Figure 5.8. AppleTalk unavailable.

Software  73

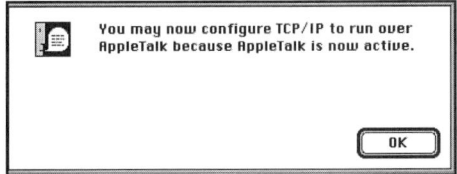

Figure 5.9. AppleTalk now available.

Open Transport lets you talk TCP/IP over an AppleTalk network. Figure 5.10 shows what the TCP/IP control panel looks like (and what you have to set up).

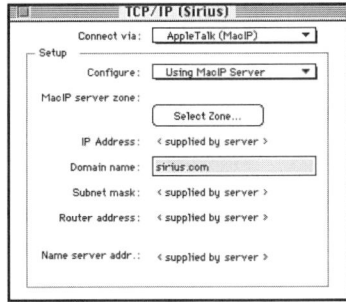

Figure 5.10. AppleTalk control panel.

Installing MacTCP

Historical note: I penned the great-great-grandmammy of this chapter in 1993, in a technical note entitled "Connecting your Macintosh to the Internet via TCP & SLIP." To see how far we've come since then, check out

`ftp://ftp.tidbits.com/pub/tidbits/tisk/info/installing-mactcp-interslip.txt"`.

Okay, on to MacTCP. Installing MacTCP is easy: drag the MacTCP control panel onto your System folder, or drag it directly into the Control Panels folder (which lives inside the System folder). Configuring MacTCP is a bit more involved.

Installing InterSLIP

Software that lets your computer speak TCP/IP over a modem is composed of an extension part (used by MacTCP) and a control part (used by you, the human).

Installing InterCon's InterSLIP requires that you place the extension part (named InterSLIP) into the Extensions folder inside the System folder, the control part (named InterSLIP Control) into the Control Panel folder inside the System folder, and an administrative tool (named InterSLIP Setup) somewhere accessible. I put it into the Apple Menu Items folder inside the System folder.

Installing MacPPP

Installing Merit's MacPPP requires that you place the extension part (named .PPP) into the Extensions folder inside the System folder, and the control part (named Config. PPP) into the Control Panel folder inside the System folder.

Configuring MacTCP

When you open up the MacTCP Control Panel you'll see something like what's in Figure 5.11. (Notice that it's not typical to have InterSLIP and MacPPP installed at the same time—especially as they seem to intermittently confuse MacTCP. You'll likely use one or the other. InterCon's upcoming InterPPP II costware will render the question moot, as it does both PPP and SLIP.)

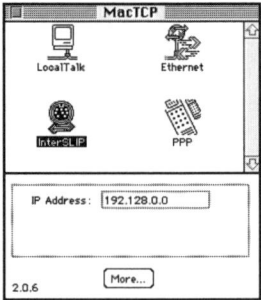

Figure 5.11. MacTCP connections options.

Select the icon that describes the way you'll be connecting. We've already mentioned SLIP and PPP. If you'll be connecting to an Ethernet network (through a built-in Ethernet—like on my PowerBook 520c—or a third-party SCSI Ethernet box) select the Ethernet icon. If you'll be speaking TCP/IP over a LocalTalk network, select that icon. In any case, you've now told MacTCP which connection method you want to use.

Look back at Table 5.1. If you'll be using Manual addressing, also known as Static or Fixed addressing, then your provider should have given you an IP address. Enter that IP address in the input area provided. Then hit the More button to bring up the MacTCP configuration dialog box, shown in Figure 5.12.

Software  75

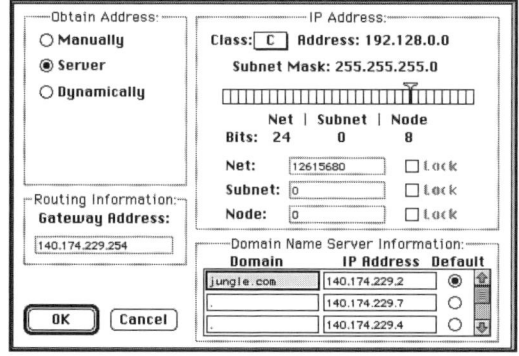

Figure 5.12. MacTCP configuration dialog box.

Let's start with the Obtain Address radio buttons. Your provider will have said that you'll get your IP address either Manually (and the IP address was already given to you) or via Server (the provider's computer gives you a free IP address from a pool of addresses). Select the appropriate radio button. Don't be confused by a strange quirk of geek-speak: a server-based address is known as a "dynamic" address (as opposed to a "fixed" address). Nobody uses the Dynamically setting—that seems to have been an evolutionary dead-end.

Move down to the Routing Information Gateway Address area and enter the gateway specified by your provider. In some cases it'll be determined automatically, but it's a required address for Open Transport, so it's best you explicitly get it.

Moving over to the Domain Name Server Information area, let's tell MacTCP which of your provider's networked machines will translate machine names (such as gildenstern.jungle.com) into a numeric IP address. You should have received, from your provider, IP addresses for a primary and a secondary nameserver.

My local domain is jungle.com. If I'm using the machine named gildenstern.jungle.com and I want to connect to rosenkrantz.jungle.com, I'm in need of name services for my local domain. This is how we set that up:

1. Enter your provider's domain where you see jungle.com in Figure 5.12.
2. In the IP address box just to the right of that box, enter the IP address of your primary nameserver.
3. Click the Default radio button.

Okay, you've now told MacTCP what nameserver to use for local requests, and you've ensured that single-word machine names, such as TT>gildenstern, will have the local domain—jungle.com in our example—appended.

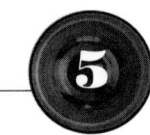 **Internet TV with CU-SeeMe**

What about requests for name services for machines outside your domain? Well, this is how you'll set that up:

1. Enter a period in the text box under your domain.
2. In the IP address box just to the right of that box, enter the IP address of your primary nameserver.

Now the primary nameserver will be consulted for requests inside and outside of your domain, just as it should.

What happens if the primary nameserver is having a bad day and has crashed or is otherwise unavailable? This is how we provide a secondary nameserver:

1. Enter a period in the Domain box on the third line.
2. Enter the IP address of your secondary nameserver.

If you have a tertiary nameserver, use the scrollbar to move to the next free line and enter a period in the Domain box and the IP address of your tertiary nameserver in the accompanying ID address box.

Lastly, let's look at the IP address area of the MacTCP configuration dialog window. Usually you'll not have to mess with this at all. If you do, ask you local Mac networking guru for some help. Between the bewildering complexity of possible network setups you may be a part of, including subnetting and supernetting (as discussed in Chapter 4), and a known bug in the network class pop-up window, comprehensive instructions on how to configure this section would require a separate volume the size of this book. But, take heart, you'll rarely have to tackle this section, and if you do, someone in your organization probably has been through it before.

When you're finished following these instructions, click the OK button to close the MacTCP configuration dialog window, and then hit the close box to close the MacTCP control panel. Depending upon the changes you've made, MacTCP will remind you that rebooting your Macintosh is necessary for the changes to take effect. That's because MacTCP updates the MacTCP DNR (Domain Name Resolver) and MacTCP Prep files when your Mac is starting up. (Sometimes these files can be corrupted by a computer crash. When I troubleshoot my MacTCP connection, I restart every time I've changed my MacTCP configuration, whether it prompts me to or not. When things are behaving erratically I throw these files away and restart. When things are really higgledy-piggledy I throw away all MacTCP files—including the Control Panel—and reinstall from scratch.)

The next step in getting online is to configure your chosen SLIP or PPP; there is quite a variety of freeware and costware software packages available. I've chosen two of the more popular freeware choices: InterCon's InterSLIP and Merit's MacPPP.

Configuring InterSLIP

Open up InterSLIP Setup, which will be in the Apple Menu if you've followed the installation suggestions. Figure 5.13 shows the setup window with the "see more" triangle pointing downwards. ("See less" by clicking once on the arrow.) In the example shown you see four configurations I have set up, two each for my local Internet service provider in San Francisco (Sirius) and for a provider when I visit my godchild, Kaeli, in Tucson, Arizona (Primenet). (The Metricom versions have extra control information for a Metricom wireless modem—a necessity when my Kaeli decides to run for it.)

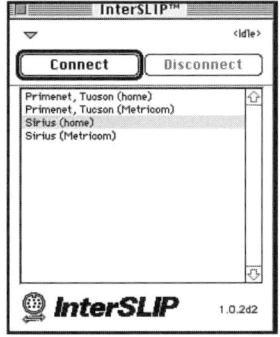

Figure 5.13. MacTCP settings.

Choosing New from the File Menu will result in a new configuration name dialog box (see Figure 5.14).

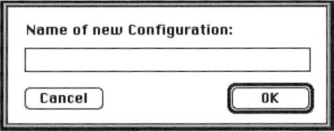

Figure 5.14. InterSLIP asks for a new configuration name.

When you enter a name and click the OK button you'll be presented with a configuration window (see Figure 5.15). (There's no Delete button; the configuration files are kept in an InterSLIP Setup folder in your Preferences folder—delete a configuration by dragging it to the Trash.)

 Internet TV with CU-SeeMe

Figure 5.15. InterSLIP's configuration window.

Going counterclockwise, let's examine and set each of the controls.

The Serial Port should be set to indicate where you've attached the modem. This can be the Modem Port (the most common choice), the Printer Port, an Internal Modem, the Printer-Modem port (if you have a PowerBook 5xx), or the Upper or Lower Card Slot on Macintoshes that have PCMCIA capability.

The Baud rate refers not to your modem speed, but the communication speed between your Macintosh and the modem. All my 14.4 kbps and 28.8 kbps modems are driven with a serial port speed of 57600 bps. Your mileage may vary.

Most Internet service providers use 8 data bits, 1 stop bit, and no parity bit.

The Hardware Handshaking checkbox should be checked if you have a v.32bis modem—all my 14.4 kbps and 28.8 kbps modems came with a hardware handshaking cable; yours probably did, too.

The Speaker on while dialing checkbox should be set on until you've gotten everything debugged, after which time the novelty of piercing schrieks will doubtlessly wear thin and you can turn it off.

The Disable Automatic Connections checkbox prevents InterSLIP from automatically dialing your Internet service provider whenever a program on your Mac wants to speak out. This sounds like a great service to have, but I've found that it's a great bother in practice. ("In theory, there's no difference between theory and practice. In practice, however, ...")

The Dial Script pop-up menu should most likely be set to a Hayes-Compatible modem. I have yet to see a modern modem that wasn't, but then I steer away from the bargain-basement el cheapo special modems. If your modem isn't basically Hayes-compatible, your life will quickly become an unenviable misery. (Well, maybe it's not that bad—InterSLIP supports other modems through the Connection Control Language (CCL) scripting language. Adam Engst, the author of several great books and the e-zine TidBits, has assembled a collection of CCL scripts for a variety of modems at

```
ftp://ftp.tidbits.com/pub/tidbits/tisk/tcp/
```

Their names begin with "scr" (for script) and include the modem they're written for. Figure 5.16 shows the folder hierarchy for InterSLIP; place any dialing scripts you've obtained into the Dialing Scripts folder.

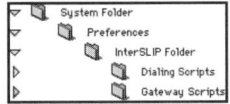

Figure 5.16. InterSLIP hierarchy

The next three items, Dial, Phone No., and Modem Init, become available for you to configure when you set the Dial Script option.

Most people (in the United States) now enjoy touch-tone dialing.

The dial-up telephone number should have been given to you and is hopefully part of your Table 5.2 cribsheet.

The modem initialization string can often be left blank. AT&F will usually set your modem to the factory-default settings. Your modem manual will have a comprehensive (if bewildering) list of all the settings your particular modem supports. For most folks, the sticking points (if any) are turning hardware handshaking on and software handshaking (also known as XON/XOFF) off.

The Gateway pop-up menu specifices how you'll navigate your provider's SLIP harbor. Simple Unix/Telebit works for many folks, but as my provider uses a non-standard system, I had to write my own CCL script. It's completely commented (the closest thing I've found to a CCL instructional manual) and available at

```
ftp://ftp.jungle.com/...
```

Adam has also collected gateway scripts for your enjoyment. Again, the names begin with "scr" (for script) and include the name of an Internet service provider, university, or terminal server manufacturer such as Cisco. Gateway scripts are placed into the (surprise!) Gateway Scripts folder.

Specify your user name (also known as a login name) given to you by your provider in the User name text input box. Type it exactly as it was given to you, as UNIX is case-sensitive. "MSATTLER," "MSattler," and "msattler" are three different user names.

Here comes a security issue. You can divulge your password to InterSLIP, but then anyone who has access to your computer can find out that information. Whether you'll use this option depends upon whether you are able to maintain "site security" (in the parlance of the security world). If you're the sole user of your Macintosh (perhaps it's a home machine or you have a PowerBook that's

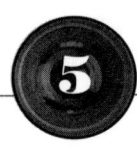

Internet TV with CU-SeeMe

always at your side) or you trust the other users (your significant other and your cat), then it may make sense to entrust your password to InterSLIP. If your computer is at your office, or part of a school computing laboratory, it may make less sense to do so (a lot less sense). (Of course my password isn't "Mac*Bigot," or anything remotely like it.)

I leave the IP address and Nameserver address areas blank (because MacTCP already knows that information).

Because I want to maximize every last bit of data throughput that I can from my modem connection, I've asked my network administer to serve me using compressed TCP packet headers and I've appropriately set the RFC 1144 TCP Header Compression checkbox. This is an all-or-none setting; both you and your provider must be in sync about this. A mismatch in either direction will cause strange connection behavior and possibly no connection at all.

Lastly, you'll need to enter the Maximum Transmit Unit size from your Table 5.2 cribsheet.

Then click the OK button to save your configuration. Repeat this process for every configuration you want to set up. If you're like most folks, and have only one Internet service provider (and therefore only one configuration), you can click the "show less" arrow to shrink the InterSLIP Setup window (see Figure 5.17). This takes up less screen "real estate", making it easier to see other windows. (If you place InterSLIP Setup onto a second monitor—if you're lucky enough to have one—and then move (or remove) that monitor, InterSLIP setup may crash and burn. The work-around is to delete the InterSLIP Preferences file. Since it only contains the now-invalid window position and which configuration file was selected, it's easy to re-create.)

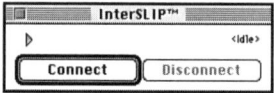

Figure 5.17. InterSLIP shrunk down.

Using InterSLIP

Users of Apple's Control Strip or Mice and Men's Desktop Strip can use Infinity System's InterSLIP Strip Module to connect and disconnect without opening InterSLIP Setup at all. Desktop Strip and Control PPP CSM may be found at UMich and Sumex software archives.

Software  81

 **Note:** Many TCP/IP-based applications don't like to have the connection yanked out from under them, even if you're not sending or receiving data. Quit those applications when you're done with them, then disconnect. You'll become familiar after a time with which applications behave well and which lash out; you'll know because your SLIP connection will be dropped due to a noisy phone line or somesuch and your TCP/IP-based applications will be open.

Configuring MacPPP

MacPPP is quite popular because of its simple initial configuration; there are far less things to set than in InterSLIP.

This becomes evident when you open the MacPPP Control Panel (see Figure 5.18).

Figure 5.18. MacPPP Control Panel.

The Port Name pop-up menu should be set to indicate where you've attached the modem. This can be the Modem Port (the most common choice), the Printer Port, an Internal Modem, the Printer-Modem port (if you have a PowerBook 5xx), or the Upper or Lower Card Slot on Macintoshes that have PCMCIA capability.

The Idle Timeout pop-up menu specifies after how much idle time (no activity on your part) MacPPP will automatically close your connection. (It will warn you, and give you a choice to postpone closing, unless you've turned on the Quiet Mode checkbox.) Some TCP-based applications don't like to have their connection cut off, even if they're idle. They may crash, or cause your Macintosh to be rebooted. If you have MacPPP automatically closing your connection, save your work early and often. That's why I set my Idle Timeout to None; I don't need to look out for more trouble.

Internet TV with CU-SeeMe

The Echo Interval pop-up menu specifies how often MacPPP should query the connection. If it receives no response to three successive queries it considers the connection dropped, and will ask you whether you want to Close PPP, Ignore, or Restart (PPP). I don't have any problems with my connection dropping, so I leave Echo Internal set to Off.

The Terminal Window checkbox controls whether MacPPP will do the work of connecting (the default) or whether you'll perform each step (something you'll want to do when you're debugging a connection that doesn't seem to work, and you want to figure out why). You'll start with specifying a phone number to dial (ATDT555-1212), move on to typing the user name and password, and finally closing the terminal window (with the OK button) when you see PPP gibberish—the sign of a successful PPP connection.

The Hangup on Close checkbox controls whether two Hayes commands will be sent to your modem to really hang it up. The commands are the +++ escape string (to get your modem's attention) and ATH to hang up the modem. None of the modems I've ever used needed this, but it's there in case yours does.

The Quiet Mode checkbox controls whether MacPPP will request your confirmation of certain actions, such as an idle timeout closing of your connection. Because I want to know exactly what my connection software is doing at all times, I don't use Quiet Mode.

The PPP Server pop-up menu shows the configurations you (or your network administrator) have set up.

Since you're just now configuring MacPPP, select the New button to bring up the configuration window (see Figure 5.19).

Figure 5.19. MacPPP configuration window.

The PPP Server Name shows the name you've given to this configuration. The Port Speed pop-up menu controls at what speed your Macintosh and modem communicate, not at what speed your modem talks to the outside world. All my 14.4 kbps and 28.8 kbps modems have worked at 57600 bps; your mileage may vary. Set it to the highest speed that works.

The Flow Control pop-up menu controls how information coming and going (known as "traffic" in the telecommunications trade) is controlled. Try using CTS & RTS (DTR) first. If you notice your phone connection intermittently disconnecting, especially when you're receiving large amounts of incoming data, try using CTS only. (In case anyone asks, all three options in the pop-up menu are types of hardware flow control. SLIP and PPP can't use software flow control, also known as XON/XOFF.)

Select the appropriate type of dialing. Most common in the USA is tone dialing. The phone number should have been given to you and is hopefully part of your Table 5.2 cribsheet.

The modem initialization string can often be left blank. AT&F will usually set your modem to the factory-default settings. Your modem manual will have a comprehensive (if bewildering) list of all the settings your particular modem supports. For most folks, the sticking points (if any) are turning hardware handshaking on and software handshaking (also known as XON/XOFF) off.

The modem connect timeout value controls how long MacPPP will wait for your modem and your provider's modem to negotiate a connection. If, for some reason, it takes an inordinately long time, you'll have to increase this value (although I've actually never seen a negotiation session last more than 90 seconds).

Lastly, at the bottom of the configure server dialog window, are the four horsemen of the apocalypse. Whoops. That'd be the four configuration buttons of MacPPP.

I'll start with the most commonly-used button, Authentication. Most likely your provider's PPP server will use the Password Authentication Protocol (PAP) to authenticate your identity. PAP is the reason for PPP's great popularity—it does all the dirty work. PAP requires that you provide your username and password. You do this by clicking the Authenticate button, waiting for the authentication dialog window (see Figure 5.20) to appear, and typing your username in the Auth. ID field and your password in the Password field.

Figure 5.20. MacPPP authentication window.

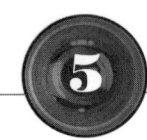

Internet TV with CU-SeeMe

The Retries value controls how many times MacPPP will dial your provider if the line is busy. The Timeout value controls how long PAP has to work; three seconds—the default—has always worked for me.

If your provider's PPP server doesn't support the Password Authentication Protocol, you'll have to provide a script that describes your provider's back-and-forth authentication negotiation. The Connect Script button brings up the connect script window (Figure 5.21), where you see a typical connection script.

Figure 5.21. MacPPP connect script window.

Each script line has three controls: radio buttons that controls who's "speaking" the line, a text field that contains what's being said, and a checkbox for sending a carriage-return after an output line (almost always necessary).

1. Send a carriage return upon connection. (The Out radio button is selected, there's no text provided, and the box at the right is checked.)
2. You wait for your provider's computer to respond with a string that contains "ogin:" —it may be "Login" or "login", since we don't know which we specify the part we do know.
3. Send your username and a carriage return to your provider's computer.
4. Wait for a response that contains "word:"—it might be "Password:" or "password:," we don't know.
5. Send your password and a carriage return. (Yes, your password is stored in plain view of anyone who knows how to find it. This is a weakness of MacPPP that you'll have to be aware of if your Mac is used in a shared setting, such as a school laboratory, or where others can get at it.)

The LCP Options and the IPCP Options buttons are gateways to configuration windows that are the province of your network administrator. The vast majority of users will never have to change any of those settings.

When you're finished configuring the PPP server, click the Done button.

Using MacPPP

Now you're back at the main MacPPP control panel window. There are two ways of initiating a PPP connection: using the Open button or starting an application that wants to speak TCP/IP (which will cause an automatic connection to be started). While it seems to me that MacPPP's automatic connection ability is slightly more robust than InterSLIP's, it doesn't give me a warm and fuzzy feeling. I wish I could turn it off for good, but that's not possible. The Hard Close button is supposed to do that, but I've found that MacPPP still dials up my provider when a TCP/IP-based application has something to say (or some other spurious event makes MacPPP think it's time to reach out and dial someone).

The Soft Close button disconnects your PPP connection, but allows MacPPP to reestablish it if necessary (which it seems to do regardless of what I do).

The Stats button brings up a window containing connection statistics, something you'll do at the request of your network administrator (if you're reporting a problem making or sustaining a PPP connection).

Users of Apple's Control Strip or Mice and Men's Desktop Strip can use Richard Buckle's Control PPP Control Strip Module to connect and disconnect without opening InterSLIP Setup at all. Desktop Strip and Control PPP CSM may be found at UMich and Sumex software archives.

> **Note:** Many TCP/IP-based applications don't like to have the connection yanked out from under them, even if you're not sending or receiving data. Quit those applications when you're done with them, then close the connection. You'll become familiar after a time with which applications behave well and which lash out; you'll know because your PPP connection will be dropped due to a noisy phone line or somesuch and your TCP/IP-based applications will be open.

Installing TCP/IP for Your Windows System

Although TCP/IP comes with Windows 95, it is not installed automatically by any of the Windows 95 setup types (Typical, Custom, Portable, or Compact). During Windows 95 setup, you can install TCP/IP by choosing **C**ustom Setup, selecting Co**m**munications, choosing Protocols, and then selecting the checkbox next to TCP/IP in the list of Microsoft Protocols.

Internet TV with CU-SeeMe

Note: Windows 3.1 users should refer to the specific instructions at the end of this chapter.

After setup, you can install TCP/IP through the Control Panel:

1. Open the Network icon and click the **A**dd button.
2. In the list that appears, double-click Protocol. A dialog box appears, listing **M**anufacturers of protocols on the left and the **P**rotocols supplied on the right.
3. Select Microsoft from the **M**anufacturers list; select Microsoft TCP/IP from the **P**rotocols list.
4. Click OK to complete the installation and return to the Control Panel. Continue your installation process by configuring TCP/IP, as described in the following section.

Configuring TCP/IP

To configure TCP/IP for Internet access, follow these steps:

1. From the Control Panel, open the Network icon.
2. From the list of **N**etwork components, select TCP/IP and click **P**roperties.

In the tabs on the TCP/IP Properties dialog box, supply the information given to you by your Internet access provider. (This information is described at the beginning of this chapter.)

You do not have to complete all the tabs or fill every blank on every tab. You need enter only what your access provider requires. For a typical account, you need to do the following:

- On the IP Address tab: Enter your IP address (click the **O**btain an IP Address from a DHCP Server button if your provider assigns IP addresses dynamically).
- On the DNS Configuration tab: Click the **E**nable DNS radio button and enter your username—the part of your Internet address that comes before the @ sign—as the **H**ost; enter the part of your Internet address that follows the @ as the Domain. Enter the IP address of your provider's DNS server in the **D**NS Server Search Order field, and then click the **A**dd button.
- On the Advanced tab: Select the Set this Protocol To Be the Default checkbox.

- On the Bindings tab: Make sure that the Client for Microsoft Networks checkbox is selected.
- On the WINS Configuration tab: Select the checkbox next to Disable WINS Resolution; deselect the Use DHCP for WINS Resolution checkbox. WINS is a Windows TCP/IP facility not involved in dial-up Internet connections.
- On the Gateway tab: If your provider has given you a gateway address, enter it in the New Gateway field and click Add.

When you have finished filling in the tabs, click OK.

Creating a Dial-Up Networking Connection for the Internet

Once TCP/IP is configured, you need to create a Dial-Up Networking connection to initiate your modem, dial the access provider, and log on to the server. If you've configured everything correctly, this final step puts you on the Internet.

How you configure Dial-Up Networking depends on the type of server you're dialing in to:

- If your access provider uses PPP servers, you must create a Dial-Up Networking connection and choose PPP as the server type.
- If your access provider uses SLIP (or CSLIP) servers, you must install support for UNIX SLIP from your Windows 95 CD-ROM disc and then set up your Dial-Up Networking connection, choosing SLIP as the server type.

To create a Dial-Up Networking connection for Internet access, follow these steps:

1. Open Dial-Up Networking in My Computer or select it from the Accessories menu.
2. Double-click the Make New Connection icon to open it. You are prompted to name the connection (you can assign the name *Internet*, for example) and choose a modem (your default modem is preselected). Enter a connection name and, if necessary, change the modem selection. Click Next.
3. Enter your Internet access provider's dial-up number and click Next.
4. Click Finish to save your new connection. A new icon, with the name you assigned in Step 2, appears in the Dial-Up Networking folder.
5. Right-click the new icon to display its context menu; select Properties. From the Properties menu, click Server Type.
6. From the Type of Dial-Up Server drop-down list, select the appropriate server type (PPP, SLIP, or CSLIP) for your Internet connection. Make sure that only the TCP/IP checkbox is selected in the list of Allowed Network Protocols.

Note: If SLIP and CSLIP do not appear in the Type of Dial-Up Server list, you have not yet installed the UNIX Connection for the Dial-Up Networking option, described in the next section.

7. If you are using SLIP or CSLIP, or if your PPP provider does not support CHAP or PAP, deselect the **L**og On To Network checkbox. Click OK.

If you deselected the **L**og On To Network checkbox in the previous step, you must also configure the modem connection to bring up a terminal window after dialing. To configure the modem connection, follow these steps:

1. Right-click the new Internet connection icon in Dial-Up Networking and choose Properties from the context menu that appears.
2. Click the **C**onfigure button. In the Modem Properties dialog box that appears, select the Options tab.
3. Click the Bring Up **T**erminal Windows after Dialing checkbox. This option causes a *terminal window* to appear after dialing; the window shows your interaction with your provider's server. You need this window to respond to the server's prompts for your username (or login name, or user ID) and password.

Tip: If you use a non-PAP/non-CHAP PPP account or a SLIP account (both of which require a terminal window and extra steps for logging on to the Internet), you can automate the extra steps with the Dial-Up Scripting utility included in Microsoft Plus! See "Automating Your Internet Logon," later in this chapter.

Installing and Configuring SLIP

You create a Dial-Up Networking connection for SLIP and CSLIP accounts exactly as you do for PPP accounts. The only difference is that SLIP support is not installed by default as a server type; you must install it before setting up your Dial-Up Networking connection.

Note: SLIP/CSLIP support is available only from the Windows 95 CD-ROM disc, not from the floppy-disk version of the operating system.

> **Tip:** Although you can't completely set up a SLIP configuration through the Internet Setup Wizard, you can "cheat" the Wizard into doing most of the work for you when setting up a SLIP account.
>
> First, install SLIP support from the Windows 95 CD-ROM by performing the first three steps described following this tip box. Next, run the Internet Setup Wizard to create a regular PPP account.
>
> Finally, open Dial-Up Networking (open My Computer and then open the Dial-Up Networking folder, or choose Dial-Up Networking from the **A**ccessories menu) and right-click the Internet connection created by the Wizard. Select Properties from the context menu that appears and click the Server Type button. Using the drop-down list for Server Type, change the server type from PPP to SLIP. Also make sure that the Log onto Network checkbox is deselected.
>
> Click OK to return to the Properties sheet and then click the Configure button. In the Modem Configuration dialog box that appears, select the checkbox next to Bring up **T**erminal Window after Dialing. This forces Dial-Up Networking to open a terminal window so that you can properly log on to a SLIP server.

To install SLIP support, follow these steps:

1. Open the Control Panel and open Add/Remove Programs.
2. Click the Windows Setup tab. A list of installed Windows components appears. Insert your Windows 95 CD-ROM disc in the appropriate drive and click Have **D**isk.
3. Enter the following directory name and click OK:
   `d:\ADMIN\APPTOOLS\SLIP`

   A dialog box appears, listing UNIX Connection for Dial-Up Networking as a Windows component. Make sure that the component's checkbox is selected and then click **I**nstall.
4. Perform the steps for setting up a Dial-Up Networking connection described in "Creating a Dial-Up Networking Connection for the Internet," earlier in this chapter. When selecting a server type, choose SLIP for a SLIP server, or CSLIP for a CSLIP server, and make sure that you deselect the **L**og On To Network checkbox. Finish configuring your Internet connection by changing your modem configuration to bring up a terminal window after dialing.

Internet TV with CU-SeeMe

Troubleshooting Your Internet Configuration

Your Internet access provider should supply you with complete and accurate configuration information. If you've followed the instructions in this chapter and entered exactly the information your provider has given you, you should be able to connect to the Internet through the provider.

If you experience problems, your first step should be to double-check your configuration, making sure that all your settings match the provider's instructions.

If you don't find a mistake, describe your problem to your access provider's technical support department. Often, access providers make changes to their own server configurations that require making changes in each user's configuration. Sometimes, the providers neglect to properly inform users of changes, or they distribute out-of-date instructions to new users. In addition, because Windows 95 is a new operating system, many providers are themselves still learning exactly how their Windows 95 users should configure their communications.

If you can't get help from your provider, try the following:

- Get a new provider with better technical support.
- If you've configured your PPP account for CHAP or PAP support and find that Windows cannot log you on to the server, reconfigure for no CHAP or PAP support (bring up a terminal window after dialing). It's possible your provider doesn't actually support CHAP or PAP or has a non-standard configuration.
- On some SLIP accounts, compression settings may vary from Windows' defaults. Consult your access provider about the proper settings. Open the Control Panel and open Network; select Dial-Up Adapter and click the Advanced tab in the dialog box that appears. Change the selections for compression as necessary. Click OK.

> **Tip:** If you use a non-PAP/non-CHAP PPP account or a SLIP account (both of which require a terminal window and extra steps for logging on to the Internet), you can automate the extra steps with the Dial-Up Scripting utility included in Microsoft Plus!.

To start your Internet connection, click the Connect button. Windows initializes your modem, dials your service provider, initiates TCP/IP communications, and connects to the server through your selected protocol.

If you're using SLIP or PPP with the terminal logon option, a terminal window pops up after Dial-Up Networking has established a connection. You must complete the logon procedure as described here:

- **For PPP with terminal logon:** Enter your user ID and password when prompted to do so. After entering your password, press F7 or click Continue to close the terminal window and allow Windows to complete the PPP connection.

- **For SLIP:** Enter your user ID and password when prompted to do so. The server responds with your TCP/IP address. Make a note of the IP address supplied by the server and then press F7 to allow Windows to complete the logon procedure. A dialog box appears.

  Make sure that the address assigned to you in the terminal window is the same as the one shown in the IP Address dialog box. If it is, click OK. If not, type the assigned IP address in the IP address dialog box and click OK. In most cases, the IP address shown is not the correct one; it is simply the address you were assigned in your last Internet session.

When Windows completes the logon procedure, it displays the Internet status box and begins timing the connection. You are connected to the Internet. You can start any Windows sockets-based Internet applications to navigate to and use specific Internet resources.

Configuring Windows 3.1 for the Internet

Windows 3.1 does not include TCP/IP, PPP/SLIP support, or a dial-up networking program (all of which are standard with Windows 95). If you want to use Windows 3.1 to access the Internet through SLIP or PPP accounts, you must add these functions through third-party software packages. All required protocols are available in all-purpose Internet software packages (one example is Chameleon, which features TCP/IP, a dial-up program, and software for exploiting specific Internet resources).

Another popular solution is Trumpet Winsock, a shareware utility that supplies TCP/IP, SLIP/PPP, and dial-up functions—all you need except for the Winsock-based programs for accessing Internet resources.

To configure Trumpet Winsock for Internet access, start the program and choose **F**ile, Se**t**up. A screen appears, in which you enter the required information as supplied by your service provider.

> **Note:** Your service provider may also require a login script for Trumpet Winsock. The login script, LOGIN.CMD, is stored in a simple text file (you can edit it with Notepad) in your Trumpet Winsock directory. Your service provider should supply you with this file, already properly set up, or give you instructions for completing it.

Once Trumpet Winsock is properly configured, your PC connects to the Internet

 **Internet TV with CU-SeeMe**

each time you open Trumpet Winsock. You can run the same Windows sockets-based Internet programs under Windows 3.1 as you can under Windows 95.

CU-SeeMe User's Guide

CHAPTER 6

After you read this chapter, you will know

- How to install CU-SeeMe on your Macintosh or Windows computer
- How to start CU-SeeMe and configure the preferences
- The different ways of connecting to another party
- How to create nicknames for people and sites that you connect with often
- Where to retrieve a Nicknames file and how to use it
- How to use the controls on your local video window, other users' remote video windows, and the audio window
- Two ways of typing text to another user
- How to use CU-SeeMe's menus

Quick Start

CU-SeeMe is a self-contained application. There are few things to install and configure, yet many people have a difficult time running CU-SeeMe for the first time. Reasons for this include

- A non-functioning TCP/IP connection

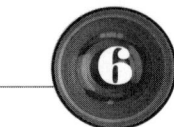

Internet TV with CU-SeeMe

- Incorrectly installed or missing system software
- Incorrectly installed or missing hardware
- Not having read the documentation

TCP/IP connectivity is addressed in Chapter 5. In general, Macintoshes require MacTCP or Open Transport as bedrock, SLIP or PPP as foundation, and a dialing program (for modem users) such as InterSLIP, MacSLIP, MacPPP, or InterPPP II as the dwelling. Windows requires a TCP/IP stack that is Winsock v1.1-compliant. Don't worry, most TCP/IP stacks today are v1.1-compliant. Windows 95 and Windows NT both have TCP/IP stacks built in and numerous others are available.

System software varies, based on the operating system, computer hardware, and camera. The manuals that come with your computer and camera have more details. In general, Macintoshes require QuickTime and associated plug-ins for video, plus a specific video digitizer plug-in for the specific camera or video capture board that you will be using.

Windows requires Video for Windows, which is already installed on most Windows 3.1 configurations. Windows 95 and NT have Video for Windows built in. You will also need the driver software for your camera, which should come with it. Windows 95 ships with over 2,000 different drivers. If you're using Windows 95 there's a good chance the software for your camera is on the installation CD.

The hardware required includes a microphone (for audio-capable computers) and a camera or video-capture board. Hardware is discussed in Chapter 4.

The CU-SeeMe discussion lists, which are described later in this chapter, are deluged with people who haven't read the bare-bones documentation that accompanies CU-SeeMe. You, of course, won't have this problem, since you have the extended documentation in your hands—and presumably you have already read up through this chapter.

Installing CU-SeeMe on Your System

The installation of CU-SeeMe varies depending on whether you are using a Macintosh or a Windows system.

Macintosh

Once you have acquired the appropriate version of CU-SeeMe for your type of Macintosh—Motorola $680x0$ or PowerPC processor—you need to decompress it. You can use Aladdin's StuffIt Expander, which is freeware available on the

Info-Mac and UMich software archives. You will probably want to acquire a Nicknames list, described later in this chapter.

CU-SeeMe generates images that have at most 16 different shades of gray, so your monitor's display mode must be configured to show at least those 16 grays or 16 colors, also known as *4-bit video*. If your monitor can display only 16 or 256 different grays or colors, your decision is easy. If your monitor can show thousands or millions of colors, you will have to play around with your video settings, because CU-SeeMe may have problems running in those modes.

Macintosh users use the Monitors control panel, shown in Figure 6.1. You will find more information in Chapter 9, "Other Videoconferencing Technologies."

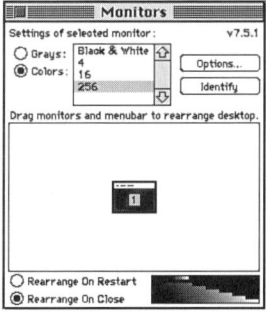

Figure 6.1. The Macintosh Monitors control panel.

On AV (audio-visual) Macintoshes, you may have to reduce the number of grays chosen to 16 in order to digitize and send video. Additionally, you may need to turn off GeoPort devices and speech recognition and to set sound sampling parameters to a lower rate, such as 11.025 KHz, with the Sound control panel to free up memory so that you can use CU-SeeMe's audio. Macintosh AV 840s default to 22 KHz sound, so make sure you check.

Some Macintosh models have speakers that are connected to the motherboard by edge-pressure contacts, which effectively disconnect the speakers when they get dusty and dirty. They are easily cleaned.

Windows

Once you have acquired CU-SeeMe for Windows, you need to decompress it with the freeware PKZIP. You will probably want to acquire a Nicknames list, described later in this chapter.

Windows users select Change System Settings from the Windows Setup control panel, shown in Figure 6.2.

 Internet TV with CU-SeeMe

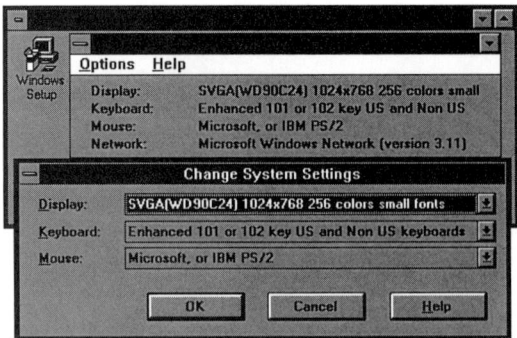

Figure 6.2. The Windows Setup control panel.

Most video digitizers for Windows will not require you to change your monitor's settings. But some digitizers do. Most monitors can be set to different color depths, i.e. black and white (1-bit), 16 colors (4-bit), 256 (8-bit), 32,768 (16-bit), and set to different resolutions, i.e. 640×480, 800×600, or 1024×768. The most common setting you might need would be to set your monitor to 16-color grayscale at whatever resolution your video card can handle.

If you need to change your Color settings in Windows 3.1, go to Setup in the Program Manager and choose Display. In Windows NT go to Control Panel, Display. In Windows 95 right-click on the desktop. Choose Properties and Settings.

You will get a list of monitor settings with color depth and resolution. Choose whatever setting your digitizer card requires and you should be all set.

Starting CU-SeeMe

CU-SeeMe requires a small amount of configuration to get up and running. The next few sections will take you through a step-by-step explanation of what CU-SeeMe needs to know.

Preferences

When you launch CU-SeeMe for the first time, the Preferences dialog box will appear, as shown in Figure 6.3. You can also change these values at a future time by selecting the Preferences item on the Edit menu. These values control how CU-SeeMe behaves and how others will see you. They are stored in a document in your Preferences folder in the System folder.

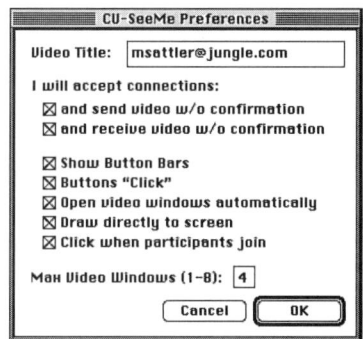

Figure 6.3. The CU-SeeMe Preferences dialog box.

- **Video Title**: The video title is the identity that you broadcast. Whereas some people choose names and locations, such as "Bob in Boston," I use my e-mail address so that others can contact me to set up conferences when I am not online. Although changing the title during a session is reflected in your local video window's title bar, others won't see the changed title until you quit and restart CU-SeeMe.

- **I will accept connections**: This section controls the automatic connection behavior of CU-SeeMe. If CU-SeeMe recognizes a valid video input device, you are offered the option to send video to others without your intervention. In all cases, you are offered the option to receive video without your intervention when someone tries to connect to your IP address. Because each video stream puts a load on your system and your network, you might not want to allow this unless you are on a fast computer on a fast network.

  If you don't check the receive checkbox, you will get a dialog box asking, `Connection request from <video title> Okay?` whenever anyone tries to connect to you. If you check the receive checkbox, your Mac simply sends and receives whenever requested; it will make an alert sound. Currently, CU-SeeMe supports only one connection at a time, so incoming connection requests are ignored if you are already connected somewhere else. The CU-SeeMe development team will soon make some improvements here so that you can use CU-SeeMe more like a telephone. It will then have a more intrusive connection alert, and you will be able to accept connection requests while already connected.

- **Show Button Bars**: This control provides all the CU-SeeMe controls and feedback tools at your fingertips, at a cost of a bit of screen real estate.

- **Buttons "Click"**: This control provides audio feedback for button use. I like this because it gives me additional confirmation that my request has been processed by the computer.

- **Open video windows automatically**: This control is operational when you are connected to a reflector. It determines whether CU-SeeMe automatically opens windows for new incoming video sources or whether they must be manually selected from the Participants menu. A new video source is any video stream that you have not already closed. Because each video stream places a load on your system, this control is important for people with slow connections. Having it unchecked prevents your modem's buffer from being overrun—that is, clogging up—and connections from timing out as your system copes with video streams coming in as they please.
- **Draw directly to screen**: When this option is selected, CU-SeeMe tries to draw directly to the screen whenever the entire video rectangle is exposed. If the video is partially obscured, the QuickDraw CopyBits routine is used, and a black border is drawn around the video to alert the user to this fact, which can entail a substantial performance penalty in many cases. If this option is not selected, CopyBits is always used and no black borders are drawn.
- **Click when participants join**: This control helps you know what is going on even when you are not looking at your monitor. A click alerts you that another person has joined the conference that you are monitoring, giving you the chance to glance up and see whether the newcomer is someone with whom you wish to speak.
- **Max Video Windows (1–8)**: This option provides a restraining hand for your network usage. Because each open window uses system and network resources, this option prevents uncontrolled automatic connections within CU-SeeMe from completely overwhelming your network. Remember, though, that having only three windows open instead of the maximum eight can still place a heavy strain upon your network. Be considerate and speak with your system and network administrator before bringing your local network to its knees.

Connecting

Now that CU-SeeMe is up and running on your system, you can reach out to others. There are two ways of doing this: manual addressing and Nickname files.

Manual Addressing

Choosing Connect... from the Conference menubar item causes the Connections dialog box to appear (see Figure 6.4).

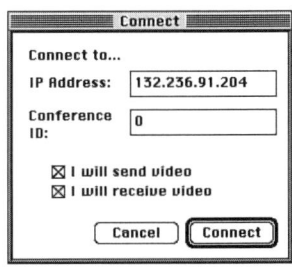

Figure 6.4. The Connect dialog box.

- **IP Address**: The IP address can be that of a digitizer-equipped Macintosh or Windows computer running CU-SeeMe or a reflector. Domain Name Services (DNS) are supported in the Connections dialog box but not yet in the Nicknames file, so you may type a host name instead of an IP address. Cornell University runs a reflector for connection testing. To test your setup, try entering its IP address (132.236.91.204) or host name (pro60-test2.cit.cornell.edu). The Cornell University Public Reflector is usually very busy, so consider not having the Open video windows automatically preference item selected. If you choose to Open video windows automatically, your network—and all the network links on the way to you—might receive quite a blast of data.
- **Conference ID**: This value will typically be 0, the default. The Conference ID is a security feature that the reflector operator can configure. A reflector will reject all petitioners from connecting if the Conference ID specified doesn't match the ID that it has been configured to accept. A zero value enables all petitioners if the system has room for you. If you are told to specify a particular ID for a given event, you must enter it or you will be refused admission to the reflector.
- **I will send video**: This checkbox is available to you if CU-SeeMe recognizes a video digitizer and camera. It controls whether you initially send a video stream to the other party. If you are send-capable, you can change this with the Conference menubar items. Sending video is not appropriate when you are connected to one-way reflectors, such as NASA TV—it places a load on their system and makes it difficult for them to transmit to you.
- **I will receive video**: This checkbox controls whether you initially receive a video stream from the other party—person or reflector. You can change this with the Conference menu items.

If you followed the instructions in the preceeding paragraphs and all is well on the other side, you should see one of the following behaviors:

Internet TV with CU-SeeMe

- If you are connecting to another computer in point-to-point mode to which no one else is already connected that has a properly-configured digitizer and camera, you will see the image as it begins to transmit.
- If you are connecting to another computer in point-to-point mode to which no one else is already connected but that has no video capability, you will see its name in the Participants list.
- If you are connecting to a reflector that is running, you will probably be greeted by a Message of the Day screen.

> **Note:** The Message of the Day (MOTD) is provided by the reflector operator. Useful MOTDs include the e-mail address of the reflector operator, a location of a Web page that gives more information about the site, acceptable usage ("Set your transmission cap to 80"), and perhaps one or two upcoming events.

If you are the only one connected, you will see no windows until someone else connects. If other sending parties are connected—receive-only "lurkers" might be present—their video images will appear on your screen or you will be informed of their presence, depending on how you set up your automatic receive preferences. If the reflector does not immediately respond, the status will show CONNECTING. If the reflector times out—that is, doesn't respond after a set time—you will get a No response from message.

When you disconnect from a conference, CU-SeeMe ignores any audio or video from that IP address for one minute. This shouldn't cause any problems if you are skipping from reflector to reflector, but there is the possibility for confusion if you wind up connecting to the same machine within one minute. The delay is only one-way. If you disconnect from a conference, you can reconnect immediately, but that IP address cannot connect to you for a minute. Likewise, if you reconnect to the same reflector within a short time, you also won't be shown the Message of the Day notice screen.

Nicknames

As an alternative to repeatedly typing in IP addresses or hostnames, you can use Edit Nicknames from the Edit menu to set up Nicknames for IP addresses. Once you have done this, the Connect To menu item from the Connection menu will show the nicknames. You can also retrieve a file that contains a list of reflectors world-wide from http://www.jungle.com/msattler/sci-tech/comp/CU-SeeMe/CUSeeMe_Nicknames.txt.

Macintosh

Macintosh CU-SeeMe users should make two copies of the CUSeeMe Nicknames file. Rename one copy CUSeeMe Nicknames and move it to the Preferences folder. The Connect To menubar item will show all the nicknames that you have set up.

Consider the Nickname file shown in Figure 6.5. It contains site and usage information that has been added. Because CU-SeeMe for the Macintosh strips out these comments, the remaining copy is for you to place in your CU-SeeMe folder, should you need to contact the person running the reflector, to find out the maximum signal that the reflector will accept without kicking you off, to find out the address of that reflector's Web pages, and so on. (Reducing the number of colors to 256 or fewer on some machines greatly speeds the scrolling rate when you are searching the Nicknames list.)

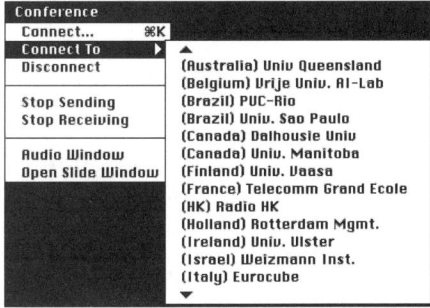

Figure 6.5. Choosing a nickname.

Windows

Windows CU-SeeMe users must do some cutting and pasting, because the Windows version doesn't accept the same format as the Macintosh version of CU-SeeMe. Edit your CUSEEME.INI file, found in the Windows directory, and add the textual hostnames—or the IP address if you really don't like being able to tell one reflector from another—to the MRU (Most Recently Used) List section. For example

```
[MRU List]
Target1=pro60-test2.cit.cornell.edu
Target2=nysernet.org
Target3=fenris.hiof.no
Target4=sunten.wiezmann.ac.il
```

Other Users' Windows

Figure 6.6 shows how another CU-SeeMe user who is transmitting might appear to you. The name that he has chosen appears in the title bar. A video image appears as he has adjusted it to appear. There is a set of buttons and a status bar below the image area.

Figure 6.6. Another—albeit scary—user.

The Video State button shows you whether the user is accepting video input or pausing the video.

The Audio button enables you turn to off sound from a particular person by clicking it until the soundwave icon disappears. When that user is transmitting audio, this button is shaded gray.

The Microphone button shows a red X if the user cannot transmit sound or has it turned off or if you clicked a user's Microphone button to do unicast audio.

Sometimes, you will see a status bar that doesn't sport any of the sound-related buttons. This happens when someone is using the older version of CU-SeeMe for Windows, which doesn't support audio (see Figure 6.7).

Figure 6.7. The other person is using an older version of CU-SeeMe for Windows, which doesn't support audio.

Consider Figure 6.8. The Transmission Statistics button, shown in Figure 6.9, shows statistics about packets, kilobytes, bytes-per-packet, and lost packets that you have received and sent.

The reset button has no effect in the Windows version and the restore is disabled.

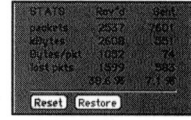

Figure 6.8. Input statistics.

Figure 6.9. The Transmission Statistics button.

Consider Figure 6.10. The Version/IP button, shown in Figure 6.11, displays the IP address of the user and the version of CU-SeeMe that he is using. This is especially helpful when you are trying to debug a problem or figure out why a user cannot get access to a feature that you are using in the current version of CU-SeeMe.

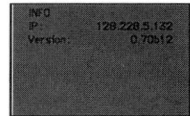

Figure 6.10. Input IP.

Figure 6.11. The Version/IP button.

Audio Window

Your ability to send audio is controlled by the Audio window, shown in Figure 6.12. You must have, of course, a microphone connected to your computer, unless it has one built in. You will not be able to transmit or receive audio over a 14.4 kbps modem link nor, most likely, over a 28.8 kbps modem. The reason is that current sound transmission requires about 32 kbps. What is being sent is already highly compressed, so it is unlikely that modem-level compression will help. At 14.4 kpbs you are going to get less than half of the segments, which is unintelligible. Charley Kline suggested that with one of the more ferocious compression methods, you might be able to push the bandwidth requirements down to about 10 kbps. For that, you would need a high-speed PowerPC processor to do the encoding and decoding. But there's always an exception. A few people on the CU-SeeMe discussion list have been able to get audio working fairly well using the delta-mod compression built in to CU-SeeMe which only needs about 16 kbps. They spent a good deal of time tweaking the CU-SeeMe transmission parameters. So if you're dedicated, a lot is possible.

- **Push to talk**: This checkbox controls whether you are required to hold the mouse button down to cause sound to be sent from your Macintosh. Hands-free operation works well in quiet locations where the microphone isn't too close to the speakers.

Internet TV with CU-SeeMe

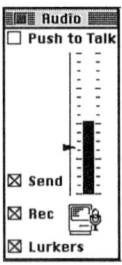

Figure 6.12. The Audio window.

- **Send**: This checkbox controls whether you send audio at all.
- **Rec**: This checkbox controls whether you recieve audio at all.
- **Lurkers**: This checkbox controls whether you accept audio from lurkers—in other words, folks without a camera.

You can move the triangle on the audio scale up or down to mark the squelch point for noisy environments. Sound levels received by the microphone below the squelch point are ignored as ambient noise. Levels above the squelch point are transmitted to the party to which you are connected. You must be connected to another CU-SeeMe user or reflector for the audio scale to show movement. Likewise, speaking into a window showing the WAITING status is pointless because you are not connected to anyone.

If you are a Macintosh CU-SeeMe user who is using a version of the Macintosh operating system before 7.5, you should get Sound Manager 3.0, which is available for free from ftp://ftp.apple.com/. Without it you will get annoying clicking during sound output, and your Macintosh will run extremely slow while you are receiving audio. MacOS 7.5—and higher—has Sound Manager built in.

CU-SeeMe's Controls

The options we'll be looking at in this section are

- The Local Video Window
- The Flip Image button
- The Status Line toggle button
- The Freeze Video button
- Picture options
- Transmission options
- Compression options
- Audio options

- Video options
- Editing a nickname

The Local Video Window

CU-SeeMe, at startup, checks the resources advertised by your particular computer configuration. If it finds appropriate hardware—such as video capture boards—or software—such as Apple's QuickTime extension and the appropriate video ditigizer component on non-AV Macintoshes, or MSVIDEO.DLL and the like for Windows—CU-SeeMe shows a video window (see Figure 6.13). If you see yourself in a video window, your camera is plugged in, operating, and pointing in the correct direction. Macintoshes with built-in digitizers, like the AV models, digitize and send video, opening a local video window even though a camera might not be connected to the Video In port. In this case, the Local Video window will be black. You will see WAITING, the current video state, below the video window until someone connects to you or until you connect to a reflector or another person. The identification name that you specified appears in the menubar. Four control buttons and the status line appear below the image.

Figure 6.13. A typical video window.

The Flip Image button, shown in Figure 6.14, causes your image to appear to be flipped, but it is not actually transmitted that way.

Figure 6.14. The Flip Image button.

The Status Line toggle button determines whether the status line is visible. From left to right, the status bar contains

- The frame rate—the number of frames per second (fps) being transmitted.
- The status of the connection to the other party
- The transmission cap—the maximum kilobytes per seconds (kbps) that you will transmit

Internet TV with CU-SeeMe

The frame rate that you can achieve depends on a number of factors: the CPU power available, the resolution, and possibly the screen depth chosen with the Monitors control panel. The frame rate is higher on a fast computer with CU-SeeMe running in the foreground, configured to use the smaller video window size—standard resolution—with the screen set to 16 grays or colors. Flipping the image or having part of the image off-screen or covered by another window will slow your frame rate.

The connection status can be WAITING, TIMED OUT, DISCONNECTED, or nothing, meaning that it is normal and active.

The transmission cap limits the bandwidth used for sending video from your machine. Depending on the amount of motion in the scene that your camera sees, the frame rate might also be affected. You can adjust the minimum and maximum values for the cap with the Transmission control. If the receivers report a packet loss in excess of five percent, the program assumes network congestion and automatically lowers the cap. It is adjusted upward toward the maximum value if loss reports aggregate to less than five percent. This system doesn't work well if a conference mixes receivers with greatly different bandwidths, such as modems and high-speed, direct-connect Ethernets.

The freeze video button pauses your video transmission. This button is often used; many times the only way to send and receive intelligible audio is to free up bandwidth used by video for the audio stream.

The Options Area toggle button determines whether you can see the CU-SeeMe options area. If you click it, a pop-up menu appears. You can then choose a digitizer (if you have more than one), change the audio, compression, picture, or transmission options.

After you click the Options Area toggle button and the pop-up menu appears, you can adjust the CU-SeeMe Picture options (see Figure 6.15). There are two slider controls. The top slider controls the image contrast, and the bottom slider controls the image brightness. These two, in combination, can make your outgoing image appear sharper, fuzzier, lighter, or darker.

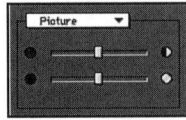

Figure 6.15. Picture options.

The CU-SeeMe Transmission options (see Figure 6.16) enable you to change the minimum kbps you send, the maximum kbps you send, and the maximum number of frames per second you send. It is customary to send no more than 80 kbps.

Indeed, many reflectors will automatically disconnect you and prevent you from reconnecting for ten minutes if you violate this boundary.

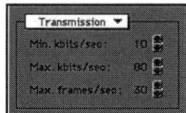

Figure 6.16. Transmission options.

The CU-SeeMe Compression options (see Figure 6.17) enable you to change the video tolerance, refresh interval, and transmission resolution. Normally, you will change only the transmission resolution—and then only for point-to-point connections. High resolution sends four times as many bits as standard resolution; consequently, it really eats up bandwidth.

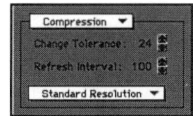

Figure 6.17. Compression options.

The CU-SeeMe Audio options (see Figure 6.18) enable you to select a transmission method and speed. Depending on your connection method, only certain audio options will be available, as in Figure 6.19.

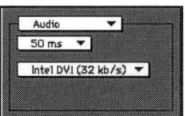

Figure 6.18. Audio options.

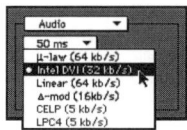

Figure 6.19. Depending on your connection method, only certain audio options will be available.

The CU-SeeMe Video options enable you to select a video digitizer resource for CU-SeeMe to use to access your camera hardware. Users of the Connectix QuickCam will see Connectix QuickCam, as in Figure 6.20. Macintosh

AV users will see Built-In AV Digitizer, as in Figure 6.21. Users of other hardware and software combinations will see yet other options.

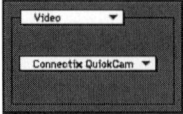

Figure 6.20. Video options.

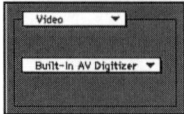

Figure 6.21. Video options.

CU-SeeMe's Menus

This section covers each of CU-SeeMe's menus.

File Menu

The File menu, shown in Figure 6.22, is a standard interface convention on the Macintosh. Basically it has the Quit command on it and a few other saving features.

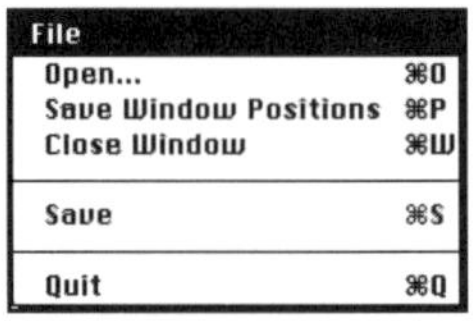

Figure 6.22. The File menu.

Save Window Positions

Save Window Positions makes a note of the current positions of some of CU-SeeMe's open windows. The next time you start CU-SeeMe, some of the windows that were open when you chose this menu item will appear in the same place. Currently, the Talk Window's position isn't remembered.

Macintosh users with multiple monitors should be aware that the remembered window positions don't currently compensate for new monitor configurations. If you remove one monitor and run CU-SeeMe, you won't be able to get at some of the windows without removing the CU-SeeMe Preferences file and restarting CU-SeeMe.

Close Window

Close Window closes the currently active CU-SeeMe window.

Quit

Quit causes all sending and receiving to stop, and the CU-SeeMe program stops running.

Edit Menu

The Edit menu, shown in Figure 6.23, implements the standard Macintosh editing and clipboard functionality. It is mostly used for cutting and pasting host names and IP addresses. CU-SeeMe's operating preferences are configurable from this menu, as are the nicknames that you have added.

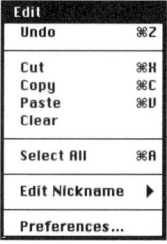

Figure 6.23. The Edit menu.

Undo

Undo returns CU-SeeMe to the state it was in before your last action. This is rarely applicable to the operation of CU-SeeMe, so it is dimmed, or grayed out, most of the time.

Internet TV with CU-SeeMe

Cut
Cut deletes selected, or highlighted, text and places a copy on the Clipboard.

Copy
Copy copies selected, or highlighted, text to the Clipboard.

Paste
Paste copies text on the Clipboard to the currently active text input area.

Clear
Clear deletes selected, or highlighted, text.

Select All
Select All causes all the text in the currently active text input area to be highlighted. Therefore, the text becomes available for the other Edit menu operations.

Edit Nickname
Edit Nickname enables you to select one of the nicknames that you previously gave to CU-SeeMe, either by entering it manually or by providing a Nicknames file. Choosing a nickname to edit brings up the Edit Nickname dialog box, shown in Figure 6.24. You use it to make changes.

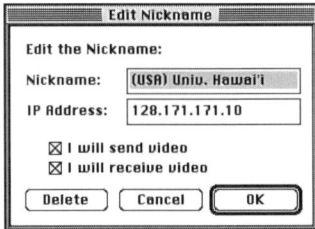

Figure 6.24. Editing a nickname.

Preferences...
Selecting the Preferences item causes the CU-SeeMe Preferences dialog box to appear. It contains all the configurable aspects of CU-SeeMe and their current

settings. You can change any of the settings that are available to you. Unavailable settings are dimmed, or grayed out, usually because you lack the hardware or software required for that particular functionality.

Conference Menu

The Conference menu, shown in Figure 6.25, contains items dealing with connecting to other CU-SeeMe users or reflectors, audio and video data control, and slides.

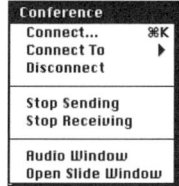

Figure 6.25. The Conference menu.

Connect...

Connect... brings up the Connect dialog box (see Figure 6.4).

Connect To

Connect To shows the pop-up list of nicknames that have been defined.

Disconnect

Disconnect causes the currently active connection to be released. When you disconnect from a conference, CU-SeeMe ignores any audio or video from that IP address for one minute. This shouldn't cause any problems if you are skipping from reflector to reflector, but there is the possibility for confusion if you wind up connecting to the same machine within one minute. The delay is only one-way. If you disconnect from a conference, you can reconnect immediately, but that address cannot connect to you for a minute.

Stop Sending

Stop Sending makes CU-SeeMe stop transmitting video and audio. Normally, you use it when you leave the room—sending empty office video is considered a breach of netiquette.

Stop Receiving

Stop Receiving tells the reflector that you don't want to have a bunch of video streams, which you won't see anyway, coming in—flooding your router, blocking access to your Web server, and wreaking havoc on your co-workers' ability to get a day's work done.

Text in the Video Window

In addition to sending and receiving video and audio, CU-SeeMe users can also type to one another. This primitive in-window text system is the original way in which CU-SeeMe users communicated via text. Macintosh CU-SeeMe users now have the Talk window, a much better tool.

Your audience—one point-to-point participant or many confrencees on a reflector—will see the alphanumeric characters that you type. The backspace key deletes the last character; you can clear the entire text with the Enter key. Text appears at the bottom of the video area; you move it to the top with the up-arrow key and to the bottom with the down-arrow key. To scroll your text, you use the left-arrow key; you stop it with the right-arrow key. (It is considered extremely impolite to leave text scrolling when you leave your desk because it changes an otherwise still image and causes CU-SeeMe to generate traffic to all the people who are watching you.)

Open Slide Window

The Slide window is a primitive whiteboard collaboration tool. It is described later in this chapter, in the "Auxiliary Data Function Modules" section.

Participants Menu

The Participants menu (see Figure 6.26) controls your interactions with others sharing the videoconference. The Show All and Close All controls show and hide all video windows. The Local Video control shows the local video window if it is hidden. The menu item is active, or black, when the local video window is showing. It is dimmed, or grayed out, when the local video window is hidden.

In Figure 6.26, the group of names with a Blank Screen icon are conference participants whose computers are capable of sending video. You can interact with these folks via video and the Talk window. The group of names with the Red X Active Window icon are lurkers whose computers are incapable of sending video in their current setup. You can interact with lurkers via the Talk window.

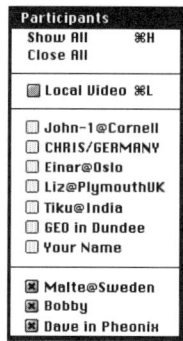

Figure 6.26. The Participants menu.

Auxiliary Data Function Modules

To most people, CU-SeeMe is a basic audio and video communications tool. To at least one of the CU-SeeMe development team, Aaron Giles, CU-SeeMe is a transport mechanism first and foremost. Out of this realization came the Auxilliary Data Transport. Auxiliary Data Function Modules, sometimes known as *plug-in* or *drop-in modules,* can extend CU-SeeMe's capabilities in ways that its developers never expected. When a module is dropped into CU-SeeMe's folder, it produces a new menubar item and gives you additional communications functionality. AuxData Transport, as it is also known, is a method of using CU-SeeMe to deliver arbitrary data. The word *arbitrary* gives a clue as to the real power of AuxData Transport.

Programmers can use AuxData Transport to package and deliver any data that they can describe programmatically in AuxData Transport Function Modules. These data are known as *items* to AuxData. Items include strings of text (used in the Talk Window Function Module) and images (used in the built-in Slide Window Function Module).

AD Trace Menu

The AD Trace menu, shown in Figure 6.27, appears only when you have placed the Auxiliary Data Trace Function Module in the same directory as the CU-SeeMe program. AD Trace FM is available from Cornell University.

 Internet TV with CU-SeeMe

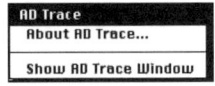

Figure 6.27. The AD Trace menu.

Trace is a debugging tool for software engineers who are creating function modules to extend the capabilities of CU-SeeMe. The Function Module Developer's Kit, also available from Cornell, consists of documentation, sample plug-ins, and a CodeWarrior project with libraries to facilitate the development of function modules.

If you select Show AD Trace Window, the AD Trace window appears (see Figure 6.28). The AD Trace window shows all AuxData items as they come and go.

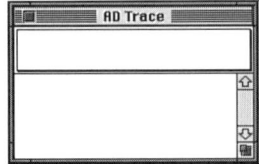

Figure 6.28. The AD Trace window.

Operation of the AD Trace window is explained in the Function Module Developer's Kit.

Talk Menu

The Talk menu, shown in Figure 6.29, appears only when you have placed the Talk Function Module in the same directory as the CU-SeeMe program. Talk FM is available from Cornell.

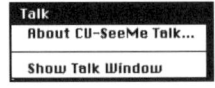

Figure 6.29. The Talk menu.

The Talk window, shown in Figure 6.30, is a sample plug-in that extends the capabilities of CU-SeeMe by providing a robust way for users to communicate with one another by typing. Low-bandwidth users, such as those connected to the network with 14,400 kbps modems, cannot use audio to communicate; therefore, text becomes especially important. The Talk window was written by Aaron Giles of the Cornell University Medical College. He developed the plug-in architecture as a demonstration of the usefulness of Auxilliary Data Transport. He succeeded.

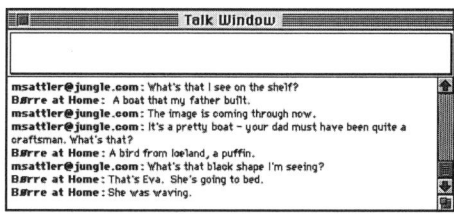

Figure 6.30. Talk window.

If you select Show Talk Window, the Talk window appears. What you type appears to others who have also installed the Talk Window Function Module. The name that you have chosen for yourself—the video title in the CU-SeeMe preferences—appears in front of each line of text you type as soon as you hit the Return key. Currently, only the menu controls—as opposed to the command keys—work for cutting and pasting to and from the Talk Window Function Module.

Slide Window

The Slide Window Function Module is now part of CU-SeeMe for Macintosh. It is a primitive whiteboard mechanism that enables you send pages of information to an audience during a presentation, just as presenters show slides through a projector. To send and receive slides, you must have QuickTime and its subsequent bug fixes and enhancements, Apple Multimedia Tuner and PowerPlug, installed because the Slide window uses QuickTimes' JPEG image compressor to lighten the transmission load.

Two conditions must be fulfilled for someone to send slides to you:

- You must have the Slide window open.
- You must have the sender's video window open.

The reverse must be true if you want to send slides to someone. Likewise, you cannot send slides if you select Stop Sending from the Preferences menu, but you can if you pause the video, which makes even more bandwidth available for the sending of slides. Sending slides uses up to seventy percent of available bandwidth, based on the current transmission capacity setting. Sharing a slide can take time if the cap is set low and the slide cannot be compressed significantly.

Using the Slide Window

Select Open Slide Window from the Conference Menu. The nonresizeable 640×480 pixel window with a button panel appears. You can now receive slides. Two modes are associated with using the Slide window: Local and Remote. When the Local button is highlighted, you are in control of which slide appears; you can grab slides, send them, and cue them for participants. In Remote mode, you just watch; and someone else controls the slides that you see.

While in Local mode, you can use the Prev and Next buttons to move backward and forward through the slides that have been accumulated.

The Discard button irrevocably deletes the current slide.

The New button enables you to preview a screen capture in the Slide window, freezing the normal video. If you press the New button, its label changes to Grab. Press Grab; the image in the Slide window freezes and the camera returns to normal CU-SeeMe mode. You can press New and Grab repeatedly to collect a series of slides and send them later during the conference. Future versions will enable you to save stacks of slides, send them in advance, and merge stacks. For now, if you quit the application—on purpose or accidentally—you will lose the whole stack that you have acquired. On a slow machine, the mode switches can be very slow, and you might find that double-clicking the New/Grab button makes things easier.

The Send button is active if anyone else in your conference or one-on-one session has his Slide window open. Press Send to transmit the image.

If you use the Prev and Next buttons to move to one of the slides that you have created, you can use the mouse to display a cursor on the slide. This cursor is larger than the normal Macintosh mouse pointer icon. When you put the Slide cursor in the Slide Window by clicking or dragging everyone who has his Slide window cued to that particular slide, a copy of the pointer moves across the slide in synchronization with yours. Get rid of the cursor by dragging it out of the window.

When you transmit a cursor, special messages go along with your video signal. At the receiving end, viewers see the top left square in your video window flicker strangely—a useful technique to show who is transmitting a cursor. After you click the cursor to position or stop dragging, whoever received it cannot accept cursor messages from anyone else for ten seconds.

Known Shortcomings and Notes on Use

Currently, the Slide window has no brightness and contrast controls. With an AV Macintosh, the same controls affect both windows. With non-AV Macintoshes you must manage the lighting directly.

The Connectix QuickCam does not produce a 640×480 pixel image. If you use the Slide Window with a QuickCam you'll get a 320×240 pixel image centered in the Slide window with unintelligible garbage—the representation of the computer's RAM—surrounding it. This can be solved by having the image expanded to fit the full size of the Slide Window.

It is possible to set up a switch with a second video camera, pointing downwards to a document table, as a dedicated slide-acquisition device. The CU-SeeMe development team has been testing a device made from $20 worth of electronics to switch cameras under software control via commands sent through a serial port. They plan on adding this as an option to CU-SeeMe.

If you have been in Local mode and then go to Remote mode, you automatically position to the last slide cued by someone else. That is, you catch up to the current state of the conference. After someone cues a slide, you cannot cue anything for ten seconds. Currently, you have no way to know when the time-out is over.

The CU-SeeMe development team has indicated their intention to improve the Slide window in the future. They plan to to improve the cursor handling so that you can point to other conferencees' slides as well as being able to tell who is pointing to whose slides.

CU-SeeMe Resources on the Internet

The CU-SeeMe user community is a far-flung supportive group of people—from experienced reflector operators to new CU-SeeMe users. Much of this book is the result of people helping others and posting their results to the CU-SeeMe discussion mailing list.

CU-SeeMe resources on the Internet are dynamic, subject to change. Instead of filling this section with Universal Resource Locators that may be stale by the time you read this book, I provide pointers to pointers. Many of us update our Web pages on a semi-monthly basis, so the information there should be up to date.

Dr. Timothy Mulkey of Indiana State University is directly responsible for much of the following being available to you on a fast Web server. Tim is a great fan of CU-SeeMe, so much so that in early 1994 he graciously donated one of his computers to be a repository of information for and by the CU-SeeMe user community. That machine, www.jungle.com, is an active Web server and list manager. (An honorable mention should be made of the mysterious Steve, a shadowy figure of a systems and network administrator who keeps this machine up and running. Thank you, Steve.) This machine is host to several mailing lists, searchable archives of all the CU-SeeMe-related mailing lists, and several megabytes of Web pages.

Internet TV with CU-SeeMe

Mailing Lists

There are several mailings lists devoted to the discussion of various aspects of CU-SeeMe. One of them is sure to cover your interests. To subscribe to a mailing list

1. Replace the words *firstname* and *lastname* with your first and last name.
2. Place your `subscribe` request in the body of the e-mail message, not on the subject line.
3. Save the acknowledgement e-mail message from the list server. It has information that you will need to refer to in order to send e-mail postings to the people who read the list and to e-mail commands to the list server—to unsubscribe, for example.

Cornell University's CU-SeeMe Announcement List

The Cornell University CU-SeeMe development team maintains an e-mail list devoted to announcing significant advances in the technology, new releases of the software, and the like. This list has very light traffic.

To subscribe to Cornell University's CU-SeeMe Announcement List, send e-mail to `listserv@cornell.edu` that reads

```
subscribe CU-SeeMe-Announce-L firstname lastname
```

Cornell University's CU-SeeMe Discussion List

The Cornell University CU-SeeMe development team maintains an e-mail list devoted to ongoing technical discussions about the software, reflectors, troubleshooting installation, related software and hardware, and events that involve CU-SeeMe. Event information is migrating to the Events List, however. This list has very heavy traffic. It is a superset of Cornell University's CU-SeeMe Announcement List, so you don't need to subscribe to both.

To subscribe to Cornell University's CU-SeeMe Discussion List, send e-mail to `listserv@cornell.edu` that reads

```
subscribe CU-SeeMe-L firstname lastname
```

CU-SeeMe Events List

Tim runs a CU-SeeMe Events mailing list. It provides announcements and discussions of broadcasts and events over the Internet that use CU-SeeMe. The goal of this list is to provide information concerning public broadcasts in which CU-SeeMe users may wish to participate or lurk. The Events list might be replaced by John Lauer's excellent CU-SeeMe Event Guide Web pages (http://www.umich.edu/~johnlaue/cuseeme/events.htm) by the time you read this.

This list is not for the discussion of hardware or software problems. Problems and technical questions should be sent to Cornell University's CU-SeeMe Discussion List.

To subscribe to the CU-SeeMe Events List, send e-mail to list-admin@www.indstate.edu that says

subscribe CUSM-Events *firstname lastname*

If you would prefer to receive a daily digest of the messages to the CU-SeeMe Events List, send e-mail to list-admin@www.indstate.edu that reads

subscribe CUSM-Events-Digest *firstname lastname*

CU-SeeMe Reflector Operator's List

Tim also runs the CU-SeeMe Reflector Operator's mailing list, which is used to coordinate reflectors for public broadcasts and events over the Internet and to provide a forum for information exchange and assistance between reflector operators. The information exchanged on this mailing list is geared to reflector operators rather than the CU-SeeMe end user.

This list is not for the general discussion of events—other than the logistics of the events as important to the operators of coordinating reflectors—nor for the discussion of hardware or software problems. Problems and technical questions should be sent to Cornell University's CU-SeeMe Discussion List.

To subscribe to the CU-SeeMe Reflector Operator's List, send e-mail to list-admin@www.indstate.edu that reads

subscribe CUSM-Reflector *firstname lastname*

If you would prefer to receive a daily digest of the messages to the CU-SeeMe Reflector Operator's List, send e-mail to list-admin@www.indstate.edu that reads

subscribe CUSM-Reflector-Digest *firstname lastname*

Official and Unoffical Sites

Cornell University maintains the official CU-SeeMe Web pages at http://cu-seeme.cornell.edu/. Our unofficial CU-SeeMe Web pages are at http://www.jungle.com/CU-SeeMe/. I am the curator of both sets of Web pages.

Internet TV with CU-SeeMe

World Wide Web Pages

Numerous web sites with information relevant to CU-SeeMe pop up all the time. Here's a list of current sites that are useful.

The CU-SeeMe Event Guide

A list of events happening on the Internet with CU-SeeMe. This list is submittable, so if you are showing an event you can post it and interested parties will see it.

http://www.umich.edu/~johnlaue/cuseeme/

The People Pages

A telephone book for CU-SeeMe users. This list is also submittable so you can tell the world that you use CU-SeeMe.

http://www.umich.edu/~johnlaue/cuseeme/people.htm

Go CU-SeeMe Go Auto Web Launcher

This program for the Windows version of CU-SeeMe allows you to click on a link on a Web page (namely the Event Guide and People Pages) and it will automatically launch CU-SeeMe and connect it to the IP address.

http://www.umich.edu/~johnlaue/cuseeme/gocusmgo.htm

White Pine Software

The company that teamed up with Cornell to work on CU-SeeMe.

http://www.wpine.com/cuseeme.html

List of CU-SeeMe Reflectors

You will find the definitive list of CU-SeeMe reflectors worldwide in BinHex 4 format (for Macintosh) at http://www.jungle.com/msattler/sci-tech/comp/CU-SeeMe/CUSeeMe_Nicknames.hqx or in ASCII format (for Windows) at http://www.jungle.com/msattler/sci-tech/comp/CU-SeeMe/CUSeeMe_Nicknames.txt. Instructions for using the list are included in the document.

CU-SeeMe User's Guide

Frequently Asked Questions and More

Frequently Asked Questions, configuration information from your fellow CU-SeeMe users, and the URLs for some fairly incredible World Wide Web pages—Eva and Børre Ludvigsen's home-on-the-Net pages come to mind—are available at http://www.jungle.com/msattler/sci-tech/comp/CU-SeeMe/. You will also find a gallery of images, including a Rogues' Gallery of CU-SeeMe users.

Searchable Archives

Searchable archives of the CU-SeeMe Discussion List, CU-SeeMe Event List, and the CU-SeeMe Reflector Operator's List can be found at http://www.jungle.com/CU-SeeMe/all_archives.html.

Miscellaneous

The current and historic load on www.jungle.com is available to you in a great variety of forms. Interested in seeing how many people are hitting this server and where they come from? Check out the multigraph statistics page at http://www.jungle.com/stats.html.

REFLECTOR OPERATOR'S GUIDE

CHAPTER 7

Much of the power of CU-SeeMe videoconferencing is the capability of having group conferences. This is done by having participants, running the Macintosh or Windows CU-SeeMe client software, connect to a CU-SeeMe reflector, maintained by a reflector operator.

This chapter is for you, the reflector operator. You are a very important link in the CU-SeeMe chain; it's the work you do, and the events you choose to broadcast, that give CU-SeeMe its public persona. Chapter 8, "History, Culture, and Usage," shows many of the ways CU-SeeMe reflectors have been used in the past. Many of these uses were innovative, bringing people together in ways heretofore impossible. These uses are also responsible for the flattering press that CU-SeeMe has received. You have some big shoes to fill; this chapter is designed to make sure you have the technical know-how.

After you read this chapter you'll know

- The purpose and operation of a CU-SeeMe reflector.
- How to install, configure, and maintain a CU-SeeMe reflector.

 **Internet TV with CU-SeeMe**

- How to interoperate a CU-SeeMe reflector and MBone (the Internet Multicast Backbone).
- What steps you'll need to take when broadcasting an event.

So You Want To Run a Reflector in a Hurry

There are times when you'll be in a (pardon the pun) reflective mood, ready to read documentation and get an entire concept in mind before moving on. At other times you'll turn to the manual only when several frenzied attempts fail miserably. This section is for those latter times. The following steps will, if you're extremely lucky, get a reflector up and running on your UNIX box. If it doesn't, you'll have to read the remainder of this chapter (which I'll endeavor to make relatively painless).

1. **Start with a well-connected UNIX box.** Reflectors, by their very nature, shuffle around lots of bits and therefore require lots of bandwidth. If you're running a reflector on your corporate LAN, you'll need lots of bandwidth there too. You'll be desconsolate if you try to operate a reflector over a modem or antiquated LAN; don't try to, and don't ask me why it won't work for you. You can't put ten pounds of manure into a five-pound bag.
2. **All UNIXes are equal, some are just more equal than others.** The CU-SeeMe reflector will work on many versions of UNIX, from Santa Cruz Operations (SCO) UNIX to Linux (far and away the preferred UNIX).
3. **Obtain the CU-SeeMe reflector software.** The current versions of the CU-SeeMe reflector executables are available for you to obtain via FTP from

    ftp://cu-seeme.cornell.edu/pub/CU-SeeMe/Reflector/

    You'll see that the reflector has been compiled for you, for a variety of UNIXes; get the one that corresponds to the UNIX system you'll be using to run the CU-SeeMe reflector software. If your UNIX kernel supports multicast then get the version with the "MC" extension.
4. **Edit the reflector configuration file.** The reflect.conf file controls the behavior and operation of the CU-SeeMe reflector; it's very important for you to know how to edit this file to customize your reflector. For starters, we'll provide only the most necessary features; set up your reflect.conf like this:

    ```
    //MOTD Welcome to my reflector.
    //MAX-PARTICIPANTS 8
    //MAX-SENDERS 8
    ```

Reflector Operator's Guide

5. **Fire up the CU-SeeMe reflector.** To start the CU-SeeMe reflector in the background, type

   reflect &

   at the UNIX shell prompt.

That's it. With luck you're now up and running. If not, read on.

What's a CU-SeeMe Reflector?

CU-SeeMe allows you to initiate and accept point-to-point sessions between one other party and yourself. A reflector provides you with the ability to have multi-party CU-SeeMe sessions between several other participants and yourself. You can all see each other (assuming you're all using cameras) and talk, wave, or use sign language in real-time.

Why Is a CU-SeeMe Reflector Needed?

To date there are no ways of having Windows- or Macintosh-based systems reflect video and audio streams in a way that allows multi-party CU-SeeMe connections. So the CU-SeeMe development team wrote a UNIX-based piece of software to do the job—the CU-SeeMe reflector.

As it turns out, having the CU-SeeMe reflector software running on a separate machine is good thing. A high-end Macintosh or Windows machine uses most of its processor time dealing with video and audio digitization and compression; earlier machines are overwhelmed by the burden. Running the reflector on the same machine would make the performance unacceptable.

For example, one reasonably satisfying CU-SeeMe connection requires about 80 kbps of bandwidth. For eight people to communicate requires 640 kbps. But that's just for the reflector to receive everyone's data—the reflector must also "reflect" that data to every other member. For eight participants the reflector needs 5120 kbps of bandwidth (that is, 5.12 mbps (megabits per second)). That's only a conservative example; Cornell's CU-SeeMe reflector typically has over 30 participants!

Why UNIX?

Reflecting CU-SeeMe audio and video streams requires lots of processor power and network bandwidth. Historically, UNIX boxes have had better network connectivity (a built-in capability in all but the earliest UNIXes) and much more

Internet TV with CU-SeeMe

processor power. Historically, UNIX machines have been able to stay operational for much longer periods of time than have personal computers. Since it was desirable to have the CU-SeeMe reflector available around the clock, UNIX was a logical choice. Previously, only UNIX had the ability to multicast (send packets to multiple destinations simultaneously). As multicasting is an integral part of the CU-SeeMe reflector's operation, this was a deciding factor in the decision to adopt UNIX as the operating system of choice. The fact that UNIX is available for almost every piece of computing hardware only made the choice a better one.

Modern Macintoshes and Windows machines are capable of being reflectors, what with faster processors and robust network connectivity. Since porting the CU-SeeMe reflector to these operating systems takes time and money, and since the UNIX-based reflectors are quite serviceable, it's not a high priority.

What Can the CU-SeeMe Reflector Do?

This chapter explores the many features of the CU-SeeMe reflector. Since there is no graphic front end available to control the CU-SeeMe reflector, you'll have to edit the reflect.conf text file to affect changes. This may feel akward to people used to working only on Macintosh or Windows, but I'll try to provide all the information you need to painlessly control the CU-SeeMe reflector.

Many-to-Many

The most common CU-SeeMe reflector configuration is a many-to-many scenario, where many people join a conference (an oasis in cyberspace) at one time. Due to present-day bandwidth and processor limitations of computing systems, the CU-SeeMe reflector has artificial limits placed upon its operation: a maximum of 40 people may join a conference and any participant may see only seven others (although you may choose which seven). As network connections and processor speeds evolve you should expect these numbers to grow.

One-to-Many

A less common, but still popular, CU-SeeMe reflector configuration is the one-to-many scenario, where the reflector operator selects some information to broadcast to an audience. NASA Select TV is perhaps the best-known one-to-many provider. (Information about NASA Select TV may be found in Chapter 2, "Typical CU-SeeMe Usage.")

The ability to chain reflectors (explained below) and interoperate with MBone (also explained below) affords reflector operators the ability to reach a worldwide audience. While it's not yet possible to rival the for-profit television networks, it's a definite improvement over e-mail.

Multicast-to-Unicast

The CU-SeeMe reflector can listen to a multicast connection (such as MBone) and reflect those multicast packets onto unicast packets, the form required by current Macintosh and Windows machines. (Multicast capability is forthcoming for both those platforms.) This brings a great deal of video "programming" to an audience that wouldn't otherwise be able to recieve it.

Unicast-to-Multicast

The CU-SeeMe reflector can take a unicast audio and video stream that a Macintosh or Windows user generates and multicast it to many participants (or other reflectors). This is the only way that current Macintosh and Windows users can participate in conferences.

MBone: The Multicast Backbone

The Multicast Backbone is a very popular form of videoconferencing sent across the Internet that predates CU-SeeMe. MBone operators set up ad-hoc MBone networks by stringing together reflectors and "tunnelling" each other's data, broadcasting events to "huge" audiences. MBone is also used to run cross- or intercontinental multiparty conferences.

Audio-only conferences

Most of my descriptions are about using audio and video together, but the CU-SeeMe reflector can reflect an audio-only stream. Since not everyone has a system capable of transmitting video, or the budget to purchase a camera (although serial-port cameras now cost less than $100), we end up with a class of users known as "lurkers." (Chapter 6, The "CU-SeeMe User's Guide," shows how to identify lurkers on a conference.) There are several ways of transmitting an audio-only stream: configuring CU-SeeMe to send only audio, using Maven (software by Charley Kline), and others. Because audio requires far less bandwidth (typically on the order of 10 kbps), it's possible to have a satisfying conversation via a 14.4 kbps modem.

Requirements for Running the CU-SeeMe Reflector

For reasons listed above, UNIX is the operating system required to run the reflector.

Native UNIX box

The CU-SeeMe development team wrote the CU-SeeMe reflector to be portable and run on most UNIXes. The team and White Pine (the commercial licensee of CU-SeeMe) provide the CU-SeeMe reflector as compiled executables for the IBM's AIX and Sun Microsystem's SunOS flavors of UNIX. The source code is made available to those who use another UNIX.

Intel-based UNIX box

If you don't have a Sun SPARC or IBM RS/6000, you can always have an Intel-based computer run UNIX. There are many UNIXes available; the most notable are Linux and FreeBSD. Both of these are free.

Linux

Linux is a cooperative effort by hundreds of programmers all over the world, all being loosely coordinated by Linus Thorvald. Operating system hackers tease, tweak, and torture the best performance out of each facet and then send the improved code back to Linus, who incorporates it into the next release of Linux.

Linux may be found on the Internet at

ftp://ftp.cdrom.com/pub/linux/

Even though the SlackWare installer does pretty much everything for you, there are many "how-to" documents available that explain the many facets of Linux.

Linux also is available on a CD-ROM, and as part of a huge book entitled *Linux Unleashed*.

FreeBSD

FreeBSD is an implementation of the Berkeley Software Distribution of UNIX. It's available on the Internet as well, at

ftp://ftp.cdrom.com/pub/FreeBSD/

FreeBSD is one of the UNIXes for which the CU-SeeMe development team and White Pine provide reflector executables. There are also CD-ROMs that contain FreeBSD and many free applications.

Reflector Operator's Guide

Windows NT

Some people have claimed to have compiled the CU-SeeMe reflector on Windows NT, but to date the executable hasn't made it back to any site that I've found. The rumor is credible, since Windows NT provides multicast capibility and its networking is Berkeley-compliant (what's required by the CU-SeeMe reflector).

Until this question is settled, I can best serve by pointing you to the best source-code compilers available, those of the GNU (GNU's not UNIX) project. These may be found all over the Internet, including

`ftp://ftp.cc.utexas.edu/pub/microlib/nt/gnu/`

Here you'll find the GNU C complier, plus the header files the CU-SeeMe reflector source code requires. (If you don't know what header files are, buy a local programmer a nice dinner in exchange for assistance in compiling the CU-SeeMe reflector.) You might have to change the networking portion around so it uses WinSock (Windows Socket) instead of the typical UNIX network header files.

Macintosh

Because of its inherent support for bitmapped graphics and high-quality audio, CU-SeeMe was developed first for Macintosh. While it would be nice to have the CU-SeeMe reflector run on Macintosh, that's currently not feasible. (Once the multicast-capable version of Open Transport is released, expect to see a Macintosh-based CU-SeeMe reflector.) Just as owners of Intel-based computers have UNIXes they can use, so do Macintosh owners. Sadly, however, none of the free UNIXes have been ported to Macintosh.

A/UX

A few hardy souls have gotten the reflector compiled and operating properly on an Apple Workgroup Server running A/UX (Apple UNIX). Since Apple is no longer supporting A/UX, this may not be the best investment of your time. I'd suggest asking around on Usenet newsgroups before trying to reinvent this particular wheel. (Specifically, I recall that changes in the file buffering code is required, and that configuring the CU-SeeMe reflector via the reflect.conf doesn't work—you'll have to be satisfied with the default settings. Or you can hack the source code with wild abandon.)

MachTen

Tenon MachTen, a commercial version of UNIX, runs on top of the Macintosh operating system (instead of taking over the hardware completely, the canonical way of UNIXes). There have been no claims of getting the CU-SeeMe reflector working on MachTen, but in the interests of completeness I mention it. The MachTen distribution includes the GNU compilers and libraries. Information about MachTen may be found on the Internet at

http://www.tenon.com/

A Fast Network Connection

Earlier in this chapter I touched upon the great amounts of bandwidth CU-SeeMe can use. (CU-SeeMe doesn't need to be a network hog; you can change its behavior to be more network-friendly, something covered in Chapter 6, "The CU-SeeMe User's Guide.") Figure 7.1 shows the flow of data in a five-person CU-SeeMe conversation through the CU-SeeMe reflector (the box in the middle).

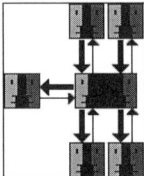

Figure 7.1. A five-way conversation.

Each of the thin arrows represents 80 kbps of data, one CU-SeeMe audio/video stream; the thick arrows represent four times that amount (the data each participant receives to see and hear the other four participants). 80 kbps is a typical CU-SeeMe setting, far from its maximum of 500 kbps. The reflector is sending and receiving 400 kbps for each participant, for a total of 2000 kbps (2 mbps). It becomes readily apparent why the processor and network capability of the participant's computers and the CU-SeeMe reflector's computer need to be powerful.

Chapter 4, "Hardware," discusses the capabilities of different networking connection options. We've already ruled out running a reflector over a modem connection. Figure 7.2 summarizes the remainder of this subsection. Please note that Figure 7.2 refers to medium and large multi-party conferences. One-way broadcasting and small multi-party groups are quite workable via ISDN.

Table 7.1. Connections and capabilities.

Connection	Bandwidth (kbps)	Will it Work?	Considerations
Modem	14.4	No	Even point-to-point is daunting at this speed
Modem	28.8	No	Still not enough throughput
ISDN	(1 bearer channel) 64	No	You will still be disappointed if you try to have a conference at this rate
ISDN	(2 bearer channels) 128	Sort of	Depending on cap rates, this type of connection has possibilities
T1	1500	Yes	Multiple users can send 80 kbps comfortably
Ethernet	10000	Yes	Unless your Ethernet is saturated with other data, things will work well
T3	45000	Yes	Now we have to consider if the reflector machine can handle all the traffic that this bandwidth can throw at it
Fast Ethernet	100000	Yes	Now we lament that CU-SeeMe can "only" transmit 500 kbps

A typical industrial-strength reflector needs a connection that affords at least 1.5 mbps of throughput. If your local area network is connected to the Internet (or your company-wide network, depending upon the intended audience) over a T1 line or better, you'll be able to run a satisfying conference, given a reasonable number of participants who each transmit a reasonable amount of data.

Internet TV with CU-SeeMe

ISDN is unlikely to support an enjoyable conference since a single bearer channel provides only between 0.056 to 0.064 mbps (56 to 64 kbps). Home ISDN supports two bearer channels, for a total throughput of between 0.112 and 0.128 mbps. (I'm using mbps for the moment for comparison with our target 1.5 mbps.)

Ethernet is the connection method of choice. A local area network running on Ethernet will flourish in its 10 mbps capacity. Remember that a connection to your reflector is as fast as its slowest link. If you're on a Fast Ethernet local area network connected into the Internet over ISDN, the Internet participants will only have 56 to 128 kbps to work with. That's not much of anything in the videoconferencing world.

The Reflector Software

As mentioned before, Cornell University is the definitive source for the latest releases of the CU-SeeMe client software and the CU-SeeMe reflector software. The URL (Uniform Resource Locator) for the reflector software is

`ftp://cu-seeme.cornell.edu/pub/CU-SeeMe/Reflector/`

When this book was written the directory containing the latest reflector release (4.0 beta 1) looked like Figure 7.2.

Figure 7.2. The reflector directory.

The CU-SeeMe Development Team no longer releases the source code for the reflectors except under license; the reflector sources are provided in the same way as are the sources to the CU-SeeMe clients). When a new reflector version is ready for release, binaries for SunOS 4.x.x, for BSDI, and for AIX will be provided immediately at Cornell. Within a day or so, binaries for other platforms will be compiled by White Pine and posted there and at Cornell. White Pine's FTP site is at

`http://www.wpine.com/CU-SeeMe/`

If you are using a UNIX for which neither Cornell nor White Pine are making executables, you will be able to get sources under an Internal Use Only license or under a license that permits free redistribution of modified binaries if you give the modifications back to Cornell and White Pine. Both of these licenses will be free or nominal-cost (administrative charge). You can get a commercial license from White Pine.

You'll also find many compiled versions of an earlier CU-SeeMe reflector (version 3.0b3) at

`ftp://248.138.med.umich.edu/pub/reflector/`

This site has executables for platforms not supported by White Pine or the CU-SeeMe Development Team.

MC or NO MC

To multicast or not to multicast, that is the question. If your UNIX supports multicast (ask your system or network administrator), then download the "MC" version.

Source Code

If you can't find a CU-SeeMe reflector executable for the UNIX you're using, you can plead your case with the CU-SeeMe development team. They've got a policy of releasing the source code if you have a good reason. Compiling it for another UNIX, especially if Cornell can add it to the ftp site, probably qualifies.

Running the Reflector

Here's the easy part. To actually run the reflector all you need to type is

`reflect`

The reflector will then read the reflect.conf file, echo the parameters to the screen, configure itself, and begin operating. Any errors that are found in reflect.conf will be noted in the on-screen output.

Once the reflect.conf has been read in, the CU-SeeMe reflector will quietly sit, doing its job. If you're connected through telnet, and you disconnect at this point, UNIX will stop the reflector (because when you log off all sessions started are discontinued). To have the CU-SeeMe reflector continue operating after you leave, use an ampersand when you invoke the reflector to put the job in the background, as in:

`reflect &`

Configuring the CU-SeeMe Reflector

The directives presented in the remainder of this section are important; they're how you'll configure the CU-SeeMe reflector to work its best. The directives are not presented in alphabetical order, they're presented in the order you're most likely to use them.

> **Multiple Configurations**
>
> You don't have to use the name reflect.conf for the CU-SeeMe reflector configuration file; that's just the default name. If you're playing around with several configuration files, you can give each of them a different name and tell the reflector which file you want it to use, as in:
>
> `reflect config-try-6 &`

SAMPLE parameter
```
Sample directive
Default values go here
```

Each directive in this section will be presented in this format. The directive itself will appear in uppercase, optional parameters appear in lowercase following the directive. The lines that follow contain the directive's purpose and default value. Lastly, a paragraph of text will explain how to use the directive.

General directives

MOTD message-string
```
Message of the day
Default = Disabled
```

The MOTD, the message of the day, is the greeting that participants to a CU-SeeMe conference see when they first connect. The MOTD is important; it sets the tone of conduct for participants. A good MOTD welcomes the participant, makes them feel comfortable, and provides them with vital operating information. A MOTD should present most of the following:

- the geographical location of the CU-SeeMe reflector
- the organization that owns the reflector
- the name of the reflector operator
- the e-mail address of the operator

- the URL of a web site that contains more information about this reflector site
- the maximum data transmission rate and the consequences should you send at a higher rate
- the earliest version of CU-SeeMe you can use to connect to this CU-SeeMe reflector
- the VAT port number

For example, here's the MOTD entry that was recently used by one CU-SeeMe reflector site:

```
MOTD Welcome to internetRADIO, the first radio station
dedicated to the internet broadcasting 24 hours/day.
We're located in Ann Arbor, MI on a T3 connection.

You must connect in receive only mode. This reflector
supports up to 40 lurkers. You can also listen through
VAT and NV on port 3334.

If you have any comments or suggestions please email
internet.RADIO@umich.edu.

Have a nice internetRADIO!
//
```

Note the two trailing forward-slashes on the last line, appearing all by themselves. This ends the message text. You'll need to remember to terminate message strings in the directives that use them. (Fortunately, the CU-SeeMe reflector's error-checking code is quite good at noticing this error.)

DEBUG

Debugging messages enabled?
Default = Disabled

In debug mode the CU-SeeMe reflector prints out more information during its operation. This directive is invaluable if you are having trouble with a configuration or just want to see what's going on behind the scenes.

SELF-REFLECT

Reflect your own video stream back at you
Default = Disabled

During the initial phases of configuration debugging it's useful to see what you're sending to the CU-SeeMe reflector. You'll see yourself twice, once in the local window and once as a participant. Because of the load each video stream places upon the CU-SeeMe reflector, this directive is rarely used once the CU-SeeMe reflector is put into operation.

Internet TV with CU-SeeMe

Security Directives

CONF-ID conference-id message-string
```
Restrict conference to invited participants
Default = 0
```

You may want to run an invitation-only CU-SeeMe reflector session; perhaps a stockholder's meeting. You accomplish this by choosing a conference identifier (an integer between 1 and 32,768 that you choose at random) which you send to the invited parties. They'll need to provide the conference identifier when they attempt to connect to the CU-SeeMe reflector.

Should someone attempt to "crash your party," or mistype the proper conference identifier, they'll be greeted by the rejection message string you've specified. The directive might appear like this:

```
CONF-ID 22222 We are currently holding a private
session on this reflector.  Try again later.
//
```

If you choose a conference identifier in the range of 32,769 to 65,535, users will not be turned away (although they will see the message), they'll only be allowed to receive audio and video streams. This mode is ideal for broadcast reflectors such as NASA Select TV or internetRADIO.

CONF-MGR ip-address
```
Dynamically set the conference identifier
Default = Disabled
```

Rather than provide a fixed conference identifer, you may choose this directive to give you the ability to change the conference identifier whenever you connect to the CU-SeeMe reflector. This way you can make the reflector private at a moment's notice.

You provide your IP address as the parameter to this directive. When you connect to the CU-SeeMe reflector it takes note of the conference identifier you've specified and dynamically changes the current conference identifier to that value. Participants that subsequently connect must provide the same conference identifier you just did; any who don't will be treated to the rejection message specified with the CONF-ID directive.

To make the conference once again open to all, you must connect with a conference identifier of 0.

ADMIT ip-address message-string

```
Admit participants based upon their IP address
Default = Disabled
```

The conference identifier doesn't provide particularly strenuous security; an annoying person can break in by trying all 32,767 choices. This directive allows you to admit participants based upon their IP address, a much better form of security. The downside of using this directive is that it's more work to specify each participant's IP address to the CU-SeeMe reflector configuration file that it is picking a random conference identifier. (Please look at the ALLOW and DENY directives, below.)

When a participant attempts to connect to your reflector, their IP address will be checked against the list of approved addresses. A match lets them in, otherwise they're shown the message string specified in the last ADMIT directive found. For example:

```
ADMIT 141.211.10.45 Unused but required message string
//
ADMIT 141.211.10.46 Unused but required message string
//
ADMIT 141.214.10.47 Unused but required message string
//
ADMIT 1.2.3.4 We are currently holding a private
session on this reflector.  Try again later.
//
```

ALLOW ip-address message-string

```
Allow participation based upon an IP address range
Default = Disabled
```

This directive allows you to permit a specific IP address or a range of IP addresses to participate in your CU-SeeMe reflector session. An asterik '*' denotes any value for that address portion. For example:

```
ALLOW 128.127.203.72
ALLOW 204.192.15.*
```

DENY ip-address message-string

```
Deny participation based upon an IP address range
Default = Disabled
```

This directive allows you to deny a specific IP address or a range of IP addresses to participate in your CU-SeeMe reflector session. An asterisk '*' denotes any value for that address portion. For example:

```
DENY 128.127.203.72
DENY 204.192.15.*
```

 Internet TV with CU-SeeMe

REFMON ip-address
```
Which machine will run the Reflector Monitor?
Default = anyone
```

Without this directive in your CU-SeeMe reflector configuration file, anyone with the Reflector Monitor program may connect. Because this is a security hole, it's typical to specify the IP address of the reflector operator's favorite computer, or to disallow all uses by specifying an IP address of 0.0.0.0.

Reflector and Bandwidth Load Directives

CAP cap penalty-time message-string
```
Set the maximum permitted transmission rate
Default = 80 kbps, 1 minute penalty
```

The transmission cap you set will certainly have an effect upon the behavior of your CU-SeeMe reflector. (See the beginning of this chapter for a discussion of reflector load.) A participant that transmits a greater rate than what you've set (or by default, 80 kbps) will be thrown off the reflector for penalty-time minutes after being shown message-string. For example:

```
CAP 40 2 I only have enough money to afford an ISDN connection with two B
channels.  So you must set your cap rate at less than 40.   Sorry.
//
```

MAX-PARTICIPANTS number-allowed message-string
```
Set the maximum number of participants
Default = 20
```

In order to manage the load on your machine (and your network), use this directive to limit the number of people who congregate on your CU-SeeMe reflector. The reflector has a built-in limit of 40, so to get more you'll have to string a few reflectors together.

This directive controls the maximum number of participants, whether they be senders or lurkers. The MAX-SENDERS and MAX-LURKERS directives (below) control the maximum number of each type of participant.

Rejected participants will be shown message-string. For example:

```
MAX-PARTICIPANTS 8 Too many participants now.
//
```

MAX-SENDERS number-allowed message-string
```
Set the maximum number of participants that are sending audio and/or video
Default = 20
```

This directive controls the number of participants that are sending audio and/or video. There is a built-in maximum of 40. This setting is only consulted after the MAX-PARTICIPANTS directive has been checked.

Rejected participants will be shown message-string. For example:

```
MAX-SENDERS 8 Too many video senders now.
//
```

MAX-LURKERS number-allowed message-string
```
Set the maximum number of lurkers
Default = 20
```

This directive controls the number of participants that are not sending any signal. There is a built-in maximum of 40. This setting is only consulted after the MAX-PARTICIPANTS directive has been checked.

Rejected participants will be shown message-string. For example:

```
MAX-LURKERS 8 Too many lurkers now.
//
```

Log File Directives

LOG Filename
```
What log file should the reflector use?
Default = reflect.log
```

The CU-SeeMe reflector log file is where rejected entry attempts are noted, etc. To use another log file, you'll specify a path and filename. For example:

```
LOG /usr/guildenstern/logs/whats-up.log
```

LOG-LIMIT maximum-lines
```
The maximum number of lines in the log file
Default = 10000
```

An unbounded log file would fill up a hard disk. This directive allows you to control the maximum size of the CU-SeeMe reflector log file. The maximum is 65535 lines. A value of 0 prevents the log file from being created. One LOG-LIMIT is reached, the entire log file is deleted and started anew.

Feed directives

ADMIT-BCC-CLIENT ip-address
```
Link this reflector to another
Default = Disabled
```

This directive is used to link CU-SeeMe reflectors, usually for event broadcasting. The maximum number of total possible participants is increased and the load on the reflectors can be distributed. Each reflector specified will receive a "blind carbon copy" of all CU-SeeMe streams on this reflector. Any number of "downstream" reflectors may be specified. For example:

```
ADMIT-BCC-CLIENT 35.1.1.91
ADMIT-BCC-CLIENT 10.65.7.9
```

OBTAIN-BCC ip-address
```
Specify an "upstream" reflector that's feeding you
Default = Disabled
```

There are times you'll be asked to use your reflector to help broadcast someone else's feed. That reflector operator will specify your CU-SeeMe reflector with an ADMIT-BCC-CLIENT directive in its reflect.conf. You, in turn, specify that reflector's IP address with this directive, which can appear only once in your reflect.conf (you can't simultaneously receive feeds from multiple reflectors).

Figure 7.3 shows a main CU-SeeMe reflector with two downstream CU-SeeMe reflectors specified with ADMIT-BCC-CLIENT directives and those downstream CU-SeeMe reflectors each specifying the main reflector with OBTAIN-BCC directives.

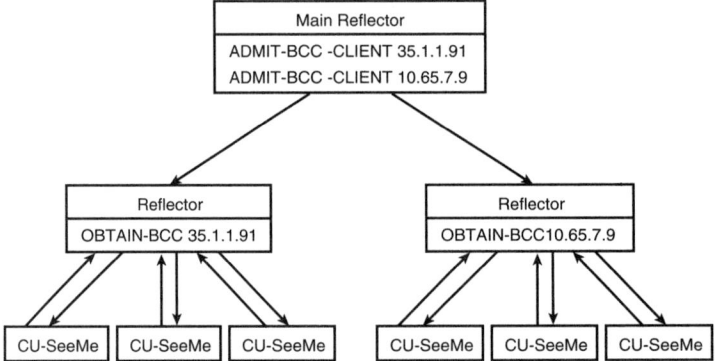

Figure 7.3. Chaining reflectors.

ADMIT-GENERAL-BCC max-reflectors conference-id
```
A less secure way of chaining reflectors
Default = Disabled
```

Using the ADMIT-BCC-CLIENT directive requires some maintenance of the reflect.conf but affords a higher measure of security. The ADMIT-GENERAL-BCC directive provides lower security but requires less configuration maintenance. You specify the maximum number of reflectors you're willing to feed and a conference identifier (which you divulge to reflector operators you wish to feed). Any reflector that knows the conference identifier will be given a feed, up to max reflectors. The maximum number of reflectors is 65,535. The conference identifier may range from 1 to 65,535.

```
ADMIT-GENERAL-BCC 9 222
```

OBTAIN-GENERAL-BCC ip-address conference-id
```
Specify an upstream ADMIT-GENERAL-BCC reflector
Default = Disabled
```

When someone else's CU-SeeMe reflector is feeding yours (with the ADMIT-GENERAL-BCC directive) you must use this directive to point back at them. You must also specify the correct conference-id. This directive may appear only once in your reflect.conf (you can't simultaneously receive feeds from multiple reflectors).

```
OBTAIN-GENERAL-BCC 35.1.1.91 222
```

Figure 7.4 shows a CU-SeeMe reflector hierarchy that's been assembled with the ADMIT-GENERAL-BCC and OBTAIN-GENERAL-BCC directives.

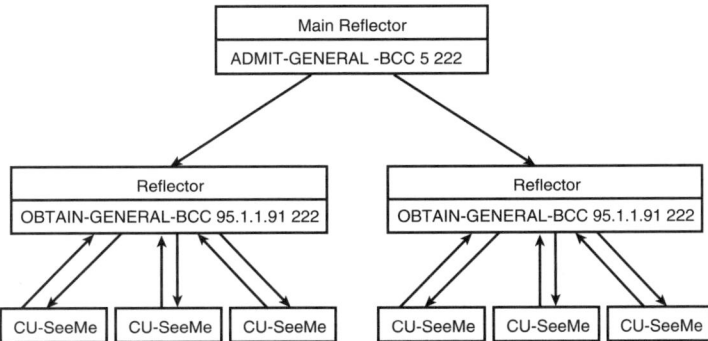

Figure 7.4. Chaining reflectors with GENERAL directives.

MC-OUT time-to-live multicast-ip-address

```
Feed a multicast broadcast
Default = Disabled
```

If your UNIX kernel and CU-SeeMe reflector executable have multicast capability, you can use this directive to feed a multicast. Multicast, which sends one stream across the Internet instead of multiple streams to specific reflectors, is by far the more efficient way of broadcasting. Each of the client reflectors must have multicast capabilities. CU-SeeMe currently doesn't, but look to this as a great growth area for future development.

The time-to-live parameter defines how far the multicast stream will reach, how long it will "live."

```
MC-OUT 64 128.127.203.74
```

MC-IN multicast-ip-address

```
Receive a multicast feed
Default = Disabled
```

Just as you can provide a multicast feed with the MC-OUT directive, you can receive a multicast feed with this directive. These directives are mutually exclusive; you can't give and take at the same time. Make sure the upstream multicast source has a time-to-live value that's high enough to ensure its signal "lives" long enough to reach you.

```
MC-IN 128.127.203.74
```

Figure 7.5 shows a multicast reflector hierarchy.

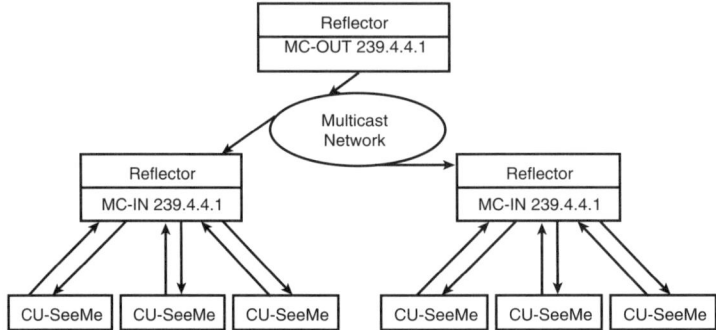

Figure 7.5. A multicast reflector hierarchy.

NO-LOCAL-SENDERS

```
Allow participants only to view, not interact, while on a reflector receiving
an MC-IN or OBTAIN-BCC feed
Default = Disabled
```

This directive puts all participants into receive-only mode, which helps to limit the load on the reflector, to obtain better quality and to prevent disruptive interferences by participants. It's like setting the CONF-ID between 32,768 and 65,535, or setting MAX-SENDERS to 0, but this directive is specific to reflectors that are receiving MC-IN or OBTAIN-BCC feeds. Somewhat redundant, it allows flexibility in configuring your CU-SeeMe reflector.

Figure 7.6 shows an MC-IN feed with NO-LOCAL-SENDERS set. Compare this with Figure 7.5.

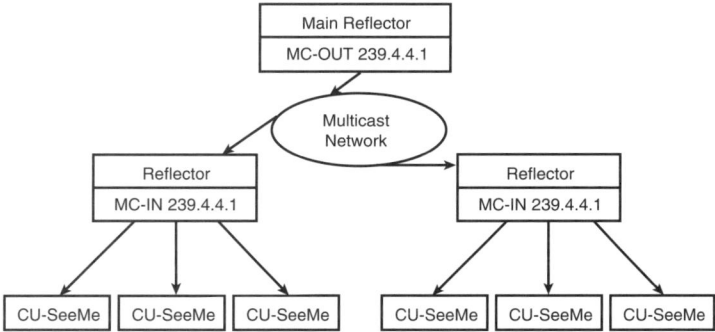

Figure 7.6. The effect of NO-LOCAL-SENDERS.

ADMIT-SENDER ip-address

```
Allow certain participants to override NO-LOCAL-SENDERS
Default = Disabled
```

This directive allows you to permit certain local participants to provide a CU-SeeMe stream when all others can't. This is useful for staging a debate, for example, where only a few participants debate while others watch.

```
ADMIT-SENDER 41.21.1.3
ADMIT-SENDER 35.1.1.92
```

Synchronization directives

UNICAST-REF ip-address

```
Specify one or more unicast reflectors to act as peers
Default = Disabled
```

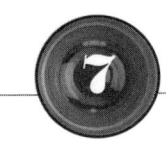

Internet TV with CU-SeeMe

Up to this point I've described reflector hierarchies, where upstream reflectors provide feeds and downstream reflectors receive feeds. This directive specifies one or more unicast reflectors that will act as peers; participants on one peer reflector are able to interact with participants on any other peer reflector. CU-SeeMe reflectors are unicast reflectors; use the MC-GROUP directive to specify multicast peer reflectors.

When participants are spread out across the country or the world, setting up a group of reflectors through this method is much more efficient than having all the participants connecting to one reflector. Only one stream of data is being sent to each reflector from the others, instead of multiple streams to each client. The multicast version of this configuration is more efficient yet.

Don't specify your own reflector's IP address.

```
UNICAST-REF 41.21.1.2
UNICAST-REF 35.1.1.91
UNICAST-REF 10.6.72.9
```

Figure 7.7 shows one configuration of peer unicast reflectors.

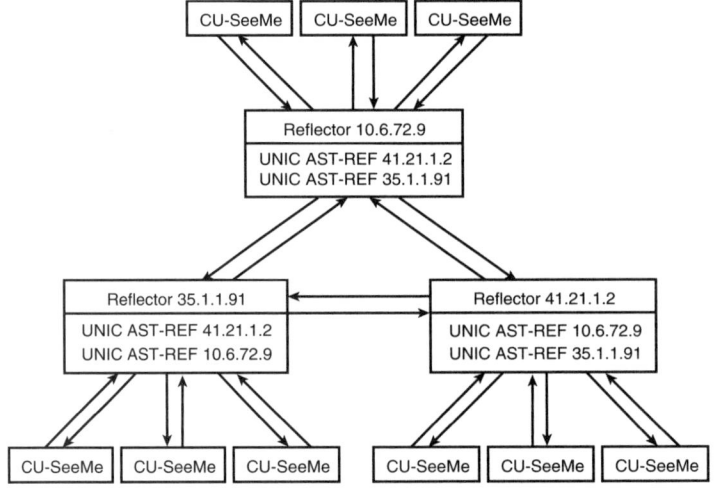

Figure 7.7. Unicast peers.

MC-GROUP ip-address

```
Specify one or more multicast reflectors to act as peers
Default = Disabled
```

Reflector Operator's Guide

Compare this directive with UNICAST-REF. Participants on one peer multicast reflector are able to interact with participants on any other peer reflector. Since multicast is more bandwidth-efficient, this configuration is preferred to unicast peering.

All peer multicast reflectors must be on the MBone or on a local area network that is multicast-capable across subnets.

```
MC-GROUP 128.127.203.74
```

Figure 7.8 shows one configuration of peer multicast reflectors.

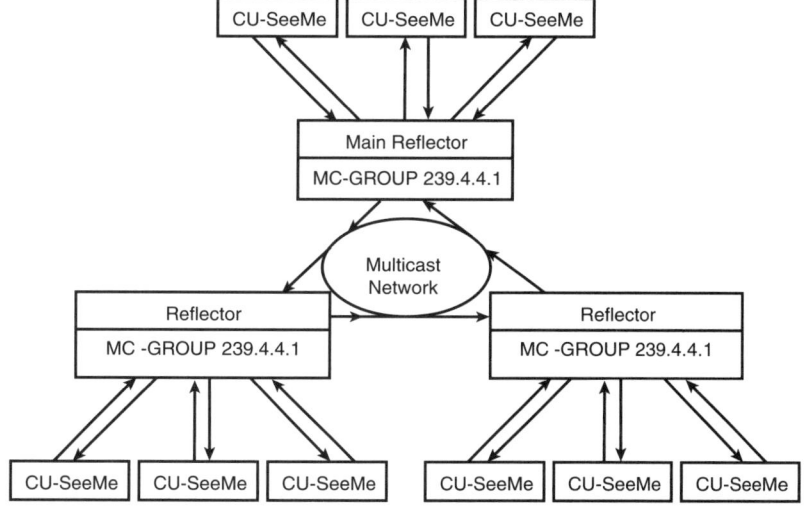

Figure 7.8. Multicast peers.

Directives for Working with UNIX Video Clients

NV-UC-PORT port-number

```
Specify the unicast UDP port number for NV clients
Default = Disabled
```

NV (Network Video) is a Unix program like CU-SeeMe. The CU-SeeMe reflector can interoperate with NV clients. Because NV doesn't have a default port that it communicates on, you must specify one. The NV client will need to know what port you choose, so this is something to note on your message of the day. You may choose any port between 1 and 65,535.

```
NV-UC-PORT 4444
```

NV-MC-PORT port-number

```
Specify the multicast UDP port number for NV clients
Default = Disabled
```

This directive is the multicast counterpart to NV-UC-PORT. Using multicast to interoperate with NV is preferred because multicast puts less of a load on your network. You may choose a port between 1 and 65,535. As ever, you must be on the MBone or have a local area network that is multicast-capable across subnets, and have a UNIX kernel and CU-SeeMe reflector executable that are multicast-enabled.

```
NV-MC-PORT 4444
```

NV-MC-IN multicast-ip-address

```
Receive CU-SeeMe streams from NV clients over multicast
Default = Disabled
```

NV is able to send CU-SeeMe streams (although you must tell your NV client to do this instead of its native encoding). This directive specifies an NV client that is sending you CU-SeeMe streams.

```
NV-MC-IN 239.4.4.1
```

NV-MC-OUT time-to-live multicast-ip-address

```
Send CU-SeeMe streams to NV clients over multicast
Default = Disabled
```

The CU-SeeMe reflector will send CU-SeeMe streams to the NV clients you specify. The time-to-live parameter determines how far your signal will travel (how long the signal will "live"). If you're using both the NV-MC-IN and NV-MC-OUT directives, both must have the same IP address as parameters.

```
NV-MC-OUT 239.4.4.1
```

NV-STREAMS number

```
Limit the number of video streams sent to NV clients
Default = 4
```

This directive limits the number of streams your CU-SeeMe reflector will send to the NV client specified in the NV-MC-OUT directive, lessening the load on the network and on the computer running the NV client. (You can limit only the number of streams; you can't pick and choose *which* streams to send.) You could limit the number of streams you're sending and choose which streams those are by selecting who may participate in your conference.

You may select up to 40 streams.

`NV-STREAMS 8`

VAT-UC-PORT port-number
Specify the unicast UDP port number for VAT clients
Default = Disabled

VAT (Video Audio Tool) is a UNIX program like CU-SeeMe. The CU-SeeMe reflector can interoperate with VAT clients. Because VAT doesn't have a default port that it communicates on, you must specify one. The NV client will need to know what port you choose, so this is something to note on your message of the day. You may choose any port between 1 and 65,535.

`VAT-UC-PORT 4444`

VAT-MC-PORT port-number
Specify the multicast UDP port number for VAT clients
Default = Disabled

This directive is the multicast counterpart to `VAT-UC-PORT`. Using multicast to interoperate with VAT is preferred because multicast puts less of a load on your network. You may choose a port between 1 and 65,535. As ever, you must be on the MBone or have a local area network that is multicast-capable across subnets, and have a UNIX kernel and CU-SeeMe reflector executable that are multicast-enabled.

`VAT-MC-PORT 4444`

VAT-MC-IN multicast-ip-address
Receive audio from VAT clients over multicast
Default = Disabled

VAT is able to send some forms of CU-SeeMe audio streams (delta-mod and Linear PCM). This directive specifies a VAT client that is sending you CU-SeeMe audio streams.

`VAT-MC-IN 239.4.4.1`

VAT-MC-OUT time-to-live multicast-ip-address
Send audio to VAT clients over multicast
Default = Disabled

The CU-SeeMe reflector will send CU-SeeMe audio streams to the VAT clients you specify. The time-to-live parameter determines how far your signal will travel

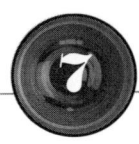

Internet TV with CU-SeeMe

(how long the signal will "live"). If you're using both the VAT-MC-IN and VAT-MC-OUT directives, both must have the same IP address as parameters.

```
VAT-MC-OUT 239.4.4.1
```

VAT-CONF-ID conference-id

```
Set the conference identifier for VAT clients
Default = Disabled
```

This directive performs the CONF-ID function for VAT clients.

```
VAT-CONF-ID 222
```

Directives for controlling CU-SeeMe clients

MIN-MAC-VERSION version-number message-string

```
Force participants to use certain Macintosh CU-SeeMe clients
Default = Disabled
```

Revisions in CU-SeeMe clients provide better algorithms, better error-checking, and the like. You may want to force conference participants to use a particular CU-SeeMe client. This directive specifies the earliest Macintosh CU-SeeMe client that will be allowed to connect.

```
MIN-MAC-VERSION 25
```

You can obtain a list that shows the mapping for some Macintosh CU-SeeMe clients and the value you'll specify to this directive. The current list is available from the CU-SeeMe Development Team.

MIN-PC-VERSION version-number message-string

```
Force participants to use certain Windows CU-SeeMe clients
Default = Disabled
```

Revisions in CU-SeeMe clients provide better algorithms, better error-checking, and the like. You may want to force conference participants to use a particular CU-SeeMe client. This directive specifies the earliest Windows CU-SeeMe client that will be allowed to connect.

```
MIN-PC-VERSION 2
```

The current list of the mapping for some Macintosh CU-SeeMe clients and the value you'll specify to this directive is available from the CU-SeeMe Development Team.

Reflector Operator's Guide

Flow Control Directives

MAX-MIN-SEND max-min-send penalty-time message-string
```
Specify the minimum transmission rate
Default = 10 1
```

This directive is used to control the minimum transmission rate the participant is allowed to request of the CU-SeeMe client software. Participants that set a large value for their minimum are going to force the CU-SeeMe client to send data even when it thinks it's unnecessary (the send rate cap will not fall below this setting regardless of packet loss).

If a client has their client's minimum transmission rate set higher than MAX-MIN-SEND they'll be thrown off your CU-SeeMe reflector for penalty-time minutes after being shown message-string.

```
MAX-MIN-SEND 40 2 Please don't set your minimum transmission
rate to more than 40 kbps on this reflector. You'll be
disconnected for two minutes until you lower your setting.
//
```

MAX-MAX-SEND max-max-send penalty-time message-string
```
Specify the maximum transmission rate
Default = 90 1
```

This directive is used to control the maximum transmission rate the participant is allowed to request of the CU-SeeMe client software. Participants that set a large value for their maximum transmission rate may flood your CU-SeeMe reflector (the send rate cap will not rise above this setting regardless of packet loss).

If a client has their client's maximum transmission rate set higher than MAX-MIN-SEND they'll be thrown off your CU-SeeMe reflector for penalty-time minutes after being shown message-string.

```
MAX-MAX-SEND 120 2 Please don't set your maximum transmission
rate to more than 120 kbps on this reflector. You'll be
disconnected for two minutes until you lower your setting.
//
```

MAX-MIN-RECV max-min-recv penalty-time message-string
```
Specify how large the minimum receive rate may be
Default = 10 1
```

The participant sets a minimum receive rate on the CU-SeeMe client software. (The reflector's rate cap will not fall below this setting regardless of packet loss.) This directive permits the participant to connect to the CU-SeeMe reflector only

Internet TV with CU-SeeMe

if that setting is below MAX-MIN-RECV. If it's larger they'll be thrown off your CU-SeeMe reflector for penalty-time minutes after being shown message-string.

The complementary directive is MAX-MAX-RECV.

```
MAX-MIN-RECV 40 2 Please don't request more than 40 kbps for a minimum
transmission rate from the reflector.  You'll be disconnected for two minutes
until you lower your setting.
//
```

MAX-MAX-RECV max-max-recv penalty-time message-string
```
Specify how large the maximum receive rate may be
Default = 10 1
```

The participant sets a maximum receive rate on the CU-SeeMe client software. (The reflector's rate cap will not rise above this setting regardless of packet loss.) This directive permits the participant to connect to the CU-SeeMe reflector only if that setting is above MAX-MAX-RECV. If it's larger they'll be thrown off your CU-SeeMe reflector for penalty-time minutes after being shown message-string.

The complementary directive is MAX-MIN-RECV.

```
MAX-MAX-RECV 600 2 Please don't request more than 600 kbps for a maximum
transmission rate from the reflector.  You'll be disconnected for two minutes
until you lower your setting.
//
```

DEFAULT-MIN-RECV default-min-recv
```
Control minimum transmission rate for old-style clients
Default = 14
```

This directive controls the minimum transmission rate from the CU-SeeMe reflector to the CU-SeeMe client software. It's used for older CU-SeeMe clients, which don't have loss-reporting capability. If you allow clients older than CU-SeeMe for Macintosh 0.80x and CU-SeeMe for Windows 0.65x to connect to your CU-SeeMe reflector, then you'll want to use this directive.

The complementary directive is DEFAULT-MAX-RECV.

```
DEFAULT-MIN-RECV 10
```

DEFAULT-MAX-RECV default-max-recv
```
Control maximum transmission rate for old-style clients
Default = 200
```

This directive controls the maximum transmission rate from the CU-SeeMe reflector to the CU-SeeMe client software. It's used for older CU-SeeMe clients, which don't have loss-reporting capability. If you allow clients older than CU-SeeMe for Macintosh 0.80x and CU-SeeMe for Windows 0.65x to connect to your CU-SeeMe reflector then you'll want to use this directive.

The complementary directive is DEFAULT-MAX-RECV.

```
DEFAULT-MAX-RECV 300
```

DEFAULT-INIT-RECV default-init-recv

```
Control initial transmission rate for old-style clients
Default = 40
```

This directive controls the beginning or initial transmission rate from the CU-SeeMe reflector to the CU-SeeMe client software. It's used for older CU-SeeMe clients, which don't have loss-reporting capability. If you allow clients older than CU-SeeMe for Macintosh 0.80x and CU-SeeMe for Windows 0.65x to connect to your CU-SeeMe reflector then you'll want to use this directive.

```
DEFAULT-INIT-RECV 80
```

RATE-ADAPT no-loss-growth loss-threshold

```
Control reflector transmission increase and data loss threshold to back off
Default = 5 2
```

When your CU-SeeMe reflector sends a stream to a client that reports zero data loss, the reflector will increase the data it sends by no-loss-growth percent until the client reports a data loss of loss-threshold percent, at which time the reflector will back off (stop the increase).

Use the OLD-RATE-ADAPT directive (below) for old-style clients.

```
RATE-ADAPT 15 5
```

OLD-RATE-ADAPT old-no-loss-growth old-loss-threshold

```
Control reflector transmission increase and data loss threshold to back off
when dealing with old-style clients
Default = 5 2
```

When your CU-SeeMe reflector sends a stream to a client that reports zero data loss, the reflector will increase the data it sends by no-loss-growth percent until the client reports a data loss of loss-threshold percent, at which time the reflector will back off (stop the increase).

Use the RATE-ADAPT directive (above) for modern CU-SeeMe clients (CU-SeeMe for Macintosh 0.80x or newer; CU-SeeMe for Windows 0.65x or newer).

```
OLD-RATE-ADAPT 15 5
```

Internet TV with CU-SeeMe

Refmon, the CU-SeeMe Reflector Monitor

Refmon is software that you'll use to monitor the operation of your CU-SeeMe reflector. You can monitor your reflector either locally or remotely. Refmon uses a command-line mode of operation much like the CU-SeeMe reflector itself, and like the reflector, runs on your UNIX box. With Refmon you'll see who is on the reflector, how long it's been up; you can kick people off the reflector, and take the reflector down.

Starting Refmon

All Refmon needs to know from you is what machine to monitor. To monitor the CU-SeeMe reflector running on flapdoodle.jungle.com you'd type:

```
refmon -s flapdoodle.jungle.com
```

You'll see Refmon trying to connect to the machine you've specified:

```
Waiting for connection to 141.214.138.248 ... Connected
>
```

and then present you with a prompt. The following commands are understood by Refmon.

Quit

Refmon ceases operation. This has no effect on the reflector it's monitoring.

Version

Refmon reports what version of the **reflector** you're running.

Who

Refmon reports the names, IP addresses, and stream settings of the participants. The stream setting will show a combination of C (connected), R (receive), and V (video-send). For example:

```
> who
CLIENT: John Lauer@141.214.138.202 CR
CLIENT: internetRADIO@141.214.138.249 CRV

Total # of clients 2   senders 1   lurkers 1
```

Maven

Refmon reports the participants connected to the CU-SeeMe reflector via Charley Kline's Maven audio software.

Uptime

Refmon reports what time the CU-SeeMe reflector was started.

Term

Refmon terminates operation of the CU-SeeMe reflector without giving any warning to the participants.

Param

Refmon reports the current configuration of the CU-SeeMe reflector. Similar to looking at the reflect.conf file, using Refmon is preferable because you'll see how the reflector interpreted your configuration commands.

Help

Refmon reports the command verbs it understands. It'll look something like:

```
> help
valid commands are: quit version help who term param maven uptime
```

The CU-SeeMe Reflector's Log File

The CU-SeeMe reflector generates a log file during its operation. The reflector writes a log entry when a user connects, disconnects, speaks, or is updated. A typical log file looks like:

```
client not found and initial message is not Open
incoming control message new msg_sock is 8
PARAM received on control socket
Client at source 130.166.109.137 is opening a connection
updating client   client count 0    seq 0
updating client Maren Steiner client count 0    seq 44
Client at source 141.214.138.249 is opening a connection
updating client   client count 0    seq 0
internetRADIO is speaking
Maren Steiner wants to receive audio from John Lauer
updating client internetRADIO client count 2    seq 9
internetRADIO wants to receive audio from John Lauer
Maren Steiner wants to receive audio from John Lauer
updating client internetRADIO client count 2    seq 9
internetRADIO wants to receive audio from John Lauer
Maren Steiner wants to receive audio from John Lauer
updating client internetRADIO client count 2    seq 9
internetRADIO wants to receive audio from John Lauer
maximum # of senders exceeded
deleting client Carroll Chiou
```

Even without using the CU-SeeMe reflector's debug option, the log file has lots of useful information about its operation. You can search for lines that say

"Client at source ... is opening a connection" to see connection activity. There are many other ways of parsing the log file, and many other trends and statistics you can derive from it.

Advanced Reflector Usage: Linking

If you've followed the chapter this far, reading (or at least skimming) each of the CU-SeeMe reflector directives, you're aware that CU-SeeMe reflectors can be linked together for huge broadcasts. You're also aware that CU-SeeMe, VAT, and NV can all interoperate to provide audio and video to participants. Streams can be sent downstream, or can be synchronized with peer reflectors. This subsection is all about different ways of linking reflectors, of making efficient use of bandwidth and distributing the load between machines.

Unicasting

The Mulicast Backbone, the MBone, is a series of routers that forward incoming packets to other networks. It's configured so that streams never traverse any wire on the network twice; it's a very efficient broadcast system. You can mimic this technique with CU-SeeMe reflectors, which are unicast (if they were multicast the routes would be automatically calculated), and by educating the participants, who must connect to the closest reflector.

For example, consider a two-reflector setup. One CU-SeeMe reflector is in New York City, the other in San Francisco. Figure 7.9 shows a correct arrangement of reflectors and participants.

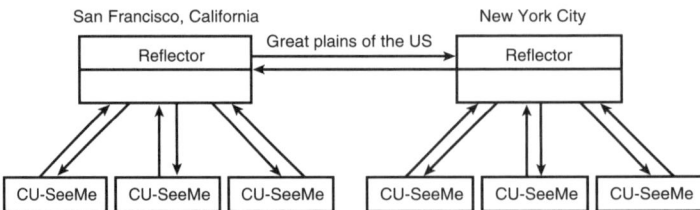

Figure 7.9. Mimicking MBone correctly.

All the San Francisco participants connect to the San Francisco CU-SeeMe reflector; all the New York City participants connect to the New York City CU-SeeMe reflector. The data are being sent between the reflectors only once, which is all that's needed.

Consider an inefficient variant, shown in figure 7.10.

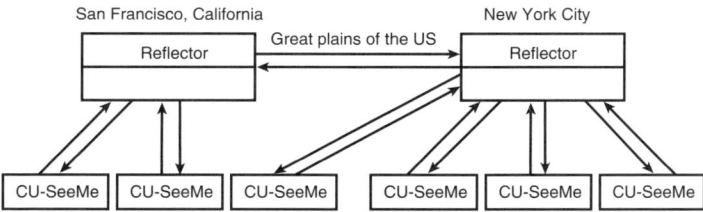

Figure 7.10. Mimicking MBone incorrectly.

One San Francisco participant has connected to the New York City reflector. Now all of the data are being sent across the Internet twice, a redundant inefficiency that puts quite a load on the network. Earlier in this chapter I showed how a small (five-person) CU-SeeMe videoconference resulted in 2 mbps of data running through the reflector. (It was figure 7.1, if you're thumbing around.) This errant San Francisco participant has, by connecting to the New York City reflector, caused 2 mbps to needlessly travel across the USA. Imagine now a dozen reflectors, with users connecting to them willy-nilly, without regard for flooding the network. Whether on the Internet or on a small-scale campus or corporate LAN, this easy-to-create inefficiency should be taken into consideration. I'm not objecting to inefficiency for its own sake, but its results: poor videoconferencing performance, poor network throughput for others sharing the network, and overall dissatisfaction.

It's vitally important for reflector operators to educate their audiences to be good net citizens.

Networks are a shared resource; being able to communicate with others is what makes them attractive. Limiting the load you place on this shared resource is a matter of some concern. The CU-SeeMe clients and the CU-SeeMe reflector use UDP datagrams, which can drown out regular TCP datagrams, such as those used by the World-Wide Web and the File Transfer Protocol. You must know the state of your LAN, and whether it can handle the load that running a CU-SeeMe reflector will place upon it.

This is true of local campus and corporate networks, but it's especially true when you send streams into the Internet. Internet service providers quickly become upset when you flood them; they become irate if they find out you're doing it unnecessarily. Efficiency is about sharing. Be knowledgeable about your networking environment. Be proactive; limit the load by properly configuring the reflect.conf file and requiring a low cap rate.

In the CU-SeeMe reflector 4.00B1 Read Me file, Richard Cogger, Tim Dorcey, and John Lynn write:

> Major changes are aimed at being "kinder to the Internet" by not sending a lot of traffic that the network would lose anyway. Reflector operators

Internet TV with CU-SeeMe

will have more control over (and responsibility for) how pushy CU-SeeMe traffic will be compared to other Internet traffic. Of course, we recommend everyone be very polite unless you know you are using only your own facilities. The effect is that a mix of modem-connected and LAN-connected participants will work much better.

Earlier versions of the CU-SeeMe reflector send complete streams to participants running the CU-SeeMe clients over a modem, participants who were destined to lose most of that data. Earlier you saw how a full reflector stream could be 500 kbps; imagine that being sent to a client on a 28.8 kbps modem. Clearly less than five percent of the data can make it through.

Multicasting

Multicasting is a most powerful tool for making efficient use of bandwidth and distributing the load. The situation portrayed above is resolved invisibly and automatically with multicast. The design of a multicast network makes redundant data nearly impossible.

Multicasting capabilities are just starting to become widespread. As it is, expect to see more use of networking technologies for data-intensive tasks such as videoconferencing. Does your operating system do multicast? Here's a list:

- UNIX: almost all support multicast
- Macintosh: Open Transport 1.1 is scheduled to support multicast
- Windows: several options support multicast
    - Windows for Workgroups with Microsoft's TCP32 stack FTP Software's PC/TCP and OnNet for Windows and DOS
    - WatTCP for Windows and DOS
    - Windows NT built-in TCP/IP
    - Windows 95 built-in TCP/IP

What is the MBone? The following blurb is taken from the MBone web pages, found at:

http://www.eit.com/techinfo/mbone/mbone.html

> MBONE stands for the Virtual Internet Backbone for Multicast IP. IP-Multicast is the class-D addressing scheme in IP implemented by Steve Deering at Xerox PARC. It was adopted at the IETF March 1992 meeting and acquired the name MBONE after the July 1992 IETF meeting.
>
> IP Multicast-based routing facilitates distributed applications to achieve time-critical "real-time" communications over wide area IP networks through a lightweight, highly threaded model of communication. The IP

Multicast routers (referred to as "mrouters") take the responsibility of distributing and replicating the multicast data stream to their destinations as opposed to individual IP hosts. The MBone topology of mrouters is designed in such a manner that it facilitates "efficient" distribution of packets without congesting any node inappropriately.

Multicast Techniques

So now you've got your Mbone feed and you recompiled your kernel on your UNIX machine. What now? Well, try receiving some multicast reflector feeds with the MC-IN, MC-OUT settings. Then try synchronizing reflectors with the MC-GROUP setting.

You could potentially transmit a high-quality video stream to the world over a simple ISDN link using multicast; with unicast and a reflector this isn't possible. THIS IS IMPORTANT FOR ALL YOU HOME ISDN FOLKS.

Figure 7.11 illustrates the problems of trying to use CU-SeeMe in unicast; each participant causes the CU-SeeMe reflector to transmit a duplicate stream, which it can't do because of the bottleneck—ISDN just isn't a big enough "pipe."

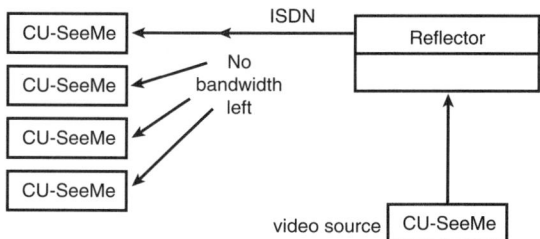

Figure 7.11. An ISDN/unicast bottleneck.

Figure 7.12 shows the same network topology, but with participants being fed by multicast. Since the stream is transmitted over the network only once, all participants can join and receive the data being broadcast.

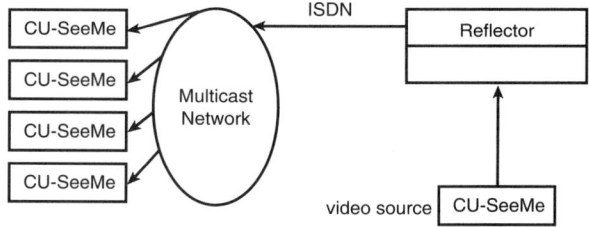

Figure 7.12. Multicast saves the day.

Internet TV with CU-SeeMe

Showing an event

Having made it this far in the chapter, it's time to go public and show an event. You have the capability to send streams to the four corners of the world. Now you can fill in the gaps; what's local to you that we would appreciate seeing? Once you find something, how do you let us know you're trying to be a junior Ted Turner?

Promoting your event

In Chapter 6, "The CU-SeeMe User's Guide," you saw the various mailing lists used by the CU-SeeMe community. Two of those lists, the CU-SeeMe Events list and the CU-SeeMe Discussion List are used for event publicity.

Remember to include the following essential information when you promote your event:

- **Who**: Who are you, and how can we get in touch with you? At a very minimum, we need your e-mail address.
- **What**: What are you going to be sharing with us?
- **Where**: What reflector (or reflectors) will be used for your presentation? (If you want to solicit reflector operators to help you in preparation or presentation, use the CU-SeeMe Reflector Operators List.)
- **When**: When should we sit down at our computers to see your presentation? Please give us the time relative to someplace we know; I don't offhand know my offset from Universal Coordinated Time (UCT), but I can convert from any time in the USA. Here's an example from this past summer that covers the USA, Europe, Australia, and Asia:

    Here's when you can see our show:

    San Francisco: Tue 25 July 1995, 1000 local time (UCT-7)
    New York City: Tue 25 July 1995, 1300 local time (UCT-4)
    Paris: Tue 25 July 1995, 1800 local time (UCT+2)
    Perth: Wed 26 July 1995, 0200 local time (UCT+8)
    Tokyo: Wed 26 July 1995, 0300 local time (UCT+9)

- **Why**: Give us some background, some context. A few paragraphs of history and notes will put us in the right frame of mind for your presentation.

Reflector Operator's Guide

In addition to the mailing lists, John Lauer has created a CU-SeeMe Events Guide on the World-Wide Web. (It was this contribution to the CU-SeeMe community that brought John to my attention, leading to John's considerable contribution to this chapter.) Located at

    http://www.umich.edu/~johnlaue/cuseeme/

the CU-SeeMe Events Guide has a forms interface (Figure 7.13) for you to fill out.

Figure 7.13. The CU-SeeMe Events Guide.

Figure 7.14. The Events Guide form.

The information you submit is compiled twice daily into a new events web page. If you've entered a one-time event it'll be listed by date. If you've entered an ongoing event, it'll appear in another section. The CU-SeeMe Event Guide doesn't yet generate a posting to the mailing lists, but we're hoping.

History, Culture, and Usage

CHAPTER 8

This is a chapter of snippets. The first section, on history, is a narrative through snippets of memos and e-mail. The second section, on usage, is a collection of snippets of event announcements, papers, and other writings about how people are using CU-SeeMe. I hope they give you the inspiration to participate in the CU-SeeMe community—and perhaps even broadcast an event or three.

After you read this chapter, you will know

- Some more specifics in the history of CU-SeeMe
- How people use Internet videoconferencing for cultural, educational, artistic, recreational, and commercial information distribution

A History of CU-SeeMe

There is a tradition of celebrating "CU-SeeMe Day" by wearing the official CU-SeeMe t-shirt and connecting with friends made on the CU-SeeMe reflectors. Jean Armour Polly, the Director of Public Services and Internet Ambassador at NYSERNet, Inc., a pioneer in CU-SeeMe use, announced in 1994,

Internet TV with CU-SeeMe

"We decided to celebrate CU-SeeMe Day on August 19 this year, since it is a work day and more people will be around than on Saturday, August 20, which we believe to be the day of the first off-campus CU-SeeMe transmission.

If you have a CU-SeeMe t-shirt, be sure to wear it tomorrow!

When is CU-SeeMe's *real* birthday? Alas, it is lost in the collective unconscious...."

From left to right, the official CU-SeeMe t-shirt, Jean Armour Polly modeling said shirt, and Dick Cogger.

Richard "Dick" Cogger, head of the CU-SeeMe Development Team, dug through his archives to reconstruct the initial CU-SeeMe product development process. He found the basic product design document and implementation plans that the team worked from.

```
Date: Wed, 17 Jun 1992 11:35:43 -0400
From: Dick Cogger
Subject: Re: Mac programming
To: Tim Dorcey

Hi Tim,

Yes, let's start as soon as possible....

The task is basically to get Mac desktop-video conferencing going as
soon as possible in any doable mode at all. I have Quicktime, a sample
video player that puts up a live video window, using either a rasterops
24stv or a video spigot, and I can step thru the program in ThinkC
debugger. So now it's a case of grabbing images, computing interframe
diffs, making packets, building UDP datagrams and sending with MacTCP,
receiving them, displaying, and whatever user-interface goodies needed
to support that. Then, we want to get audio going too. I haven't gotten
very far researching that. After next week, I'm planning to take two
weeks vacation, during which I plan to work full time plus get some of
this to happen. Your help would be extremely valuable. I figure if we
can get something working at all, we can refine it along the way and
probably get additional resources, time-committment, etc. -Dick
```

Timothy recalls,

> Things then got off to a slow start as it wasn't until the end of July that we were even able to grab a frame from the Spigot. The first network-capable version was called "WatchTim," and as near as I can figure, it was created on August 31, 1992, except that you couldn't really watch me because I didn't have a camera. Instead, you got to see a videotape of C-SPAN that I used for all of the early development. A separate application called "VideoSend" was used to transmit. Soon, there was a "WatchDick" and, I think, maybe a "WatchSteve," and before I went any further Dick suggested that I should add a way to enter IP addresses rather than hardcoding them in the application. (I had been aiming for a streamlined user interface.) Of course, what he really wanted was a single application that would both send and receive, so September 13th brought us "DigitDemo2Way." By this time, everyone was getting tired of my naming style. As a quick thinking maneuver to avoid the name suggested by our Vice President ("EZ-Pic"), Dick came up with "CU-SeeMe," on September 27, I think. So, I guess that would be the official birthday for CU-SeeMe. Or, if you want to go with the first transmission outside Cornell, I would put that around September 1, shortly after the first local transmission. This is, after all, the Internet Protocol, and if you can send it across the room, you can send it around the world!

The National Science Foundation Steps In

Less than six months after Dick's inital memo to Tim, the National Science Foundation became aware of the work being done at Cornell. Intensely excited by the possibilities of Internet videoconferencing, Steve Wolf of the NSF in December 1992 invited the Global SchoolNet (GSN), an organization that designs networks for elementary and secondary schools, to participate in a National Science and Technology Week conference to be held the following April.

Don Mitchell of the NSF proposed a collaborative environmental activity with two schools—one in Tennessee and one in Washinton, D.C. The activity was to be about environmental issues because of Vice President Al Gore's interest in the topic; the locations were the Vice President's home state and his city of work. Don was an early force in the growth of CU-SeeMe. He arranged for funding at a crucial time in its life.

Yvonne Marie Andres of GSN wanted to include a California school near her work. Because CU-SeeMe could connect only two Macintoshes in a point-to-point connection, she consulted with Dick and Tim. They were able to add multipoint connectivity in time for the event, so schools in California and London were added.

CERFNet provided a T1 line—perhaps the first time so much bandwidth went directly to a middle school. The University of London provided network access for the London side of things—but only at the university, so the school children were bussed back and forth.

On April 28, 1993, on a large video screen, with government leaders at each site, the school children demonstrated videoconferencing collaboration across the Internet. The topic chosen was groundwater pollution. Because CU-SeeMe did not yet have the capablity to broadcast audio or text, white writing tablets were used to "converse."

The event was so well recieved that the NSF provided a second grant for the network to be expanded to include seventeen schools in four "learning clusters." New topics chosen by the students included space exploration, solid waste management, alternative energy sources, and national disasters. The Global SchoolHouse (GSH) was off to a good start. Yvonne summarized GSH's history in a recent message to the CU-SeeMe discussion list.

> GSN, formerly called FrEdMail (Free Educational Mail), originated in 1985 when teachers in San Diego linked their students to classrooms on the East Coast. With no budget and minimal support, those teachers set about creating a powerful and now internationally-recognized educational information infrastructure starting at the grass-roots level. GSN envisioned and then constructed the concept of the Global SchoolHouse, where teachers, students, business, government, and the community can learn side-by-side.

Friends of the Global SchoolHouse

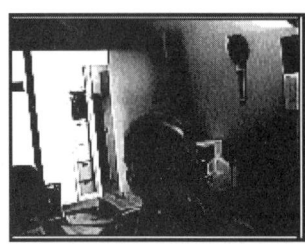  

From left to right: Don Mitchell of the National Science Foundation, Larry Duffy of the Jet Propulsion Laboratory, and Jill Charvoneau , the designer of the CU-SeeMe t-shirt.

History, Culture, and Usage

The Global SchoolHouse project is centered around children, whose faces you see throughout this book. Larry Duffy of the Jet Propulsion Laboratory was an early user of CU-SeeMe. One day, he popped into the CU-SeeMe reflector that the GSH school children were using. The kids explained what GSH was and how he could optimize his setup. In general, they charmed him. Larry, the rocket scientist, taught by high school kids, became a CU-SeeMe booster, setting up a reflector dedicated for GSH, and having many interactions with the kids—and some notables, including Al Gore, Vice President at that time.

Steven Adams, also of JPL, became a "scientist-on-tap" for the GSH kids four hours a week.

Jill Charvoneau, an Information Designer in the Advanced Technology Planning Group at Cornell University, was the designer of the original CU-SeeMe t-shirt. Jill also participated in such events as Career Day via CU-SeeMe. James Hill of QMS, an early adopter of CU-SeeMe, participated as well.

 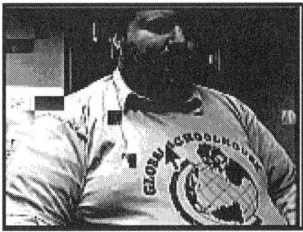 

From left to right, James Hill, an early adoptee of CU-SeeMe, and Greg German, a regular user of CU-SeeMe, demonstrating the technology in his home state of Ohio and in Hawaii.

Greg German, shown here in Ohio and on the road in Hawaii, was one of the first dozen regular users of CU-SeeMe. Greg is a friend of Charley Kline, the creator of the Maven audio software, and introduced Yvonne's seventh graders to the wonders of multipoint audio.

Images from Senator Feinstein's conference.

Internet TV with CU-SeeMe

Other Global SchoolHouse guests have included Congressman Rose and local meterologists Bob Ryan and Terry Burnhanf.

The children have spoken with politicians—such as Senator Diane Feinstein, Yvonne Cisco, and Congressman Rose—and with local personalities, including Southern California's Bob Ryan, a meterologist. Terry Burnhanf, a meterologist with KUSI-TV in San Diego, California, did a CU-SeeMe demonstration for a television program about the Global SchoolHouse entitled *The Class Act*. Peter Knight, of the World Bank, spoke with the GSH kids about how the international monetary system works and the role of the World Bank.

CU-SeeMe and the Global SchoolHouse have a long-standing relationship with scientists, the early adopters of new technologies.

Peter Knight of the World Bank.

These images are from a collaboration between four Global SchoolNet campuses during a "space cluster." On the left are NASA officials. On the right, one of the students is describing some drawing and models of space vehicles.

This image was taken during one of a series of interactions between Global SchoolNet kids and scientists of the National Energy Research Supercomputing Center at Lawrence Livermore National Nuclear Laboratory, just east of San Francisco. This program taught the GSH kids how to use one of NERSC's Cray computers. The image on the right shows the kids using Climoman, a climate-modelling simulator.

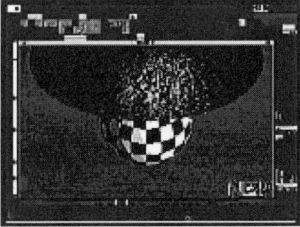

Here is a CU-SeeMe broadcast of the kids using Wireman, a three-dimensional modelling program.

Ken Hartman is a high school chemistry teacher at the Global SchoolHouse in Ames, Iowa, and the winner of a Presidential award for science and math projects. He is shown here during the NERSC collaboration.

Josh Knauer, the director of the Envirolink project at Carnegie-Mellon University is shown here speaking with school students via CU-SeeMe.

Jane Goodall, the famed cultural anthropologist known for her studies of chimpanzee communication, traveled from her field laboratory in Tanzania to the United States. While here, she visited with Global SchoolHouse kids. Dr. Goodall was supposed to become a regular visitor to the Global SchoolHouse via CU-SeeMe, but the satellite to be used has malfunctioned, and the funds to repair it are not available. The alternative communication method is to fax a message to a hotel in Tanzania, from which someone delivers it to a boat that travels three days to her field laboratory. The Global SchoolNet hasn't given up on getting Dr. Goodall "wired"!

Back to the People

One person you won't find here is H.R.H. Prince Charles, who was originally supposed to appear at the "UK-LA" event, which was planned to promote the performing arts and technology. "UK-LA" even had links from the Beverly Hilton hotel to Australia. MCI provided 500 "listening ports" through a toll-free telephone number. Sprint jumped on the bandwagon and matched that number.

Two days before the event, the promoters and CU-SeeMe reflector operators began hearing that the Prince might not be able to make it. Just ten minutes before the event was to begin, the promoters were told by the British ambassador that Prince Charles was unfortunately detained by pressing matters and would be unable to participate. Instead, he spent the day with Barbara Streisand.

From the CU-SeeMe demonstration at Interop '94.

John Morgridge, the chief executive officer of Sysco Systems, a computer networking company, arranged for a CU-SeeMe demonstration at Interop 1994. The demonstration was coordinated through major Internet sites such as CERFnet and NYSERNet. It was planned to show the network movers and shakers in the audience how end users were using their products and services. Some attendees had tears in their eyes. They were so moved by the enthusiasm of the CU-SeeMe people and the novel uses for their routers, cables, and the like.

University of Song

Jocelyn Jocya and Adam Curry, from their particpation in a CU-SeeMe singing contest.

CU-SeeMe is used in the University of Song's annual over-the-Internet singing contest. Jocelyn Jocya, a songwriter and performer who has worked with Paul Anka and Angie Dickenson, was a participant.

Adam Curry, formerly of MTV, moderated the proceedings. Adam is a regular CU-SeeMe user. He often sends an around-the-clock video feed from his home.

CU-See in Use

This section is composed of messages (sic) I've received, reproduced here to provide an insight into the various real-time CU-SeeMe interludes.

Satellite CU-SeeMe?

```
From: Martin Stoufer
Date: Sun, 9 Jul 1995,
```

The other day, I was showing a Ham Radio phreak/friend of mine how CU-SeeMe worked. The first thing he could say was, "Is this coming from a satellite feed or something?" It broke my heart to tell him it was a 28.8 modem. Then we both got thinking, "Wouldn't it be possible for someone with a satellite dish to pick up a satellite, tune to a specific frequency and start receiving CU-SeeMe A/V?"

```
From: Roger Lee Boston
Date: Mon, 10 Jul 1995 00:30:05 -0500 (CDT)
```

I think you get that at 400kbs with DirectPC, an offering from Hughes. Your modem going TO the internet, and the satellite down FROM the internet.

From: "Dr. Joe Baptista"
Date: Mon, 10 Jul 1995

I heard a while back that Hughes was offering DirecPC, with which you could hook up a PC to a modem line, have a Web browser, select a link, and then have and with a card the receiving of the data requested by a Direct-PC digital sat dish at 400Kbps for less than 20 bucks a month. For a receive-only application this would seem great, but I think they charge more after you reach a certian amount on MBits downloaded. I think you can also subscribe to services like CNN desktop too, and I think the applications (unless there is a new PCI card for the new Macs) work only with Windows PCs, but I don't know. It would seem that there could be some good applications for a configuration as a Mac with CU-SeeMe or even Quicktime conferencing broadcasts and a DirecPC link. It could also be designed for instructional video-on-demand applications. The nice thing is that it gives enough bandwidth to receive good audio, video almost anywhere, anytime. Even in business applications, you could always use a phone call to give feedback.

From: "David R. Seay"
Date: Thu, 25 May 95 13:14:08 PDT

A new service is available that provides access to the Internet via satellite (see http://www.acmeweb.com/direcpc/index.html). Data can be received at speeds up to 400kbps via a satellite dish. Maybe this could turn into a good way to broadcast CU-SeeMe videoconferences? Just something to look into.

From: JohnBalogh@psu.edu (John D. Balogh)
Date: Fri, 26 May 1995 14:30:05 -0400

From that Web page, it appears that Hughes/GM is charging for usage. They seem to have a limit of 130MB/month for the most expensive plan. If you use only CUSM and limit yourself to 100Kbps—watching only two others users at 50Kbps each—you could run for 130MB*8b(/B)/100Kb/S = 10400 seconds per month, or 2.9 hours each month.

Hmmm. I still like ISDN at the same rate without a monthly limit.

From: Little Robbie Burcham
Date: Fri, 26 May 1995 17:06:36 -0500 (CDT)

Not to mention the fact that the satellite is receive-only. That is, you get a satellite feed of up to 800 kb/s, but all your sending is done through SLIP/PPP to an 800-number terminal server.

Internet TV with CU-SeeMe

Drums and Didjerideu

From: chris blohm
Date: Tue, 4 Jul 1995 15:48:41 -0400 (EDT)

Live internet concert broadcast on CU-SeeMe and RealAudio
The spread of ideas, evolution, and flourishing creativity
Ideosphere will be the meeting point for artists, academics, and technology. This point will provide the means for the furthering of education and awareness of the new technologies, the world at large, and of ourselves. This event and all hence will introduce new talents, ideas, and engender an experience unparalleled in Vancouver.

Performing artists: Live drum circle of 15 percussionists and didjerideu, Off and Gone, Elfclan, Hellen Keller, and Deprogrammers. Featuring: James K-M, an artist and CD-ROM producer who will demonstrate "Restless Machines," the Vancouver-produced CD-ROM on the history of industrial and electronic music, as well as Dr. Stockmann, a physicist, who will give a presentation on entropy, time, and our lives as we approach the next millenium.

It will be broadcast on the internet via ISDN on CU-SeeMe and RealAudio from Multimedia.edu and on Axion Internet. The night begins at 6pm PST in the Multimedia.edu surround-sound theater, with no admission charge. Point your web browser to http://www.multimedia.edu/~cblohm/transcus.htm for general and reflector information.

Thank you,

Christopher Blohm
Multimedia.edu
cblohm@griffin.multimedia.edu

Transcendelia-Vamcouver Electronica
http://www.multimedia.edu/~cblohm/indra3.htm

CU-SeeMe in the College Classroom

From: "William Getter"
Date: Fri, 14 Jul 95 14:40:07 EST

I teach with the distance learning and continuing education programs at Embry-Riddle Aeronautical University. We have over 100 teaching sites around the world (primarily at U.S. military bases) that offer undergraduate and graduate degree programs. We are examining affordable alternatives for doing video conferencing to link classrooms throughout the system for instructional purposes. We want to be able to broadcast a lecture or presentation with the ability for students at remote sites to interact live with the instructor. Our challenge is to originate a lecture from any one of the 100-plus sites with the ability to receive at several of the other sites simultaneously. This leaves out the alternative of satellite uplink systems because of the cost of over 100 uplink sites.

Needless to say, we are very interested in the concept of compressed video/
voice over the Internet and the inroads already made with CU-SeeMe. If anyone
out there has had any successes (or failures) using CU-SeeMe for remote
classroom presentation, I would be grateful for feedback, suggestions,
lessons learned, and so on.

```
************************************************
*  Dr. William Getter                           *
*  Asst. Professor of Aeronautical Science      *
*  Embry-Riddle Aeronautical University         *
*  getterw@cts.db.erau.edu                      *
************************************************
```

From: avelon@phys.uva.nl (Ian Carr-de Avelon)
Date: Sat, 15 Jul 1995 18:20:11

I suggest you have a look at http://kmi.open.ac.uk/kmi-misc/
virtualsummer.html

This shows work using an old Macintosh version of CU-SeeMe. It is likely to
become out of date as the new versions we have been promised are released.

There is also a separate mailing list: videoconf@pul-ver.com. However, I have
lost the instructions of how to join, which will be a problem if I decide to
leave.

From: Richard Collins
Date: Sat, 15 Jul 1995 22:57:00 -0230

In response to your inquiry concerning teaching on the Net, we have done a
fair bit of exploration and testing in this area. Check out http://
mirror.det.mun.ca.

We are headed towards the economy of Internet conferencing as a teaching
tool, but because of available bandwidth this fall will see us with another
mixed bag of solutions:

Broadcast and Internet Teaching Project 95
The Division of Educational Technology, Memorial University

During the Fall semester of 1995, Educational Technology will be delivering
courses to our Provincial Colleges from Memorial's campus in St. John's.
Colleges are located in Carbonear, Clarenville, Burin, Gander, Grand Falls,
Lewisporte and Labrador City. In addition, a large lecture theater with a
capacity of 320 just down the hall from our studio will participate.

Having previously conducted experimental courses via a variety of technologies, both sattelite and computer, this is our first combination of the two.

We will be delivering broadcast video and audio of live teaching sessions via
satellite from our studio in St. John's. These will be downlinked to the
various colleges either by dishes installed at the particular college or
through the local cable system. I believe, at this point, we have been able
to access local cable systems in all but two regions.

For the interactive component, we have taken advantage of the newly established Internet links to each of these locations. There are A/V Mac 6100's equipped with the latest versions of the CU-SeeMe videoconferencing software. These Macs supply only return video. Audio is returned via traditional teleconferencing systems. All but one of the colleges have a minimum 64k frame relay link to our campus. They are connected by "cloud," and in our tests they achieve approximately 30-50kbs each. We chose the Macs because we wanted the larger picture format of 320x240. Combined with the bit rate, this allows an average of 1-4 frames per second. The exception is the site in Labrador City. This is off-island and suffers from poor line availability. The best option for the Internet connection in that area is a 19,200 line. We have yet to install the equipment in Labrador and, so, cannot comment on the quality that we will achieve through this link.

In our studio, the instructor can glance a large (21" Triniton) Mac monitor with the seven pictures displayed. This is not intended to give the instructor a detailed view. It is enough to confirm that the class has arrived and will indicate some general indication of who may be asking a question.

To achieve greatest quality, the remote machines have been configured as send-only video to a central reflector running on Linux. The reflector machine is a Pentium 90 with 32M of RAM and, most importantly, a PCI Ethernet (SMC) card. It is running within our Thin-wire (10 mbit) network. The reflector receives seven streams and sends two streams. One output stream goes to the Mac used in the studio with an extra stream sent to our second reflector. This enables others to view the event on the second reflector without slowing the main reflector.

We will be keeping up-to-date with the latest versions of reflector code and Macintosh CU-Seeme versions throughout the project.

So far everyone involved is suprised by the quality of video that we are receiving from the sites. When September comes, these classes will be taught from 10am to 1pm each day.

Last year, we taught to a single site using compressed (high-bandwidth) audio and video. This project depended upon dedicated 56k lines (7 of them) using an IMUX system. This is akin to a modem system ($50,000 worth of hardware plus $80-per-hour connections). With that came horrible connection troubles for each 50-minute session. With dedicated satellite time and the ever-present Internet, those connection problems should be more easily dealt with and confirmed well in advance of each session.

Ph.D. Defense Over CU-SeeMe

From: Paul Ruscher
Date: Mon, 26 Jun 1995 14:59:25 -0400 (EDT)

Just thought you might like to know that on June 15, we held a Ph.D. defense using CU-SeeMe. An external committee member from NASA Goddard, could not be in Tallahassee because of big meetings to help save her group from the budget axe. We used a Mac Centris 610 at Goddard and a Quadra 660AV at FSU on a point-to-point connection between the two. Part of the seminar was beamed live to her, and the entire oral defense with the graduate committee was carried via CU-SeeMe. Thanks to the folks at Cornell, we did not have to reschedule the defense or make other special arrangements. The work reported on is part of the NOAA Cooperative Institute of Tropical Meteorology at Florida State University's Meteorology Department. You can link to a related document on the WWW if you want more information about the research. The first link below is for the observational component, and the second link is for a modelling component.

http://thunder.met.fsu.edu/explores/tasbex.html
http://thunder.met.fsu.edu/gsc/cherb/cgh-citm.html

We send the Goddard group a QuickCam and the software. They loaded it up and were up to speed in no time. We also sent a videotape copy of a dry run and copies of the overheads for the seminar. The major hitch was that the entire campus network went down at 1:30 PM that day and did not come back up until 4:15 PM, just as my student was finishing the seminar. But the defense part went great! Guess Murphy was on his committee for that day only!

Paul Ruscher
FSU Meteorology
ruscher@met.fsu.edu

Come Fly With Me

From: FlyVision@aol.com
Date: Fri, 19 May 1995 21:40:29 -0400

I'm leaving tomorrow (May 20) for a three-month trip around the world. Come with me! There will be text, images, and sounds waiting to be experienced on my Web site, http://www.interport.net/~fly/trip95/. And live videoconferencing with CU-SeeMe from places around the globe...

CU soon.

Internet TV with CU-SeeMe

Web Belly: Belly Dancing on the Web

```
From: Spyder
Date: Fri, 9 Jun 1995 18:09:44 -0400 (EDT)
```

"Web Belly: The Art of Belly Dancing on the Web" debuts at @cafe in New York City on Thursday, June 15, 10:00 pm Eastern Standard time at @cafe Reflector: ip: 204.137.204.6.

You can find out more details at
http://www.nyic.com/spyder/webbelly.html

We are activity looking for additional reflectors for this entertaining and historic event.

Jonathan Sarno
Spyder World Wide Web
www.nyic.com/spyder/

"Peace for Sarajevo" Worldwide Video Conference

```
From: lignano@eurocube.it (Lignano)
Date: Thu, 20 Jul 1995 00:48:26 +0200
```

Internet Worldwide conference at Lignano Sabbiadoro (Italy) for world peace

Peace for Sarajevo

One night talking about the war

Saturday, July 22, in Italy, at the city of Lignano Sabbiadoro, during the event "The virtual week," which is dedicated to virtual reality, the Internet, and information technologies

It will be possible to get a connection with the children of Sarajevo by the Internet.

Lignano Sabbiadoro is located close to the border of Yugoslavia where, as everybody knows, a bloody civil war is destroying the lives of thousands of children.

All net users can get in touch with the people of Lignano using chat programs, email, or CU-SeeMe videoconferences. From 6 pm to midnight (Italian time), we will talk together about the war, and send some email to Sarajevo's people.

So keep in mind this day and remember to log on the Net!

```
-----------------------------------
   email     : lignano@eurocube.it
   reflector : 194.20.44.111
-----------------------------------
```

Adam Curry's SparrowCam

From: Adam Curry
Date: Sat, 17 Jun 1995 17:54:33 -0400 (EDT)

I just discovered a family of sparrows—babies and all—in my back yard. Immediately I saw a CU-SeeMe application. After a trip to Radio Shack for 100ft of video cable, the job was quickly done. Check it out on the curryco.com reflector at 199.34.33.34.

Fun and educational for the whole family :-)

Adam Curry
On Ramp, Inc. 1-800-2-ONRAMP
adam@metaverse.com

Journey to Mars

From: Chris Rowan
Date: Thu, 6 Jul 1995 08:21:30 -0500 (CDT)

I have posted queries here before, and I have always received numerous helpful suggestions. I have wanted to experiment with CU-SeeMe ever since I learned of its existence a year ago. I wrote a proposal for a grant this past school year that would involve NASA engineers, scientists, and technicians in a dialogue with my fifth grade students. Much to my surprise, I was awarded the grant.

The project is a high-fidelity simulation of a journey to Mars. With the help of NASA, my students will design one or more spacecraft for the journey and engage in a realtime simulation of a roundtrip journey to Mars.

We will not spend every moment of every school day conducting the simulation. That would be impossible. But we will allocate a portion of every school day to the simulation. CU-SeeMe connectivity offers an exciting alternative to email. The herky-jerky nature of CU-SeeMe would only enhance the simulation by adding a touch of realism.

Best regards,
Chris Rowan
1995 NASA NEWEST Participant, Kennedy Space Center

Model Lunar Rover

From: Jon Pike
Date: Wed, 26 Jul 1995 18:37:15 -0700 (PDT)

I am coordinating a videoconferencing event at a local convention. We will have a teleoperation/VR display known as the LTM-1. It is a model Lunar rover

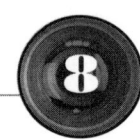

that drives across a model moon. Normal operation is via a dial-up modem and special software. You drive it with your arrow keys and watch the video.

For the event, the entire LTM-1 will be transported to the site, where people can wear a head mounted display, use data gloves, and watch others driving. I am also setting up for a CU-SeeMe link out to share the event with the Net. Should be much fun!

Singapore National Day Parade (NDP) '95 Internet Broadcast

From: CU-SeeMe Postbox
Date: Fri, 28 Jul 1995 15:27:53 +0800 (WST)

Singapore will be celebrating its 30th National Day on 9 August 1995. This year is going to be a special one because many exciting performances and programmes are being lined up from 5pm to 8pm at the Padang, outside City Hall. Besides the usual live televised broadcast of the event nationwide, we will also be broadcasting it on the Internet through MBONE and making use of CU-SeeMe for the PC and Mac. Look to our Web page http://www.nus.sg/NDP30.html for more details.

The National University of Singapore and the Television Corporation of Singapore (TCS) are organizing this project. We are already setting up mirror (reflector) sites in the U.K. and Australia for the CU-SeeMe broadcast. We thank those people who volunteered to join hands with us in this event.

The combined project team, comprising the National University of Singapore Computer Centre, Technet Unit, and Internet Research and Development Unit (IRDU) and the Television Corporation of Singapore will be proudly presenting to you the audio and visual images on the Internet by using the World Wide Web, MBONE, and the CU-SeeMe desktop videoconferencing software.

We welcome overseas sites to participate as reflectors site on the days of transmission.

Any queries and comments can go to ndp95@irdu.nus.sg. You can also send your greetings to us at the above URL.

Daughters at Work Day

From: Yvonne Marie Andres
Date: Thu, 27 Apr 1995 07:59:30 -0700 (PDT)

The Global Schoolhouse will have our student "ambassadors" available to answer questions and interact with "daughters" on Thursday, April 27, 1995.

Our students will be available from 8:00-10:25 AM and 11:00-12:40 PM on the JPL reflector, 137.79.6.31.

We will be unavailable from 10:30-11:00 AM, as we will be participating in a private CU-SeeMe conference related to Daughters at Work Day.

In addition, both I (President and Curriculum Director for Global SchoolNet) and Josephina Cicero (Director of PAACE) will be available to answer questions.

For your information, the PAACE (Personal Achievment and Career Awareness) program prepares kids for the job environment. Josephina is a very dynamic speaker.

We look forward to interacting with your daughters today.

```
>>>>>>>>
Yvonne Marie Andres, Global SchoolHouse/Global SchoolNet Foundation
        7040 Avenida Encinas 104-281, Carlsbad, CA 92009
    URL  http://www.aldea.com    (select Global SchoolHouse from menu)
Voice (619) 433-3413    FAX (619) 931-5934  email: andresyv@cerf.net
>>>>>>>>
```

Simulated Shuttle Mission

From: lt055@nptn.org (Jud Elliott)
Date: Wed, 26 Apr 1995 11:20:55 -0400

Today, the National Educational Simulations Project Using Telecommunications (NESPUT) schools are running a simulated space shuttle mission.

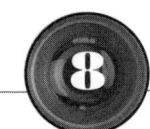

Internet TV with CU-SeeMe

As part of that program, Willoughby Middle School is transmitting a simulated shuttle tracking map through the University of Kansas reflector (129.237.247.160).

We are using a Connectix camera, a magnifying glass, and the Orbitrak program (NASA Spacelink) to generate and transmit the image.

We are SLIPped here, but the rate of change in the map (1 orbit every 90 minute) is very forgiving for the frame rate that we can use.

Stop in until 4:00 EDT, have a look, and send comments to jse@nptn.org.

Questions about the simulated space missions are also welcome, but they won't be answered until the mission ends tomorrow morning.

Judson Elliott, Computing Coordinator
Willoughby Middle School
Willoughby, Ohio

Dan Goldin, NASA Administrator

From: axduh@asuvm.inre.asu.edu (Douglas A. Howard)
Date: Fri, 21 Apr 1995 10:42:19 -0700

Today (4/21/95) Dan Goldin, NASA administrator, will be visting our facility, the Mars Global Surveyor Space Flight Facility at Arizona State University. This is an informal visit in conjunction with a formal visit to the city of Scottsdale, Arizona, for the Remote Sensing Land Use and Planning Project. I will try to introduce this new technology (CU-SeeMe) to Dan Goldin and reflect through our reflector. All interested are welcome to connect. He is due to arrive at 3:45pm (AZ time, MST) and will be here for about 90 minutes. Maybe he will be interested and talk to some folks out there.

ASU GEOLOGY REFLECTOR 129.219.145.149

I have yet to have an official open house for this reflector, but I plan to on the 1st, 2nd, and 3rd of May. Because this is a special event, I thought I would open the reflector to the public for today.

Hope to CU this afternoon.

Douglas A. Howard
Research Associate
Mars Global Surveyor Space Flight Facility
Thermal Emission Spectrometer
Department of Geology
Arizona State University
e-mail: D.Howard@asu.edu

Cancer Update for Physicans

```
From: "Sunni Hosemann"
Date: 17 Apr 1995 18:41:49 U
```

This telecast will be available on our CU-SeeMe reflector. Continuing Medical Education credit available free for CU-SeeMe viewers. We want viewers' comments!

When: Wed., April 19, 1995, 12noon-1pm (CST)

CME Satellite Teleconference:
Cancer Update for Primary Care Physicans—Breast Cancer. Description: This is a live television program for continuing medical education, delivered direct via satellite to licensed sites. This telecast will also be available to a limited number of viewers on the Internet via the University of Texas M.D. Anderson Cancer Center CU-SeeMe reflector. The reflector's IP address is 129.106.60.32. Please encourage physicians and other interested parties to tune in.

The panel are MD Anderson faculty. They will discuss screening and diagnostic mammography, current treatment options including mastectomy versus lumpectomy/radiation and breast reconstruction, and adjuvant therapy.

There will be a live question-and-answer period.

CME: 1 hour AMA PRA Category 1 and AAFP Prescribed Credit

CME credit will be offered FREE for CU-SeeMe viewers.

For more information, e-mail us:
teleconf@utmdacc.mda.uth.tmc.edu

Meeks, Stone, and Yoshide

 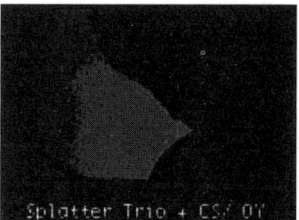

Musical performances on CU-SeeMe.

```
Date: Wed, 31 May 1995 14:17:31 -0700 (PDT)
From: "Eric S. Theise"
```

This Thursday and Friday, June 1 and 2, we'll be experimenting with CU-SeeMe to broadcast two prerecorded Bay Area events of note.

Brock Meeks (unplugged): Recorded at Modern Times Bookstore in San Francisco

on March 29th of this year, this two-hour presentation features the noted CyberWire Dispatch writer and editor talking about telecom politics as usual inside the Washington Beltway.
Background: http://cyberwerks.com/cyberwire

Carl Stone and Otomo Yoshide: Recorded at Beanbenders in Berkeley on April 12th of this year, this hour-plus concert features electro-acoustic musician/composer Stone and turntable artist/guitarist Yoshide, whose recent collaboration Monogatari: Amino Argot is available on the Trigram Records label. Vocalist Min Xiao-Fen joins the duo.
Background: http://www.tmn.com/0h/Community/cstone/home.html

Thursday: 7 pm (PDT): Stone/Yoshide, 9 pm (PDT): Meeks (unplugged) Friday: 7 pm (PDT): Meeks (unplugged), 9 pm (PDT): Stone/Yoshide —Eric S. Theise Liberty Hill Cyberwerks, P.O. Box 460177, San Francisco, CA 94146

Cornerstone Album Release Concert on Internet Video

Posted on behalf of Chris Stuart and Cornerstone, adapted from the Cornerstone Web page, http://www.cfe.cornell.edu/cstone/cstone.html, which also contains pictures and song clips from the new album.

From: slw1@cornell.edu (Steve Worona)
Date: Tue, 9 May 1995 11:20:10 -0400 (EDT)

Kidneystone, cortisone, ah yes, Cornerstone. A little bluegrass, a little swing, a little Cajun, a little old time, a little paprika, a little humor, a little cornmeal, a lotta help from Folk Era Records, simmer for five years and voila—our latest recording, Lonesome Town.

Cornerstone is hosting an Album Release Concert on May 13, 1995, at 8pm in the Statler Auditorium on the campus of Cornell University in Ithaca, New York. You can pay the measly $5 ticket price, or you can watch it for free over the Internet via CU-SeeMe. CU-SeeMe is a videoconferencing tool developed at Cornell. All you need is a Mac or a PC and a fairly fast Internet connection (Ethernet), and you're ready for an evening of Cornerstone. You'll need to connect to IP 132.236.91.204 with a conference ID of zero.

NYSERNet BirdCam

From: jpolly@nysernet.org (Jean Armour Polly)
Date: Thu, 18 May 1995 19:09:29 -0400

We're at the nysernet.org reflector (192.77.173.2). The NYSERNet birdcam is a bird mobile that we have the camera on all night when no one is here. It moves very slowly, so it is good for doing demos from low-speed connections.

I know it's hard to believe, but people LOVE the birdcam. I get a lot of mail, I thought it was time to let birdcam have its own mbox. :-) NYSERNet birdcam fans: You can now send email to the birdcam at birdcam@pat.nyser.net

History, Culture, and Usage

Local Telementor at K-12 School

From: rkrupp@edcoe.k12.ca.us (Renee Krupp)
Date: Fri, 7 Apr 95 09:26 PDT

I am at a K-12 site. Actually, I am in charge of educational technology at Charter Community School, under the auspices of the El Dorado County Office of Education. My site spends a lot on technology. I have a terrific lab with high-end machines, enough RAM to function, scanners, CD-ROMs, laserdisks, video....

I am also a local telementor, which means that I was selected and trained by the state to provide Internet assistance to other teachers. I've been teaching/administrating since I was 20 (started young), and am in my 28th year in education. I have an M.A. and about six teaching credentials. I started using educational technology in 1980 or so and have used/been absolutely immersed in technology since then.

We use the Internet, but have had CU-SeeMe for about only a month. This last Saturday, I spearheaded a technology conference at our county office for about 200 people. It was a full day with eight different sessions; the people selected six 45-min sessions to attend. One session was the Internet (hands-on in my lab), and another session was CU-SeeMe in a small group demonstration. The entire day went well, but the Net really wowed them. I had a cadre of students positioned right behind the "non-techie" adults to help them navigate and negotiate the equipment and software. It was a hit.

Now that this last Saturday is gone, I will be moving my attention to classroom/lab use of the Net and CU-SeeMe.

Foreign Language Materials via CU-SeeMe

From: Bob Dixon
Date: Fri, 28 Apr 1995 10:52:19 -0400 (EDT)

We are now sending foreign language materials continuously via CU-SeeMe. A Mac located at our Satellite Dish facility is fed programs from foreign satellites, and it transmits the audio and video to the Ohio State University reflector. The language changes each day, and has included Spanish, Italian, Russian, Arabic, Japanese, French, and German so far. The window is labelled "The World." This is an experiment to see if it is useful for instructional purposes and to provide a continuous CU-SeeMe demonstration.

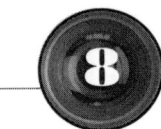 Internet TV with CU-SeeMe

Save 25 Cents

```
From: Eric Lease Morgan
Date: Wed, 31 May 95 21:21:50 0400
```

Michael,

I have written a script you may or may not be interested in. For a good time try:
http://152.1.24.177/save-25-cents/save-25-cents.cgi

The CGI script at the other end is supposed to take a live picture of my office using a QuickCam. Everything should be (well) documented at http://www.lib.ncsu.edu/staff/morgan/save-25-cents-cgi.html

The script works most of the time. When it doesn't, it hangs my whole computer. If someone could tell me what I am doing wrong, I would be most grateful.

Eric Lease Morgan
NCSU Libraries
http://www.lib.ncsu.edu/staff/morgan/

Timed Video Grabber

```
From: "Allon Stern"
Date: Sat,  4 Mar 1995 05:16:47 -0500
```

I've written a program for the Mac called the Timed Video Grabber, or TVG for short. TVG lets you set up your Mac to grab a frame of video every n seconds/minutes/hours/days and shuffles it off to a JPEG file.

You can then set up your web server (if it's on another machine) to FTP that file from your Mac when it gets updated and have a current picture on your web page!

Cool, eh?

http://spiderweb.yoyodyne.com/allon/tvg.html

Sixth Joint European Networking Conference

```
From: "Halvor Kise jr."
Date: Mon, 15 May 1995 06:09:05 +0200 (MET DST)
```

The 6th Joint European Networking Conference (JENC6), "Bringing the World to the Desktop," held May 15-18, 1995, in Tel Aviv, Israel, will be broadcast on the Internet, on the Mbone and with CU-SeeMe at the following times (GMT):

```
Monday May 15 11:00-12:30
Tuesday May 16 13:00-14:00
Thursday May 18 08:00-09:30
```

```
In addition to the plenary sessions, we plan to broadcast the following
sessions:

1-1: Mobile Computing and intermittent connectivity (15/5 13:00-14:30)
V-2: Views and visions of European service providers (16/5, 06:00-07:30)
1-4: Technical developments from an industrial view point (16/5, 08:00-09:30)
1-2: Network performance issues (16/5, 11:00-12:30)
IV-3: Electronic publishing and information retrieval (18/5, 06:00-09:30)

The primary CU-SeeMe reflector will be 158.36.33.6, but in the interest of
saving Internet bandwith, please use a reflector located as close as possible
to your own site.

*** MEMENTO MORI ***
PGP-key by fingering halvork@frodo.hiof.no
Halvor's
```

NHK Show About AIDS

In November 1994, the NHK, the national broadcasting corporation of Japan, did a television program on services available on the Internet, including CU-SeeMe. Here is the call for participation:

```
From: Jim Cooper
Date: Mon, 21 Nov 1994 12:01:57 -0500
```

I am working with NHK in Tokyo on a television program dealing with what is available on the internet. One of the services that we would like to profile is CU-SeeMe. NHK is the national brodcasting corporation of Japan. It operates without commercials and is supported by the government. The theme of the program is "Earth, Humans, and the Future" (rough translation). Other topics we will be discussing are space-related issues (for example, Jupiter SL-9), technology for future society; Bosnia and Uganda report; and AIDS (a film crew reports from San Francisco. This report will be followed by an example of using the Internet as a forum for discussion of important world topics.

Our on-air time may be a little inconvenient: Japan time 3:00 PM to 6:00PM on Friday November 25, 1994. That will be 1:00 AM to 4:00 AM EST on Friday. (All other U.S time zones will still be in Thursday, November 24, 1994.) This will be a live broadcast.

Because of the nature of live TV, we ask that you can sign on and be configured by 5:00 PM (3:00 AM EST) and plan to remain on line until the end of the program (one hour). The live portion will actually hit the air at about 3:45 AM EST.

We will feature a six-minute segment of the discussion. An NHK newscaster will be speaking from a position live in the studio, and during that time we will send the live feed over the CU-SeeMe link.

Any person who would like to participate, please email.

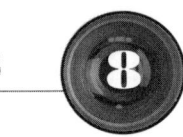

Internet TV with CU-SeeMe

Here is the post-broadcast report:

From: Jim Cooper
The NHK broadcast Earth, Humans, and the Future 25-11-94

Arthur C. Clarke introduced the program from a garden somewhere in, I believe, Sri Lanka. The program started with a quote of his: "Any sufficiently advanced technically civilization is indistinguishable from magic." Clarke spoke after each report during the three-hour program; he was the connecting thread.

The program went out from 15.00-18.00 JP time (6.00-9.00AM GMT). I connected at 5.30AM GMT, and the producer and the interviewer did a brief CU-SeeMe session to let me know the format. The entire program was fed through on the net. While the programme was going out, there were three CU-SeeMe windows: the broadcast, mine in Plymouth, and NHK's staff's.

Adam, an HIV-positive volunteer, phoned me the night before to say that he was willing to talk on the program. I had never met him before. He said he would meet me at the roundabout at the end of the street at 8AM. We had no idea whether he would turn up or not; we knew nothing about his condition. When he did arrive it was 20 minutes to air-time, and we had to communicate his information to NHK via keying in text on the CU-SeeMe window and talking to Jim, who translated into Japanese. Adam had not seen the technology before and didn't want to be screened; he stayed off camera and I keyed in text as he spoke. The timing was very tight, and he agreed to speak over the phone with his voice modulated only 5 minutes before going live!

We watched the Teen AIDS report from San Francisco via CU, and then we were interviewed on the content.

Section on AIDS and HIV:

Adam (not his real name) has been HIV-positive for 9 years and has provided support for many people both with HIV and AIDS. A report on Teen AIDS in San Francisco was shown. A young girl interviewed explained that she could not find a way to tell her parents. Adam has not told his parents and said he was glad because his mother has since died from cancer. He is grateful that this problem did not add to her suffering. His father still does not know.

He said that he thought it was marvelous that the Net could be used to educate people in different countries and provide comfort through support.

As I was the only CU-SeeMe person, they blew my screen up on a large wall and I was interviewed; I responded by keying in text. I said that as a technician in the Social Science department at the University of Plymouth, I thought that there are great opportunities to use this technology as a means of educating (especially) third world countries and preventing suffering. I related that educators in my department were currently using satellite communications to train social workers in Romania.

I shared with them that there were a number of sites for information on safe sex on the Internet, and that AIDS and HIV newsgroups provided a means of support and comfort for sufferers both on a private basis and through group discussion.

We were on air live for six minutes. The interviewer spoke in Japanese and then translated into English. The text I keyed in (in English) was translated into Japanese; the telephone conversation was translated into Japanese.

Party Girl

From: Jay M. Williams
Date: Wed, 24 May 1995 22:16:40 -0500

We will be broadcasting the full-length motion picture Party Girl live in conjunction with the preview at the Seattle Film Festival on June 3, 1995, at 9pm PST. We're working with Apple Computer, Silicon Graphics, and many others to put this on, and we need reflector sites to tie into our main site and act as feeds to the rest of the world. We are getting a lot of media attention, and I have various local reports looking for carriers in their areas to do stories on. If you are interested in being a downstream reflector site, please email me directly off list. We are currently looking for sites in New York and continental Europe, but we'll consider others if you have the bandwidth to spare. Thanks.

For more information on viewing the broadcast, check out
http://www.polis.com/firstlook/party/default.html

jmw@polis.com — Jay M. Williams — Williams Enterprises
Wide Area Network Design and Internet Consulting
voice:713-416-2216 fax:713-688-1194 http://www.polis.com

Voices for Diversity

From: roberson keith
Date: Tue, 16 May 1995 08:47:23 -0400

Keith and Kirsten invite you to join us in...
VOICES FOR DIVERSITY / The Collabarena Internet Festival

Opening ceremony: "Finding a Rhythm" (drumming circle via NetPhone, CU-SeeMe)
At dusk, evening of Friday, May 19, 1995 (approximately 7:30EST or 12:30am GMT)

You are invited to bring drums, musical instruments, singing voices, and anything else to contribute to a communal rhythm. We will find a rhythm and maintain it for as long as it needs to breathe. As the rhythm finds its silence, we will light the flame.

Conferencing circle: "Seen and Heard"
Night of Friday, May 19, 1995

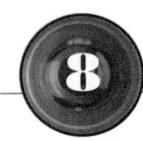

Internet TV with CU-SeeMe

All participants are invited to take a turn speaking. We will move from each individual in the physical circle to individuals on the global projection until we come full-circle. Participants are invited to read a short poem, story, or article; sing or play a short song; dance a brief movement; or hold up a drawing, painting, or object that reflects her/his identity.

Closing ceremony: "Carry the Flame"
Through the morning of Saturday, May 20, 1995

As the flame fades within the arena, participants will receive a totem of the flame as a symbol of the power of diversity.

If you are in the the Baltimore area, please join us within the Collabarena at the University of Maryland Baltimore County, UMBC Fine Arts Amphitheatre, Visual Arts Building.

Members of the global Internet and UMBC community are invited to participate in a global video conference to dialogue on issues of identity and diversity. The goal of this event is to promote visible diversity over the Net and on this campus via video links with individuals and universities here and abroad that share concerns.

Bring sleeping bags and food for your overnight stay. Coffee and beverages will be provided in the Collabarena. Reservations are not required but are encouraged.

For complete details, see
http://imda.umbc.edu/imda/keith/net_event/netevent2.html

or contact

Keith Roberson
(410)455-2150
Kirsten D'Andrea
(410)455-2150

The Virtual Human Body: Performance Art

Date: Thu, 4 May 1995 18:53:42 -0500

```
VIRTUAL HUMAN BODY
A CU-SeeMe, Internet-based Performance of the Human Body
LIVE VIDEO / AUDIO AVAILABLE OVER THE INTERNET!
**************************************************
*********** A 24-HOUR PERFORMANCE: ***********
**************************************************
STARTING: Wednesday, May 17, 1995 @12:00 am (CST)
ENDING: Wednesday, May 17, 1995 @11:59 pm (CST)
```

On the EDEN MATRIX Reflector (199.171.21.8), available using CU-SeeMe Internet teleconferencing software. For more information about this performance, try the performance homepage, http://yar.cs.wisc.edu/~void/

History, Culture, and Usage

The VIRTUAL HUMAN BODY is a 24-hour live performance art event created and performed exclusively on the Internet. It involves the broadcast of digital video/audio data over the Internet and can be experienced anywhere on the planet that supports an Internet connection and can run CU-SeeMe teleconferencing software.

*************** FOR A 24-HOUR DURATION ***************

I will broadcast images of by interactions with technologies.
I will welcome and accept comment, critique, and discussion via email or CU-SeeMe.
I will explore, in part, my relationship with technology—past, present, future—and ponder the role techology might play in a society dedicated to technological advancement and innovation.

This performance will be broadcast on the EDEN MATRIX multiconferencing reflector site. You can reach the EDEN MATRIX homepage at http://www.eden.com/

Flyvision and Spyder World Wide Web

From: Jonathan Sarno
Date: Sat, 13 May 1995 07:48:22 -0400 (EDT)

Saturday May 13th 1995 - Starts 9:00 pm EST

"Flyvision" and "Spyder World Wide Web" cordially invite you to New York's first CU-SeeMe WORLD PARTY TOUR, featuring the Cyberspace premiere of the French techno-film masterpiece "Vibroboy."

http://www.imaginet.fr/~relig/vibro.html

Join the WORLD PARTY TOUR virtually!

The tour's itinerary is available at
http://www.escape.com/~spyder/INTERNETTVHP.HTML
http://www.interport.net/~fly/CU-SeeFly/index.html

Join the WORLD PARTY TOUR physically!

On a large video projector, we will travel together with fellow CU-SeeMe fanatics from around the world, checking out CU-SeeMe reflector sites in Europe, North America, and Asia.

New York Cyber Salon physical location:
130 West 3rd Street, Apt# 4
(Off Sixth Avenue)

A project by members of Navigating Global Cultures:
Artists, Educators, and The New Technologies.
(http://www.interport.net/~fly/NGC/index.html)

New York University
Commission on Experimental Aesthetics

Internet TV with CU-SeeMe

Simulcast Interview of Daniel Fortune

From: daniel fortune
Date: Wed, 31 May 1995 13:15:15 -0600

This past Sunday, we performed an experimental simulcast with CU-SeeMe and KSJS 90.5 FM radio in the San Francisco Bay Area. The format was an hour-long interview of Daniel Fortune on multimedia, technology, and CU-SeeMe.

We broadcast the live interview via FM transmitter, and we transmitted the image via the Internet. Listeners to the show could call in and ask questions, or they could dial up CU-SeeMe on the Cornell reflector and ask questions via a talk window while listening to the broadcast on 90.5 FM.

It was an interesting experience to interact with the people on CU-SeeMe while being interviewed live. People on CU-SeeMe who were listening to the broadcast could ask questions via a talk window, or they called into the show.

The goal of the experiment was to acquaint people with digital video transmission via the Internet with CU-SeeMe, which as you all know is in its infancy. I guess we take for granted the fact that because we know how the technology works, everyone else should as well.

However, it is new technology. As such, we should not make the assumptions that people are as far up the learning curve as we are. We are the pioneers.

My conclusion is that many people are interested in the technology, as it truly is an exciting way to communicate with other people, but they have to learn about the technology first.

Imagine if mainstream public and commercial radio provided a simple way for the listeners to "watch" and participate with simple technology such as CU-SeeMe. I believe that as digital video transmission becomes an accepted norm, we will experience a slow but steady cultural revamping of how we view traditional media sources.

For more information, go to http://www.fortune.org/simulcast.html for a review of the show. For a transcript of the interview, email me at dfortune@best.com.

```
*         http://www.fortune.org
*         Great spirits have always encountered
*           violent opposition from mediocre minds...
*                              Albert Einstein
```

History, Culture, and Usage

Project BillVision

```
Date: 03 May 95 11:58:26 EDT
From: John.S.Erickson@Dartmouth.EDU (John S. Erickson)
```

On Sunday, June 11, President Bill Clinton will be delivering the commencement address at Dartmouth's graduation. This message is to announce "Project BillVision," an effort by students at the Thayer School of Engineering and the staff of the Kiewit Computation Center to carry that address live on the Net using CU-SeeMe.

For more information, check out the Project BillVision home page:
http://picard.dartmouth.edu/~oly/BillVision.html

We have over 15 reflectors set up worldwide to mirror the Dartmouth transmission. Those reflectors connected as mirrors will receive packets from Dartmouth and rebroadcast to the viewer. To help viewers find the various mirrors, we have created a custom BillVision nicknames file that you put into your preferences folder before starting CU-SeeMe.

General information:

The Office of Instructional Services at Dartmouth will be providing multicamera coverage of President Clinton's speech and will supply a live feed to various campus buildings and local cable. Project BillVision, based at the Thayer School of Engineering, will separate video and audio, feeding both into a Macintosh Quadra 840AV running CU-SeeMe. At Dartmouth's Kiewit Computation Center a high-end server running the CU-SeeMe reflector will receive this transmission and rebroadcast the packets to all connected clients. These could be users running CU-SeeMe or, preferably, reflectors set up to mirror the Dartmouth transmission.

```
              John Erickson
Interactive Media Lab Dartmouth Med School
Hanover, NH 03755     VOICE: 603-650-1821
oly@dartmouth.edu     FAX:   603-650-1164
http://picard.dartmouth.edu/~oly/oly.html
```

The Lobster Lives

```
From: Borre Ludvigsen
Date:  Wed, 22 Mar 1995 15:46:36 -0500
```

Two years ago, a group of my multimedia students took one of those skeletal models of animals made of plywood (a lobster I had bought at the educational toy store on Harvard Square during a visit to the U.S.), built a double-scale model painted red, made an animated replica on their Macs and used them as a "mascot" in their stand at the annual software exhibition in Oslo.

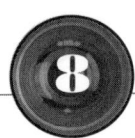

The model has been hanging in the ceiling in their lab ever since. The other day, someone, somewhere in this world, moved our remote-controlled CU-SeeMe camera a bit too far to the right. So we decided to try to make that the camera's home position.

That's what you see in the mm94@hiof.no CU-SeeMe window at the 158.36.33.3 reflector. mm94 is the class; hiof is Norwegian for Ostfold Regional College; and no is Norway. And, yes, that is the email address to that class of students. And the URL in the bottom of the window does allow you to run the camera. But please be kind and patient. You might be sharing it with someone else. (Anyone want to do the AppleScript code to restrict usage to one IP address for 5 minutes?)

Just in case you were wondering what it all was.

Japan-Stanford Videobridge

From: Michael Bayle
Date: Tue, 25 Apr 1995 20:18:45 -0700 (PDT)

Hi Michael,
Essentially TEPIA is a MITI-funded organization in Japan that has a large exhibit hall. The annual exhibit opens on Friday in Japan, but we (Stanford University) always get a sneak preview of selected exhibits via videoconference. It is our goal this year to try and provide as much video as possible over CU-SeeMe. This is technically a challenge, as we have many video feeds coming in and out of our auditorium on campus. Given that you are in the Bay Area, if interested, I could fax you a map of the campus, should you wish to come in person. We will have many high-level people here including Becky Morgan (original founder of Smart Valley), Harry Saal (CEO of Smart Valley), Bill Wong of COmmerceNet, and so on, not to mention our "virtual audience" in Japan.

Here's the announcement:

The following will be broadcasted on CU-SeeMe live this Wednesday, 4/26/95 at 6PM-8:15PM PST (10AM-12:15PM Japan Thursday). It will be available on 36.4.0.111.

An agenda follows. Please note that for two of the presentations, our broadcast will be temporarily halted as the speakers require a quick connection to the Net. (We are only using one machine for this.)

Please join us if you have the chance.

The US-Japan Technology Management Center presents a LIVE VIDEO-BRIDGE WITH JAPAN! Wednesday 4/26 5:30-6pm refreshments outside, 6pm-8pm video bridge, 102 Thornton Hall (directly West of Terman). In this live two-way videobridge

with the TEPIA convention center in Tokyo, Japan, we will get a pre-opening
view of the multimedia exhibition, which doesn't open publicly until the next
day.

```
6:00  MC in Japan:  Miss Kuniko Yamashita
         Opening message from President Shigeru Harada
         Greeting from  MITI, Mr. Hideo Morimoto
      MC at Stanford: Mr. Richard Dasher
         Opening message from Dean Dwain Fullerton
         Greeting from Dr. Masahiro Kawahata
         Greeting from Professor Joseph Goodman
      Presentations from Stanford
         Dr. Harry Saal - Smart Valley
         Dr. William Wong - CommerceNet (5 min. blackout on CUSEEME)
         Mr. Burt Lee - Japan Window (10 min. blackout on CUSEEME)
7:05  Introduction of exhibition hall and exhibitions from TEPIA
      1. TEO - Another Earth
         Presented by Mr. Atsushi Yagi from Fujitsu, Ltd.
      2. Video on Demand
         Presented by Mr. Hideki Sakamoto from NTT
      3. Hi-Vision Interactive Images
         Presented by Mr. Toshiyuki Takarada,NHK Enterprises
      4. Virtual Skiing
         Presented by Mr. Kunihiro Nakagawa from NEC
      5. Automated Building Construction System
         Presented by Mr. Yoshihiro Ichioka from Obayashi Corp.
7:30  MC in Japan
         Discussion (Q&A session; 2-way video, 2-way audio
8:15  End
```

Michael Bayle
US-Japan Technology Management Center
Department of Computer Science

CNN via CU-SeeMe at the Aerospace Corporation

From: Louis McDonald
Date: Tue, 25 Apr 1995 07:10:50 -0700

Within our firewalled network, I am using CU-SeeMe to run a feed of CNN for Headline News. The output of the cable/VCR is going into a Mac AV that connects to our reflector. A number of users like having Headline News because it is "news on the half hour."

We also use this set up to broadcast corporate VTCs that use the VTC network on ISDN (we branch the video out to another Mac AV).

Louis McDonald
The Aerospace Corporation.

From: GENE@JOHNSON.CORNELL.EDU
Date: Wed, 10 May 1995 11:14:28 -0500 (EST)

Michael, I have been using CU-SeeMe for about 18 months. In November 1993, I started something I call the "virtual office project." I belong to a national

Internet TV with CU-SeeMe

association of business school computing directors who meet two or three times a year and between meetings communicate electronically. The project put seven people from this organization on CU-SeeMe; they share a private reflector that I run here at Cornell.

We all come to work in the morning and connect to the reflector, and stay parked on the others' screens much of the day. The "we" includes my compatriots at MIT, Emory, UCLA, Vanderbilt, Dartmouth, and Purdue. We started it just to see what sorts of interaction opportunities presented themselves because of the ready availability of the technology. It has been really interesting. I had it in mind to write the story anyway, but had not decided on the media.

On a related note, we are planning to use CU-SeeMe for a pilot project for HelpDesk Consulting next year.

```
    _/_/_/_/   _/_/_/_/   _/       _/   _/_/_/_/      GENE ZIEGLER, alias Dr.Z
       _/         _/        _/      _/  _/         Director of Computing Services
      _/  _/_/   _/_/      _/  _/  _/  _/_/         Johnson School of Management
     _/     _/    _/      _/    _/_/  _/                Cornell University
    _/_/_/_/   _/_/_/_/   _/       _/  _/_/_/_/          (607)255-3217
```

The Oklahoma City Bombing

From: Matthew Sanderson
Date: Sun, 23 Apr 1995 00:54:45 -0400 (EDT)

I'm posting this as an aid to those who truly need the information, not as a tourist attraction. Please use discretion.

From web page http://www.ionet.net/explode.shtml:

For live feed from KOCO Channel 5 (ABC) in Oklahoma City, go to 204.96.200.5 with CU-SeeMe. The feed from Channel 5 is up. This feed is throttled for 1 fps to conserve bandwidth. Please do not transmit to our site; receive only.

```
/ Matthew Sanderson   CIS: 70733,2700   'net: matthews@hookup.net \
\ http://www-bprc.mps.ohio-state.edu/cgi-bin/hpp/matthews.html    /
```

Machine Room Surveilance

Date: Mon, 08 May 95 09:25:18 CET
From: Espen Lyngaas

The Norwegian School of Management tried CU-SeeMe as a machine room surveilance system. This worked fine. Then we installed a video camera in the students' computer lab so that students (from home) could see how many people

History, Culture, and Usage

were using the lab. For example, if there were queues, they wouldn't have to travel go to school until more computers were vacant.

I know that these uses were not that "serious" and probably not what CU-SeeMe was made for. However both things worked great. Unfortunately, we've had to take them down due to the massive bandwidth that CU-SeeMe uses. We only have one 64Kbps line to the outside world.

```
Espen Lyngaas                             Norwegian School of Management
Computer Systems Administrator            Computing Center
EARN: edb88002@nobivm                     Internet: edb88002@vm.bi.no
Phone: +47-67570708      Cellular: +47-94341160      Fax: +47-67570555
```

Giving Consumers a Choice: The New World of Telecommunications

```
From: "Chuck Poulton"
Date: Wed, 17 May 1995 10:03:02 EST -0500
```

Jacqueline F. Woods, president and chief executive officer of Ameritech Ohio, will present "Giving Consumers a Choice: The New World of Telecommunications" this Thursday, May 18th, 12:30 pm EDT (16:30 GMT) at the monthly meeting of the Akron Roundtable in Akron, Ohio. The audio from this talk will be carried live via the MBONE and CU-SeeMe.

CU-SeeMe users can connect via our reflector at 131.123.89.8 (mozart.wksu.kent.edu). The MBONE session will be announced via sd.

Questions for the speaker can be mailed to roundtable@wksu.kent.edu, and further information can be found at http://www.wksu.kent.edu/rt.html. A RealAudio version of the speech will also be available at the above URL soon after the event has concluded.

Feedback on audio quality to the above email address is always appreciated.

The Buckman School

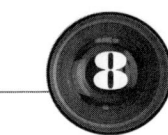

Internet TV with CU-SeeMe

From: Larry Helseth
Date: Wed, 3 May 1995 09:55:58 -0700

We've used CU-SeeMe to allow the kids to interview people from our classroom. Interviewees have included Craig Hickman, the creator of Kid Pix; Jeff Price, a graphics researcher at Virginia Commonwealth University; and Borre Ludvigsen, a professor from Norway.

The Buckman School's Room 100 QuickCam Page

http://buckman.pps.k12.or.us/picturecam.html

provides a view of what the kids are doing every 10 minutes throughout the day. It runs a common gateway interface program and serving up a picture for each log-in as a web page. Pretty nice application. They've also got a pointer from their home page to a page with images of people they've met using CU-SeeMe,

http://buckman.pps.k12.or.us/cuseeme/cuseeme.html

Check it out!

We're just beginning to set up CU-SeeMe with a secure reflector for use for internal communinication within our corporation. I'll send you more info on our plans when I get time. We got started after my wife saw the "Cyberscope" announcement in Newsweek last August describing CU-SeeMe.

Good luck with the book. It will be a hot seller at Baxter!

Supporting Baxter Healthcare's Biotech Community
Larry Helseth, Ph.D.
Baxter Healthcare-Round Lake, IL   60073-0490
(708) 270-5384 [VOICE] (708) 270-5381 [FAX]

Earth Day 1995

Date: Wed, 3 May 1995 14:35:06 -0400
From: Tim_Dorcey@cornell.edu (Tim Dorcey)

Hi Michael,

I've been following your progress with the book deal. I thought I'd sift through some old email, and forward anything that might be of interest. Believe me, I have produced a lot of verbiage on CU-SeeMe over the past couple years.

What follows here is a press release for an event we did at Cornell. Of course, CU-SeeMe is not really designed for this kind of "big event," (a 500-channel cable TV system would be much better suited), but it does illustrate the global nature of CU-SeeMe. I guess the process of collecting the seven video signals was distinctly CU-SeeMe-ish, whereas the idea of creating a show that lots of people will simultaneously watch is not characteristic of CU-SeeMe, if that makes sense.

Here's what we used as the reflector message of the day to set the stage:

> Welcome to Earth Watch 95! This is the Earth. Not a video game or other treat for the senses, but simple scenes from around the world as it exists live at this moment in 1995. It is not a very big place anymore. You have friends in some of these places, or you will someday soon. We are all connected. Let your eyes roam our home for a time. Then learn something new about the Earth today. You might want to start at http://www.cfe.cornell.edu/.

And here's the press release:

> Chris Stuart, cs10@cornell.edu, Information Systems Manager
> Center for the Environment, 200 Rice Hall, (607) 255-3972
> Cornell University, Ithaca, NY 14853
> http://www.cfe.cornell.edu
> environment-L@cornell.edu
>
> FOR EARTH DAY, CORNELL WILL CONNECT SEVEN CONTINENTS WITH LIVE VIDEO VIA THE INTERNET

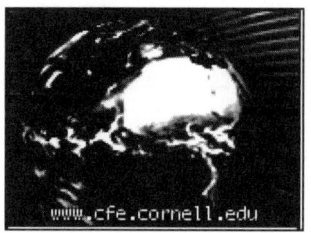  

> ITHACA, NY - Visiting all continents on the first Earth Day would have required a fast (and air-polluting) jet. Environmentally-conscious celebrants of Earth Day '95 will make the same trip, from the comfort of their computers, in an Internet videoconference sponsored by Cornell University's Center for the Environment.

> Beginning about 12 noon EST, on Friday, April 21, live video from New York City; Tokyo; Rio de Janeiro; Salzburg, Austria; Cape Town, South Africa; Adelaide, Australia; and Antarctica's McMurdo Research Station will appear in seven separate windows on computer screens connected to "EarthWatch '95."

 **Internet TV with CU-SeeMe**

The global view is available to anyone with an Apple Macintosh or an IBM or compatible PC running Microsoft Windows, an Internet connection, and a freely available piece of videoconferencing software called "CU-SeeMe," which was developed at Cornell.

"This will be something like the 1950s, when Edward R. Murrow heralded the age of television by delivering live views of the Atlantic and Pacific oceans simultaneously to homes across the country," said Chris Stuart, the Cornell Center for the Environment director of computing who is coordinating the connection. "The idea is to show how technology has made the world seem smaller while pointing out what has always been true: that we are all interconnected ecologically."

The North American video camera will show the New York City skyline, Stuart said. Live from South America, videoconference viewers will see a rain forest scene, while the European view will originate outside a Salzburg cathedral. The Adelaide camera will be set up on the quadrangle of Flinders University of South Australia to show Earth Day events there. "We're not sure what Tokyo is showing, and there probably won't be much excitement in Antarctica," Stuart said, "although a few penguins may wander by." Video camera operators were recruited from the worldwide legion of CU-SeeMe users, he noted.

EarthWatch '95 will close its video eyes Saturday, April 22, around midnight EST.

The Center for the Environment is an interdisciplinary research, education and outreach program at Cornell University. CU-SeeMe was developed by Tim Dorcey, a senior programmer at Cornell Information Technologies. The "reflector" computer for the videoconference, a Sun SPARC station, is located at Cornell.

 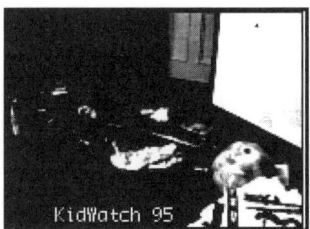 

Instructions for connecting to EarthWatch '95 and a free download of the CU-SeeMe software are available on the World Wide Web or by anonymous ftp.

```
EarthWatch 95: All right, Hansen!
EarthWatch 95: We appear to have lost Salzburg, but I'm working on getting it back or a Switzerland site.
EarthWatch 95: thank you Geneva!
```

Beijing Spectrometer Experiment

From: Joseph M. Izen
Date: Wed, 3 May 1995 10:51:12 -0500

I have been using CU-SeeMe to host weekly analysis meetings between grad students and faculty collaborating on the Beijing Spectrometer experiment. People make GIF versions of their plots and put them out on the WWW. You're welcome to spy on our meetings as long as you understand that the actual physics results should not be discussed with others. I host the meetings; Colorado State and the University of Hawaii and (sometimes) the University of Washington and Cal Tech join in.

We have also experimented with netcasting monthly collaboration meetings when we are all in one place. It takes someone to grab a frame in a slide window and transmit it, and it works only with an AV Mac and a real camcorder. The QuickCam images are too small.

This summer we are going to experiment with using it over the Internet link to China, which was created for my experiment that actually is in Beijing. The ESnet people have warned us to expect audio dropouts, because the total bandwidth to China is 64 Kbaud. I suspect CU-SeeMe will be the application that will force the bandwidth issue so that we can get the link upgraded. At present, we have occasional phone conference calls to China that are always initiated (for financial reasons) on the U.S. side. If CU-SeeMe works, my Chinese collaborators can initiate calls themselves. I think this will have an extremely healthy impact on the collaboration.

Best regards,
Joe Izen
Assoc. Prof. of Physics.

Chapter 9

Other Videoconferencing Technologies

CU-SeeMe isn't your only choice for videoconferencing. This chapter provides you with enough information to evaluate these many systems; some of these technologies may better meet your requirements. Their prices range from nothing to several thousand dollars per participant.

Software to enhance and automate CU-SeeMe operation on the Macintosh also is covered in this chapter. Similar software for Windows is sure to follow the release of the Connectix QuickCam for Windows, in the autumn of 1995.

Overview of Other Technologies

This section covers a variety of videoconferencing technologies. Pictures and logos that appear here have been taken from the web pages for that product. The summary information, compiled by Leigh Anne Rettinger of the SUCCEED project, was checked at the time of this printing. In some cases, very little information about a software package was known, but contact information is provided anyway. If you have videoconferencing tales to tell, please let me know.

Avistar

Provider: Avistar Conference

Minimum requirements: Intel, Macintosh, or Sun platform.

Notes: Multipoint (up to 4 simultaneous participants), collaboration (shared window with annotation capability.)

For more information: Avistar Systems, 555 Hamilton Avenue, Palo Alto CA 94301, +1.415.617.1350, +1.415.617.1351 (fax), info@avistar.com, http://www.avistar.com/avistar-adr.html

Being There

Provider: Intelligence at Large

Minimum requirements:

- Macintosh: Mac 68040 or Power Mac, MacOS 7.1, 8 MB RAM, 3.5 MB available disk space, QuickTime video capture, video input (S-VHS, NTSC, PAL, SECAM), audio input.

Notes: Modem use requires 28.8 kbps for audio, video, and collaboration (9600 bps sufficient for collaboration only). LAN Protocols: Appletalk and AppleTalk Remote Access (ARA), TCP/IP. Audio encoding: QuickTime. Video encoding: Quicktime, National Semiconductor Video Codec Interoperability Standard Support. Multipoint capability in some configurations. Collaboration: full document window sharing, real-time updates of shared documents, drag-and-drop interface for file transfer, file and clipboard transfer, object-based whiteboard markup. Demon version available from their web page.

Cost: $299 for Standard, $599 for PRO, $149 for Starter kit (includes 2 Standard kits, limit one per site).

For more information: Intelligence at Large, Inc., 3508 Market Street, Suite 230, Philadelphia PA 19104, +1.800.425.7638, +1.215.387.6002, +1.215.387.9215 (fax), info@beingthere.com, http://www.beingthere.com/

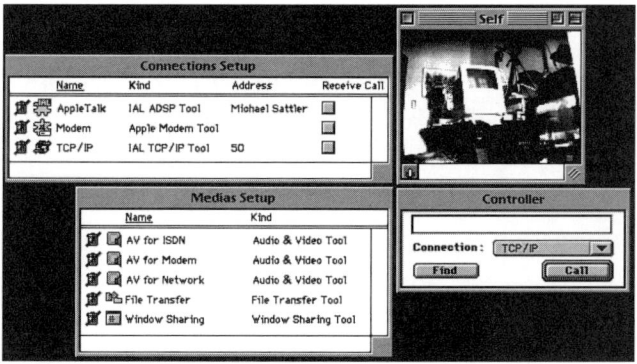

Figure 9.1. Being There in action.

Bitfield Video Communication System (BVCS)

Provider: Bitfield Oy

Minimum requirements:

- **Intel:** Windows 3.1, external monitor or video overlay board (any of Bitfield DVP, Creative Labs VideoBlaster, Fast Electronic Screen Machine, New Media Graphics Super VideoWindows, Omnicomp M&M Basic, VideoLogic DVA, Adda AVer Video Commander, or other products supporting Microsoft Media Control Interface (MCI))

Notes: LAN protocols: TCP/IP and NetBIOS. Interoperability: H.320. Video encoding: H.261. Audio encoding: G.711, G.722, G.728.

For more information: Bitfield Oy, Ukonvaaja 2, FIN-02130 ESPOO FINLAND, +358.0.5024220, +358.0.4552240 (fax), general information: info@bitfield.fi, technical support: techsupp@bitfield.fi, http://www.bitfield.fi/. Bitfield USA, 1960 E. Grand Ave., Suite 550, El Segundo CA 90245, +1.310.322.9863, +1.310.322.9867 (fax).

C-Phone

Provider: Twincom

Minimum requirements:

- **Intel:** Windows 3.1, 386SX, 4MB RAM, VGA, graphics board with feature connector

Notes: Interoperability: H.320. Video encoding: H.261. Audio encoding: G.711, G.722, G.725, G.728. The C-Phone Multi-Point Controller add-on (from Target Technologies, +11.800.666.2496) will allow a 4-person multipoint conference for $4000. Collaboration: file transfer. Software can image capture and record full-motion video and audio, up to 30 fps given sufficient network bandwidth.

Cost: $1,995 (for LAN user), includes Sony video camera and Primo microphone.

For more information: Twincom, Wilmington NC, +1.910.395.6100

Cameo Personal Video System

Provider: Compression Labs Inc.

Category: AV for high-bandwidth environments

Minimum requirements:

- **Macintosh:** MacOS 7.0, video card (RasterOps 24STV, 24LTV)

Notes: Video over Switched 56, ISDN, and Ethernet; audio requires separate ISDN or analog phone line. Video encoding: Proprietary CLI PV2 compression algorithm. Audio encoding: Proprietary CLI PV2 compression algorithm. Collaboration: file transfer.

Cost: $1595 without camera, $2095 with camera.

For more information: Compression Labs Inc., 2860 Junction Ave., San Jose CA, 95134, +1.800.CALL.CLI, +1.408.435.3000

Communicator III

Provider: EyeTel Communications Inc.

Minimum requirements:

- **Intel:** Windows 3.1, Novell Netware 3.11, 386SX, 4 MB RAM, Super VGA w/256 colors and feature connector, audio input/output, 5 MB hard disk space

Notes: LAN protocols: NetBIOS, TCP/IP, IPX. Interoperability: H.320. Video encoding:H.261. Audio encoding:G.711, G.722, G.728. Has multipoint capability. Collaboration: whiteboard, file transfer.

Cost: $6995, includes camera, microphone, speakers, CODEC and video capture board. Optional motion estimation board $995

For more information: EyeTel Communications Inc., #206 - 267 W. Esplanade, N. Vancouver, B.C., Canada, V7M1A5, +1.800.736.3236, +1.604.984.2522, +1.604.984.3566 (fax)

Communique!

Provider: InSoft

Minimum requirements:

- **Intel:** Windows 3.1, 3.11
- **IBM:** AIX 3.2.5, 4.1.1
- **Sun:** SunOS 4.1.3, 4.1.4, Solaris 2.3, 2.4
- **HP:** HP-UX 9.0.3, 9.0.5, 10.0
- **DEC:** OSF/1, OSF/2, OSF/3
- **Silicon Graphics:** IRIX 5.3

Notes: LAN protocol: TCP/IP. Video encoding: CellB, JPEG, Indeo (more info at http://www.intel.com/IAL/indeo/indeo.html). Collaboration: whiteboarding, shared applications, file transfer, "groupware" tools. H.261, G.711 planned in future versions. Upon official release of Windows NT 3.51, Communique! will be available for NT both on Intel and Alpha-based PCs.

Cost: $995

For more information: InSoft, 4718 Old Gettysburg Rd. #307, Mechanicsburg PA 17055, USA, phone: +1.717.730.9501, info@insoft.com, http://www.insoft.com/

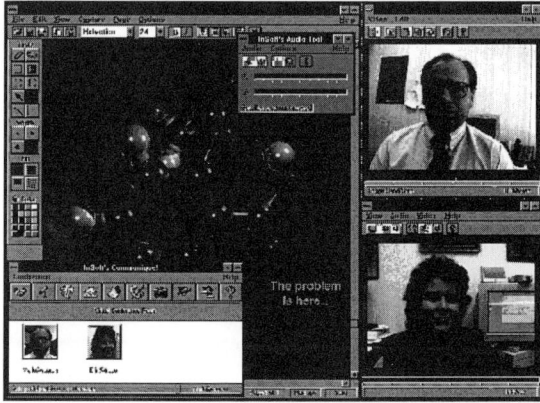

Figure 9.2. Communique!

Connect 918

Provider: Nuts Technologies

Minimum requirements:

- **Macintosh:** no additional information

Notes: Interoperability: H.320. Video encoding: H.261. Audio encoding: G.711, G.722, G.728. Point-to-point only. Collaboration: whiteboard, screen sharing. Intel version promised.

Cost: $3000-$5000 depending on ISDN or LAN options.

For more information: Nuts Technologies, 2374 Walsh Ave., Santa Clara CA, 95051 USA, phone: +1.408.980.7800, `NUTS.USA@applelink.apple.com`

DECspin (DEC Sound Picture Information Network)

Provider: Digital Equipment Corporation

Minimum requirements:

- **DEC:** DECstation 5000, ULTRIX 4.3 or higher, TURBOchannel, DECmedia hardware (DECvideo, DECaudio), XMedia Tools Runtime license, 24-32 MB RAM, 500 MB - 1G B disk storage.

Notes: LAN Protocols: TCP/IP, DECnet. Multipoint capable, to 8 participants.

For more information: Digital Equipment Corporation `http://www.dec.com/`, `ftp://ftp.digital.com/pub/Digital/info/DTJ/mm-08-decspin.txt`

Eris Personal Video Communications System

Provider: RSI Systems Incorporated

Minimum requirements:

- **Intel:** Windows 3.1
- **Macintosh:** MacOS 7

Notes: Eris is a self-contained SCSI or PCMCIA device (no board is required). Interoperability: H.320. Video encoding: H.261 (QCIF,CIF). Audio encoding: G.728, G.711, G.722. Collaboration: file transfer, window sharing.

Other Videoconferencing Technologies

Cost: $4495 includes desktop unit (with built-in 28,800 baud V.34 modem, integrated speakerphone) and color video camera

For more information: RSI Systems Incorporated, One Corporate Plaza, 7400 Metro Blvd # 475, Edina MN, 55439, +1.800.496-4304, +1.612.896.3020, +1.612.896.3030 (fax)

Face 2 Face

Provider: Electronic Studio

Minimum requirements:

- **Macintosh:** no further information

Notes: Point-to-point only. LAN Protocols: Appletalk. Collaboration: text and image exchange.

Cost: $995 video, $995 text and image exchange, $1495 both.

For more information: The Electronic Studio, 7 Fitzroy Square, London, W1P 6HJ, Great Britain, +1.408.974.0784.

ICU Video Services

Provider: Uni-Data and Communications, Inc.

Minimum requirements: Category 3 UTP for video within a campus

- **Intel:** Windows 3.1
- **Macintosh:**
- **Sun:**

Notes: Uses separate network (up to 300 meters in total length) of unshielded twisted-pair wire to send television-quality images and distribute VCR, CATV, and broadcast TV. Interoperability: H.320. Video encoding: H.261. LAN Protocols: TCP/IP. Collaboration: white pages, directory services, text messaging, frame-grabbing. Multipoint in stages of 4-, 9-, and 16-way audiovisual conferencing.

For more information: Uni-Data and Communications, Inc., 174th Street, Flushing, NY 11365, USA, +1.718.445.5600, +1.718.445.5604 (fax); 2/9, Mason's Avenue, London, EC2V 5BT, England, +44.171.600.4124, +44.171.600.5412 (fax).

InPerson

Provider: Silicon Graphics, Inc.

Minimum requirements:

- **SGI:** IRIX 5.3
- **Windows:**

Notes: Audio encoding: Intel/IMA DVI ADPCM, CCITT/ITU-T G.711u-law PCM, CCITT/ITU-T G.728, GSM 06.10 RTE/LTP. LAN Protocols: UDP; whiteboard uses TCP/IP; IP multicast used for more than participants. Multipoint-capable. Video encoding: H.261, RGB8, HDCC (SGI compression algorithm). Collaboration: text and image sharing, 3D model sharing, whiteboarding, a *shared shelf* for visual file transfer between participants in a call. Optional board (for Indy) provides G.728 audio compression and acoustic echo cancellation. InPerson whiteboard is available on Windows from NetManage (+1.408.973.7171, sales@netmanage.com). Internezzo Technologies (+1.415.561.5171) promises InPerson on Suns and HPs.

Cost: $495

For more information: Silicon Graphics, Inc., 2171 Landings Drive, Mountain View CA 94043, +1.415.390.3900, +1.415.960.0197, inperson@sgi.com, http://www.sgi.com/Products/inperson_main.html

Interact

Provider: Applied Communication Concepts, Inc.

Minimum requirements:

- **Intel:** Windows 3.1, Intel 386SX, 4MB RAM, VGA display

Notes: Interoperability: H.320. Video encoding: H.261. Audio encoding: G.711, G.722, G.728. Multipoint-capable, but only two of eight participants are visible at one time.

Other Videoconferencing Technologies

Cost: $5,995 includes variable-focus proprietary person and document camera with built-in speakerphone/handset. Collaboration: shared drawing areas, shared clipboards, file transfer, OLE links. This system allows remote control of others' cameras, can record full-motion, and can generate up to 15 fps.

For more information: Applied Communication Concepts Inc., Research Triangle Park NC, +1.919.549.0874.

INTERVu

Provider: Zydacron, Inc.

Minimum requirements:

- **Intel:** 386 or higher, Windows 3.1

Notes: Interoperability: H.320. Video encoding: H.261 (QCIF,CIF). Audio encoding: G.711u/a, G.722, G.725, G.728. Multipoint capable. Collaboration: file transfer.

For more information: Zydacron, Inc., 670 Commercial St., Manchester NH 03101, +1.603.647.1000.

InVision

Provider: InVision Systems Corp.

Minimum requirements:

- **Intel:** 486/33, Windows 3.1, 8 MB RAM, 3 MB hard disk space, high density 3.5" disk drive, 256-color VGA or SVGA (local bus recommended), Windows-compatible mouse or pointing device, Wave-compatible sound card, Video for Windows compatible compression board, camera and microphone.

Notes: LAN Protocols: TCP/IP, IPX. Video encoding: DVI (ActionMedia II or MediaShare Mambo). Point-to-point video only. Uses VisionGraphics document-sharing software, which includes a whiteboard and supports OLE. H.261, H.320, and MPEG support under development.

Cost: $595

For more information: InVision Systems Corp., 317 S. Main Mall, Suite 310, Tulsa OK 74103, +1.800.847-1662, +1.918.584.7772, +1.918.584.7775 (fax), info@invision.com

INRIA Videoconferencing System (IVS)

Provider: RODEO Project, INRIA Sophia Antipolis

Minimum requirements:

- **Sun SPARC:** Parallax, SunVideo, VideoPix, or VigraPix video cards
- **Silicon Graphic:** IndigoVideo, GalileoVideo, VinoVideo
- **Intel Linux:** SCREENMACHINE II
- **Intel FreeBSD 2.0:**
- **DEC 5000:** VIDEOTX
- **DEC Alpha:**
- **HP:** VideoLive

Notes: LAN Protocols: UDP/IP, IP Multicast. Video encoding: H.261. Audio encoding: PCM, ADPCM, VADPCM. Multipoint: Yes. Collaboration: None. Multihost conferences require kernel support for multicast IP extensions (RFC 1112).

Cost: Free. Available by anonymous ftp from `ftp://zenon.inria.fr/rodeo/ivs`

For more information: RODEO Project, INRIA Sophia Antipolis, France. `Thierry.Turletti@sophia.inria.fr, http://zenon.inria.fr:8003/rodeo/personnel/Thierry.Turletti/ivs.html`

Mediafone/Fonewatch

Provider: Fiber & Wireless, Inc.

Minimum requirements:

- **Intel:** 486DX/33, 4MB RAM, 256 K external cache, 12 MB hard disk space

Notes: Multipoint: yes. Collaboration: whiteboard, application sharing.

Cost: PC kit includes video capture and VGA board, feature connector, and AV/VGA cable. Other configurations are available including a software-only package, a complete laptop system, and a software-only laptop kit.

For more information: Fiber & Wireless Inc., 2200 Amapola Court #102, Torrance CA 90501, +1.310.787.7097, +1.310.787.7099 (fax).

Meet-Me

Provider: SAT usa/Sagem

Minimum requirements:

- **Macintosh:** Macintosh AV or PowerPC Macintosh AV (except 660AV and 6100AV), 1 free NuBus slot.

Notes: LAN Protocols: AppleTalk. Interoperability: H.320. Video encoding: H.261. Audio encoding: G.711 and G.728. Collaboration: file transfer, shared whiteboard. H.320 codec (for QuickTime Conferencing) with Planet ISDN daughterboard.

Cost: $3000

For more information: SAT usa, 20370 Town Center Lane #255, Cupertino CA 95014, +1.408.446.8690, +1.408.446.9766 (fax), http://catalog.com/satusa/

MINX

Provider: Datapoint Corp.

Minimum requirements:

- **Intel:** 386SX, 4MB RAM, VGA display, Windows 3.1

Notes: Interoperability: H.320. Video encoding: H.261. Audio encoding: G.711, G.722, G.728. Multipoint: yes (maximum of 54 parties, software automatically switches view to current speaker). Collaboration: Shared drawing areas, file transfer, external applications.

Cost: $5,000, includes microphone and camera

For more information: Datapoint Corp., San Antonio TX, +1.800.334.9968, +1.210.593.7900

Ntv

Provider: Peregrine Systems

Minimum requirements:

- **Intel:** 386 DX/25, 4MB RAM, Windows 3.1

Notes: Collaboration: Application sharing.

For more information: Peregrine Systems, Inc., 1959 Palomar Oaks Way, Carlsbad CA 92009, +1.800.638.5231, +1.619.431.2400, +1.619.431.0696 (fax), info@www.peregrine.com, http://www.peregrine.com/

nv (Network Video)

Provider: Xerox Palo Alto Research Center (PARC)

Minimum requirements:

- **Sun 4:** Parallax, PARCVideo, VideoPix, X Window System
- **Sun 5:** SunVideo, VideoPix, X Window System
- **Sun SPARC:** X Window System
- **DEC 5000:** (Ultrix) PIP, X Window System
- **DEC Alpha:** (OSF 1) J300, X Window System
- **Silicon Graphics:** (Irix 5) SGI VL (Indy, Galileo), X Window System
- **HP 9000:** (HPUX) VideoLive, X Window System
- **IBM RS6000:** (AIX) IBM VCA, X Window System

Notes: nv provides unicast and multicast video over the Internet. It is commonly supplemented with vat (Visual Audio Tool) and wb (whiteboard) for full-featured video/audio conferencing and collaboration. LAN Protocols: UDP/IP, IP Multicast. Video encoding: Native NV, CU-SeeMe, Sun CellB. Audio encoding: N/A. Multipoint: Yes. Collaboration: None. vat and wb are available at ftp://ftp.ee.lbl.gov/conferencing/.

Cost: Free. Available by anonymous ftp from ftp://parcftp.xerox.com/pub/net-research

For more information: Ron Frederick, frederick@parc.xerox.com, ftp://parcftp.xerox.com/pub/net-research/nv-paper.ps

Person to Person

Provider: IBM

Minimum requirements:

- **Intel:** 386SX, OS/2 2.x or Windows 3.1, 8 MB RAM, ActionMedia II hardware

Notes: LAN Protocols: NetBIOS, TCP/IP, APPC, Novell IPX/SPX. Video encoding: DVI. Multipoint: Yes. Collaboration: whiteboard, file transfer, Talk window, shared clipboard.

Cost: $280

For more information: IBM, +1.800.IBM.4FAX (fax-back, in USA), +1.404.238.6726, +1.415.855.4329 (outside USA), http://www.hursley.ibm.com/p2p/index.html, http://fiddle.ee.vt.edu/succeed/p2p.html

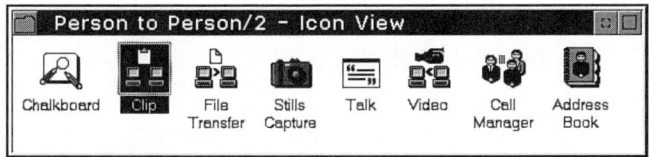

Figure 9.3. Person to Person icons.

Personal Viewpoint

Provider: ViewPoint Systems

Minimum requirements:

- **Intel:** Windows 3.1, VGA graphics, 1 available slot

Notes: LAN Protocols: TCP/IP. Multipoint: Yes. Collaboration: whiteboard, file transfer.

Cost: $1595 without camera, $1995 with camera

For more information: ViewPoint Systems Inc., 2247 Wisconsin St., Suite 110, Dallas TX 75229, +1.214.243.0634.

PICFON

Provider: Specom Technologies

Minimum requirements:

- **Intel:** 386, 4 MB RAM, 40 MB hard disk, DOS 5.0

Notes: Multipoint: Yes, to 3 persons. Collaboration: Still-image sharing. This product superceeded by Specom's TelePro.

For more information: Specom Technologies Corp., 2322 Walsh Ave., Santa Clara CA 95051, +1.408.982.1880, +1.408.982.1883 (fax).

PictureTel Live PCS 100

Provider: PictureTel

Minimum requirements:

- **Intel:** 386, 2 ISA slots, Windows 3.1

Notes: Interoperability: H.320. Video encoding: H.261. Audio encoding: G.721, G.722, G.728, PT 724 proprietary algorithm. Multipoint: Yes, to 16 persons. Collaboration: whiteboard, file transfer, screen sharing, application sharing.

Cost: $4995

For more information: PictureTel Corp., The Tower at Northwoods, 222 Rosewood Dr., Danvers MA 01923, +1.800.716.6000, +1.508.762.5000, +1.508.762.5245 (fax).

PictureTel Live PCS 50

Provider: PictureTel

Minimum requirements:

- **Intel:** 386, 2 ISA slots, Windows 3.1, VAFC graphics connection (available from PictureTel)

Notes: Interoperability: H.320. Video encoding: H.261. Audio encoding: G.721, G.722, G.728, PT 724 proprietary algorithm. Multipoint: Yes, to 16 persons. Collaboration: whiteboard, file transfer, screen sharing, application sharing. The Zenith Data Systems Z-STATION GT 575 VC, a 75Mhz Pentium system (`http://www.zds.com/htdocs/zds/htm/zstatvc.htm`), will include the PCS-50 complete with camera and speakerphone.

Cost: $2495

For more information: PictureTel Corp., The Tower at Northwoods, 222 Rosewood Dr., Danvers MA 01923, +1.800.716.6000, +1.508.762.5000, +1.508.762.5245 (fax).

Figure 9.4. Zenith's Z-STATION.

PictureTel LiveLAN

Provider: PictureTel

Minimum requirements:

- **Intel:** 486-66, video capture card, Windows 3.1, audio card

Notes: LAN Protocols: IPX. Audio encoding: Proprietary. Video encoding: Proprietary. Multipoint: No. Collaboration: Application Sharing.

Cost: $395

For more information: PictureTel Corp., The Tower at Northwoods, 222 Rosewood Dr., Danvers MA 01923, +1.800.716.6000, +1.508.762.5000, +1.508.762.5245 (fax).

PictureWindow

Provider: Bolt, Beranek, and Newman (BBN)

Minimum requirements:

- **Sun SPARC:** 8-bit frame buffer, 24 MB RAM, SunOS 4.1.1 with IPC_SHMEM option, OpenWindows 2.0 or the X Window System release 4, VideoPix card

Notes: LAN Protocols: UDP/IP, TCP/IP. Multipoint: Yes. Collaboration: No.

Cost: $495, $1495 with VideoPix and camera. A receive-only demo is available via ftp from picwin.bbn.com. Log in as picwin.

For more information: BBN, 150 Cambridge Park Drive, Cambridge MA 02140, +1.800.422.2359, +1.617.873.2000, +1.617.873.5011 (fax), `picwin-sales@bbn.com`, `http://www.bbn.com/BEN.mm.html>BBN`

ProShare Video System 150

Provider: Intel

Minimum requirements:

- **Intel:** 486/33, Windows 3.1, 8 MB RAM, 16 MB hard disk space, 8-bit VGA display (no feature connector required), network interface card, 1 full-length ISA slot, LANDesk Personal Conferencing Manager, one of the following protocol stacks: IPX (Novell VIPX, version 1.11, 1.17, 1.18), TCP/IP (FTP PC/TCP, version 2.31, FTP OnNet, version 1.1), Novell LAN WorkPlace for DOS (version 4.12), NetBIOS (Windows for Workgroups 3.11)

Notes: LAN Protocols: NetBIOS, TCP/IP, IPX. Audio encoding: GSM. Video encoding: Indeo. Collaboration: whiteboard, application sharing.

Cost: $1499, includes software, one full-length ISA card, color CCD camera, headset/microphone unit

For more information: Intel Corp., 2200 Mission College Blvd., P.O. Box 58199, Santa Clara CA 95052-8119, +1.800.538-3373, +1.503.629.7354, +1.800.525.3019 (fax), `http://www.intel.com/comm-net/proshare/`

ProShare Video System 200

Provider: Intel

Minimum requirements:

- **Intel:** 486/33, Windows 3.1, 8 MB RAM, 17 MB hard disk space, 8-bit VGA (no feature connector required), 2 full-length ISA slots, LANDesk Personal Conferencing Manager, one of the following protocol stacks: IPX

(Novell VIPX, version 1.11, 1.17, 1.18), TCP/IP (FTP PC/TCP, version 2.31, FTP OnNet, version 1.1), Novell LAN WorkPlace for DOS (version 4.12), NetBIOS (Windows for Workgroups 3.11)

Notes: LAN Protocols: NetBIOS, TCP/IP, and IPX. Audio encoding: GSM, G.711. Video encoding: Indeo, QCIF H.261 Interoperability: H.320. Multipoint: Yes, using H.320-compatible bridges. Collaboration: whiteboard, application sharing.

Cost: $1999. $1499 if user purchases either local ISDN Service from a participating LEC or long distance ISDN Service from an IXC. $999 if user purchases both local and long distance ISDN service from participating carriers. Includes software, 2 full-length ISA cards, color CCD camera, headset/microphone unit.

For more information: Intel Corp., 2200 Mission College Blvd., P.O. Box 58199, Santa Clara CA 95052-8119, +1.800.538-3373, +1.503.629.7354, +1.800.525.3019 (fax), http://www.intel.com/comm-net/proshare/

Paradise Software Video Conferencing (PSVC)

Provider: Paradise Software, Inc.

Minimum requirements:

- **Sun SPARC:** Parallax XVideo/PowerVideo boards, SunOS 4.1.3 or Solaris 2.3, OpenWindows 3.x, 1 MB hard disk space, 16 MB RAM, 16 MB swap space.

Notes: LAN Protocols: TCP/IP. Video encoding: M-JPEG. Multipoint: Yes. Collaboration: whiteboard, video mail, screen capture. Support for HP 700 series, Motif promised. PSVC is integrated into Paradise Software's new "Simplicity" virtual meeting software.

Cost: $995

For more information: Paradise Software, Inc., 7 Centre Drive, Suite 9, Jamesburg NJ 08831, +1.609.655.0016, +1.609.655.0045 (fax), support@paradise.com, http://www.paradise.com/

ShareVision Mac 3000

Provider: Creative Labs

Internet TV with CU-SeeMe

Minimum requirements:

- **Macintosh:**

Notes: Interoperable with ShareVision PC product.

Cost: $1299

For more information: Creative Labs, Inc., 1901 McCarthy Boulevard, Milpitas CA 95035, +1.800.998.1000, +1.408.428.6600, +1.408.428.6611 (fax), SHAREVIS.MKT@applelink.apple.com, http://www.creaf.com/

ShareVision PC

Provider: Creative Labs

Minimum requirements:

- **Intel:** 486SX/33, 2 available, 16-bit ISA bus slots, 8 MB RAM, 6 MB hard disk space, Windows 3.1, VGA or SVGA display

Notes: Video encoding: VATP. Audio encoding: VATP. Multipoint: No. Collaboration: application sharing, whiteboard, document sharing, file transfer. Interoperable with ShareVision Mac product.

Cost: $1599, includes software, 2 boards (Video Blaster RT300 video capture/compression card and ShareVision PC Audio card), color CCD camera, fax/modem, headset/microphone unit

For more information: Creative Labs, Inc., 1901 McCarthy Boulevard, Milpitas CA 95035, +1.800.998.1000, +1.408.428.6600, +1.408.428.6611 (fax), SHAREVIS.MKT@applelink.apple.com, http://www.creaf.com/

ShowMe

Provider: Sun Microsystems

Minimum requirements:

- **Sun SPARC:** Solaris 2.3, X Window System release 5, OpenWindows 3, 1 SBUS slot, SunVideo board, SunMicrophone

Notes: LAN Protocols: UDP/IP, TCP/IP, IP Multicast, RTP. Video encoding: CellB. Audio encoding: G.711 (uncompressed 8-bit, 8 KHz audio stream at 64 kbps). Multipoint: Yes, with and without IP Multicast. Collaboration: whiteboard, application Sharing for X Window System releases 4 and 5-based applications and WABI 1.0 supported Windows applications.

Cost: $3270, including SunVideo board and camera. Educational discount available.

For more information: Sun Microsystems, +1.800.873.7869, `sunsol-www@sunsolutions.eng.sun.com`, `http://www.sun.com:80/cgi-bin/show?products-n-solutions/sw/ShowMe/index.html`

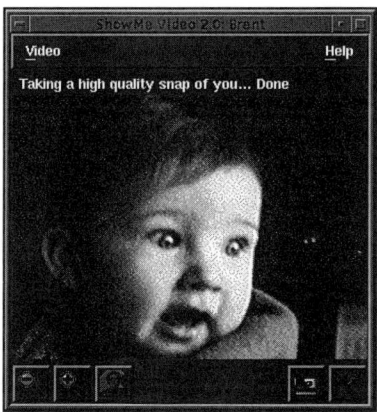

Figure 9.5. ShowMe Video.

TelePro with VisionTime

Provider: Specom Technologies Corp.

Minimum requirements:

- **Intel:** 386, 8 MB RAM, 8 MB disk space, Windows 3.1, high-color VGA card with 64K true colors, video capture card with Video for Windows drivers.

Notes: Multipoint: Optional, up to 64 users. Collaboration: document sharing of Windows applications, OLE.

Cost: $995, includes software, frame grabber card, voice/data modem, handset.

For more information: Specom Technologies Corp., 2322 Walsh Ave., Santa Clara CA, 95051, +1.408.982.1880, +1.408.982.1883 (fax).

TeleView 1000C

Provider: Video Conferencing Communications, Inc.

Cost: $3995, includes boards.

For more information: Video Conferencing Communications, Robert Medrano, +1.714.452.0800.

VC8000

Provider: British Telecommunications plc

Minimum requirements:

- **Intel:** 386, 8 MB RAM, 10-15 MB hard disk space, full-length ISA slot, VGA, SVGA or XGA non-interlaced monitor ISDN-2, Windows 3.1, DOS 5.0, BT partner application software

Notes: Interoperability: H.320. Video encoding: H.261 (QCIF moving images, CIF image capture). Audio encoding: G.711, G.722, G.728. Multipoint: H.242. Collaboration: application sharing, file transfer, whiteboard. Promised are CIF resolution for image capture, QCIF resolution for moving images, and T.120 data support.

Cost: 2700 UK pounds, includes ISA card, NTSC or PAL camera, audio unit, connection unit, AC/DC adaptor, associated leads, and accessory pack.

For more information: BT Visual Images, 360 Herndon Parkway, Suite 2200, Herndon, Virginia 22070-4820, +1.800.778.4820, +1.703.709.4231 (fax, attention John Taylor), `taylor@vaherndon1.btna.com`, technical questions to `iain@empire.bt.co.uk`

VicPhone

Provider: VIC Hi-Tech Corporation

Minimum requirements:

- **Intel:** 486/33, 16-bit ISA bus, Windows 3.1, VGA board with feature connector, CCD camera (NTSC, PAL, or S-VIDEO).

Notes: Video encoding: JPEG. Multipoint: LAN/WAN only. Collaboration: shared images, shared documents, whiteboard, file transfer, text window. H.320 promised.

Cost: $599, includes video capture/display card, videoconferencing software and additional multimedia video/audio capture/edit/playback features.

Other Videoconferencing Technologies

For more information: VIC Hi-Tech Corporation, 2221 Rosecrans Avenue, Suite 237, El Segundo CA 90245, +1.310.643.5193, +1.310.643.7572 (fax), 70544.2472@compuserve.com

VidCall

Provider: MRA Associates Inc.

Minimum requirements:

- **Intel:** 386/33, 2 MB disk space, 4 MB RAM, VGA display, Windows 3.1 or Windows NT.

Notes: Audio requires separate phone line or voice/data modem. Interoperability: No. Video encoding: Proprietary. Multipoint: LAN/WAN only. Collaboration: whiteboard, image sharing and annotation, application sharing via OLE.

Cost: $99 for two-system package. Demo available from web page.

For more information: MRA Associates Inc., 2102B Gallows Rd., Vienna VA 22182, +1.703.448.5373, f+1.703.734.9825 (fax), +1.703.448.5931 (bulletin board service), http://www.access.digex.net/~vidcall/vidcall.html

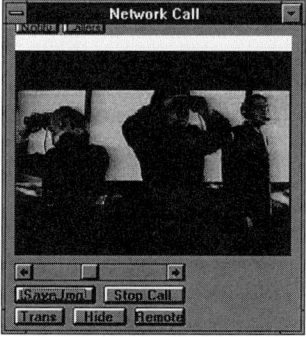

Figure 9.6. VidCall.

VideoVu

Provider: Future Communications Systems, Inc.

Minimum requirements:

- **Intel:**

Notes: LAN/WAN only, up to 8 persons.

Cost: $74.95, VideoVu Two Pak $129.95, VideoVu Complete Kit $325 (2 copies of VideoVu with the Video Logic Captivator PRO capture board). Demo available from web page.

For more information: Future Communications Systems, Inc., P.O. Box 244, Syosset N.Y. 11791, +1.516.496.7121, +1.516.496.7121 (fax), `future@i-2000.com`

VISIT

Provider: Northern Telecom Inc.

Platform requirements:

- **Intel:** 386, Windows 3.1, AT-bus expansion slot, DOS 5.0 or greater, 8MB RAM (12 MB RAM max on ISA PC, 16MB or more possible on EISA w/ memory re-mapping), 256-color VGA board and color monitor (Super VGA w/ thousands of colors support recommended).
- **Macintosh:** Macintosh II family or other NuBus-equipped Apple computer, NuBus expansion slot, System 7 or greater, 8MB RAM, Color monitor.

Notes: The current version uses H.261 video encoding. Future versions promise to provide H.320-compliant interoperation. Has whiteboarding and file transfer capabilities.

Cost: $5319, including camera.

For more information: Northern Telecom Inc., 2221 Lakeside Blvd., Richardson TX 75082, USA, +1.800.667.8437, +1.214.684.5930, +1.214.684.3866 (fax), `http://www.nortel.com/visit`

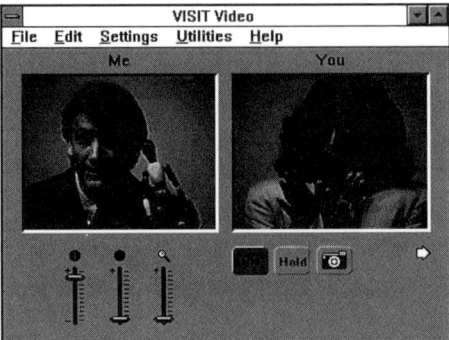

Figure 9.7. VISIT Video.

Other Videoconferencing Technologies

Vistium 1200

Provider: AT&T Global Information Solutions

Minimum requirements:

- **Intel:** 486/66 or Pentium, 8MB RAM, VGA with VESA feature connector, Windows 3.1, one ISA slot (second slot for V-BRI ISDN interface - not required for 8510 models). Provides ISDN "S/T" interface, requires external NT1 for ISDN "U".

Notes: Interoperability uses H.320 protocol. Audio encodings: G.728, G.711. Video encoding: H.261 (QCIF,CIF). Collaboration features include whiteboarding, file transfer, JPEG image capture, and Windows application sharing. Uses the AT&T Microelectronics AVP-II codec chip set to perform hardware-assisted encoding and decoding. Upcoming version promises T.120 and multipoint capability.

Cost: $2700 including camera and ISDN S/T interface.

For more information: AT&T Global Information Solutions, 1700 S. Patterson Blvd., Dayton OH 45479-0001, +1.800.225.5627, +1.513.445.5000, http://www.att.com/home64/vistium.html

Vistium 1300

Provider: AT&T Global Information Solutions

Minimum requirements:

- **Intel:** Intel 386/25, 8MB RAM, VGA with VESA, Windows 3.1+, two adjacent ISA slots (plus a third slot for network interface board - except 8510 models). ISDN models provide "S/T" interface, require external NT1 for ISDN "U" connection.

Notes: Interoperability uses H.320 protocol. Audio encodings: G.728, G.711. Video encoding: H.261 (QCIF,CIF). Collaboration features include whiteboarding, file transfer, JPEG image capture, and Windows application sharing. Uses the AT&T Microelectronics AVP codec chip set to perform hardware-assisted encoding and decoding. Upcoming version promises T.120 and multipoint capability.

Cost: $5000 including camera, AV connectors, Share Software, and network interface.

For more information: AT&T Global Information Solutions, 1700 S. Patterson Blvd., Dayton OH 45479-0001, +1.800.225.5627, +1.513.445.5000, http://www.att.com/home64/vistium.html

Vivo 320

Provider: Vivo Software, Inc.

Minimum requirements:

- **Intel:** 486 66-MHz PC, 8 MB memory, A video display adapter that uses the PC's local bus (either VESA or PCI), 2 free ISA or EISA slots, Windows 3.1

Notes: Interoperability: H.320. Video encoding: transmits QCIF (176x144), receives CIF (352x288) and QCIF. Audio encoding: G.711, G.722 7KHz. Multipoint via H.320-compliant MCU (Multi-point Conferencing Unit). Collaboration: document sharing with Databeam's FarSite 2.0, image presentation and markup.

Cost: $1995, includes Vivo320 software, Logitech VideoMan digital video camera and microphone, monitor-top and desktop stands for the VideoMan camera speaker for hands-free operation and an earpiece for privacy, Logitech MovieMan ISA-bus video capture card, IBM WaveRunner ISA-bus ISDN terminal adapter card and associated driver software, device drivers

For more information: Vivo Software, Inc., +1.800.848.6411, +1.617.899.8900, +1.617.899.1400 (fax), info@vivo.com, http://world.std.com/~vivo/

VS1000

Provider: Mentec International Ltd.

Minimum requirements:

- **Intel:** Windows

Notes: Audio encoding: G.711. Video encoding: H.261.

Cost:

For more information: Mentec International Ltd., Mentec House, 520 Birchwood Boulevard, Birchwood, Warrington, WA3 7QX, Great Britain, +44.925.830000.

Add-On Software that Adds Functionality

This section is about third-party software that adds automation or additional functionality to an existing videoconferencing system. The softwere described here are all for the Macintosh. Due to the lack of an inexpensive Windows standard product, equivalent software for Windows doesn't yet exist. The release of the Connectix QuickCam for Windows this autumn should change all that.

Cambot

Cambot, by Eric Johnston <ej@applelink.apple.com>, is a digital fun-house for videocameras. Figure 9.8 shows some aspects of Cambot. The Camera window shows at what the camera is pointed. Having the brightness control at hand is very nice (but having automatic exposure would be even nicer).

Figure 9.8. Cambot provides all the bells and whistles.

The Motion window allows one to select four areas of the image and assign motion detection warning sounds. The Kaleidascope and Bug Eye effects are self-explanatory. Promised is the ability to read Universal Price Codes (UPC) bar-codes from packages.

There are more features in Cambot to add power and functionality to your videoconferencing setup than I've listed here. Cambot is a great example of value-added software.

# Internet TV with CU-SeeMe

ShutterBug

ShutterBug, by Tim Molteno & Cannibal Island Software, is a small Macintosh application that periodically takes a snapshot through your camera. This is useful for keeping an up-to-date image on a web page. ShutterBug's claim to fame, however, is its ability to automatically cope with changes in light levels in the scene, capability still lacking in Connectix's QuickCam software. Auto-exposure makes it possible for true unattended operation; without it pictures quickly become too dark or washed out.

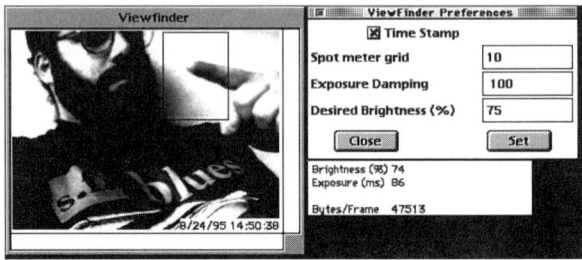

Figure 9.9. ShutterBug in action.

Figure 9.9 shows ShutterBug in operation. Things to note include the optional date/time stamp at the bottom right of the image and the ability to arbitrarily choose a rectangular area to be used for auto-exposure. (I'm pointing to the area I've chosen for this snap-shot.)

Shutterbug is available from `http://jurgen.physics.utoronto.ca:8080/~tim/Cannibal.html`

WHAT THE FUTURE HOLDS IN STORE

CHAPTER 10

Prediction is difficult, especially when it concerns the future.

CU-SeeMe has enjoyed an explosive growth since it's humble beginnings several years ago. Those involved have all learned something of value. Computer scientists have learned how people interact in an audiovisual conferencing environment. Systems and network administrators have learned the real computing and network requirements of videoconferencing. (We've learned how fragile the Internet is, and how it must expand if the masses are to use videoconferencing.) Artists have learned the pitfalls and pleasures of bringing far-flung performers to an audience. Businesses have learned the value of face-to-face meetings. People have learned how wonderful it is to reach out and connect with others, across the state or around the world. (David Watson, a CU-SeeMe presence from Australia, and his wife recently visited me in San Francisco during their high-technology tour of the USA. Only through the magic of CU-SeeMe could David and I have made and nourished a friendship, although e-mail helped cement our warm feelings.)

Where do we go from here? I believe there are two paths we'll simultaneously walk: the technological and the cultural.

Internet TV with CU-SeeMe

The Technological Path

The technology underlying videoconferencing will continue to evolve at an explosive pace, much as it has since the beginning of the computer age. Such speedy change makes long-term prognostication excruitiatingly difficult, but short-term changes are compelling, and worth visiting.

Networking

CU-SeeMe, as well as other videoconferencing tools, depends upon a network infrastructure to connect the conferencees. The real-world use of CU-SeeMe, perhaps more than any other technology, clearly shows the deficiencies in our current setup and hints at where growth need be. (Many thanks to Per G. Bilse, Senior Network Engineer of EUnet Communications Services, for spurring to life many spirited discussions about network issues.)

Network Bandwidth

There are several aspects to bandwidth usage. One is using what's there to encourage investment in growth. The other is creating network gridlock by using a networking technology not well-designed for videoconferencing.

> Tim Dorcey, in e-mail to the CU-SeeMe Discussion List, discussed the tension between new technology and the existing bandwidth limitations of the Internet:
>
>> ...we were not interested in producing a "demo." Nor was it our main objective to be "friendly to the Internet." We were interested in producing a videoconferencing tool that would be useful for some number of people today (not necessarily Everyone On The Internet). There are lots of places on the Internet where bandwidth is plentiful. For example, we have a 100 mbps campus backbone at Cornell; would it make sense to cripple CU-SeeMe in that context simply because it doesn't work well in every context? Why should those who have made the investment in bandwidth (e.g., regional nets, corporate nets, etc.) be restricted to services that are limited to the lowest common denominator? That doesn't sound like a good recipe for encouraging investment in bandwidth.

> ...the only way we are going to see increases in bandwidth capacity is if we use what's there. This is a bit of a simplification, but the folks that own the fiber plant just want to get their $100,000/month. If they think we'll use 1 mbit, they'll charge $100,000/mbit... if they think we'll use 100 mbit, they'll charge $1000/mbit. In the era of fiber optics, most of the expenses have little to do with how much data is actually moved. Of course, there are some arcane government policies and entrenched monopolies to contend with, so it's not going to be an easy transition. But, obviously, prices aren't going to come down until we demonstrate that what is lost in price can be made up for in volume.

The capacity of the Internet will have to increase just to keep up with the masses who are joining online services in droves. It'll have to increase to provide audio to the masses (as the RealAudio technology is doing today). It'll have to increase to allow for the greater bandwidth needs of color videoconferencing, more simultaneous users, and new interaction matters that we've not yet seen.

> The technology CU-SeeMe uses to send information was never designed for such uses. EUNet, the European Internet backbone provider, summed up the ways that this technology (called UDP) stresses the networks:
>
> [Videoconferencing] applications, due to their unique requirements for a constant and [large] traffic stream, do not use the normal management layers of the Internet Protocol, i.e., TCP, and therefore have a very detrimental effect on other traffic—they are able to totally "hog" links, no matter how large the link size. This has a very disruptive effect on the network performance as seen by other users, and can upset networks at any or many links worldwide between the two or more communicating application end-users.
>
> [The use of UDP to transmit high-volume real-time videoconferencing] violates the fundamental design of the Internet, which is largely based on TCP (advanced, highly adaptive, robust, flow control) for high volume, and UDP (simple, crude, unreliable, no flow control) for single, occasional datagrams.

Internet TV with CU-SeeMe

> Applications that need high volume, real-time traffic currently have no option other than to use UDP. [The] result can be, and usually is, devastating for TCP-based traffic. When a TCP connection detects packet loss, it immediately backs off. In the presence of high volume UDP traffic, the ensuing packet loss will cause TCP connections to slow down to a crawl....When TCP traffic is high on a link, all connections "back-off" thus sharing equally the available bandwidth. UDP however, does not back-off in this controlled manner, but will take all available bandwidth.

The CU-SeeMe's Development Team has been involved in making CU-SeeMe a friendlier technology right from the beginning.

> Dick Cogger explained what network communication software changes are desired:
>
> Tim and I spent some time talking about this. Probably the real issue is that the [programmer's interface] to TCP doesn't give any info about what's happening on the connection (network level virtual circuit). With real-time stuff, the sender needs to delay capturing a frame until bandwidth exists to send it end-to-end with minimal delay. This paradigm requires that the send-routines (or better, the bandwidth manager) call the data-creation routines (frame grabber) when bandwidth is available. The typical TCP implementation works the other way: a data source sends until blocked and then waits. Whatever happens on the network is invisible to the app otherwise—any delay is only reflected when the send buffers are full (of what will soon be old data).
>
> A TCP that didn't do retransmission, had a [programmer's interface] that provided callbacks when new data could be accepted and let the application control packet boundaries, etc., could be a good idea for some of the stuff we do in conferencing.

Network Cost

Arthur C. Clarke, futurist extraordinaire, predicted in his book *2001: A Space Odyssey* that all telephone calls would become local calls by the turn of the millenium. It's already true on the Internet. Ironically, just as the telephone companies are moving to fulfill Clarke's prediction, the main Internet network providers are working towards metered usage, charging customers per bit sent over the networks (and perhaps for the distance the bit travels as well).

Dick Cogger, in a discussion about these issues, said "...traffic-sensitive and distance-sensitve pricing are obsolete. We now have the technology to cover the globe with enough photonic pathways to carry everything anyone will have to send. Keeping track will cost more than giving it away. The size of the access pipe is the reasonable metric on which to price."

Dick later asked "what do you think the lower limit [to the per-bit price] is when non-telephony folks get into stringing fiber?" The entrance of cable television companies into the networking fray, what with their plans of two-way high-bandwidth connections to each set-top box, sets the stage for a frenzied price war. Hopefully the end-user will win with cheap, robust network connectivity to every place you want to call.

Video and Audio Technology

Network issues aside (most of us believe that the network will grow to meet the demand), CU-SeeMe has in part spurred the growth of other video and audio technology and made the creation and sale of communications software a viable venture.

Because CU-SeeMe has become almost commonplace, small companies such as Electric Magic (NetPhone) and large ones such as Apple Computer (QuickTime Conferencing) have brought telecommunications to market. Some of the technological advances include color videoconferencing, a multitude of audio encoding schemes for slower computers, and in the case of Philip Zimmermann, Will Price, and Chris Hall, encrypted audioconferencing via PGPfone.

The growth of videoconferencing has spurred new hardware as well. Connectix is bringing a QuickCam for Intel-based computers to market, and is speaking about a color QuickCam as well. The price of 28.8 kbps modems keeps dropping, as does ISDN hardware. Computer manufacturers are releasing all-in-one audio-visual computers (Apple for the last several years, Intel-based manufacturers started this year), and it may be only a few more years until on-board digital cameras are de rigeur.

The Cultural Path

Even more sweeping than the upcoming technological changes are the cultural and psychological changes that we users of the net are undergoing.

Internet TV with CU-SeeMe

The availability of inexpensive digital videocameras, combined with inexpensive Internet connections for the end user (here in San Francisco we can get unmetered 28.8 kbps Internet access for $9 (US) per month), have shrunk the world even more. Time zones, rather than distance or expense, are now foremost on our minds. For several years I've maintained several acquaintances (and several new friendships) soley by CU-SeeMe. The fact that one video-pal lives eighteen time-zones away is the major impediment to our conversations ("is my morning his yesterday afternoon?").

While it may be premature to claim that CU-SeeMe heralds the demise of the telephone system, it's certainly having an impact. AT&T is once again hawking its videophone technology, and cable companies are betting they can perform an end run around the entrenched Internet infrastructure. It's difficult to imagine the results of an all-out price war once there are competing high-bandwidth fiber optic networks across the USA. We'll find out in a few years; several cities are already wired by cable companies as part of a pilot project.

Businesses will most likely comprise the next great wave of consumers of CU-SeeMe and other videoconferencing technology. Internet access is becoming ubiquitous in the business world, and the advantages of face-to-face conferencing are too great to be ignored when careers and pet projects are on the line. Networking consultants will see a great rise in demand for the ability to install CU-SeeMe into a business setting and to train the workforce in its use; the number of such requests that I get increases with every passing month.

Considerations of the cultural changes brought on by videoconferencing would be woefully incomplete without mention of one of our strongest drives: sex. Just as earlier technologies have been embraced by sexually-oriented marketplaces (the exploding growth of phone sex over the years, sexually explicit digital images becoming the largest component of USENET newsgroups) videoconferencing has spawned an ever-increasing number of video-sex services.

People and couples are increasingly advertising for sexually explicit point-to-point CU-SeeMe conferences; the Internet Relay Chat CU-SeeMe channel exists soley for scheduling such meetings between consenting groups. (The nature of videoconferencing stops under-age, would-be participants from impersonating adults.) To answer the now-famous *New Yorker* cartoon: soon it will be possible to tell that you're a dog on the Internet.

Sexually explicit digital movies are beginning to show up on the USENET `alt.binaries` newsgroups. Offerings on USENET are free; teasers of for-cost video have already come, and several full-blown (pun unintended) live video-sex services have sprung (pun unintended) into being.

Last Words

The future of CU-SeeMe (and videoconferencing in general) will be much less tawdry. In the few years that CU-SeeMe has been available, we've seen inspiring organized educational uses and ad-hoc cultural exchanges of desktop video surfers worldwide. As more and more people are connected to the Internet, and as inexpensive video hardware becomes available for Windows, I suspect we'll see more of the best (and worst) of humanity. It'll be an adventure.

CU there.

Troubleshooting Q&A

APPENDIX A

This chapter contains the answers to questions frequently asked by newcomers. Answers have, for the most part, been provided by the CU-SeeMe community and the CU-SeeMe Development Team. This chapter covers the following:

- CU-SeeMe in general
- Macintosh
- Windows
- QuickCam

Questions About CU-SeeMe in General

"Empty Office" Video Bothers Me. What Can I Do?

If you don't like something you see, close that window. That'll cause the reflector to stop sending that video stream to you. If no one else is watching that stream, the reflector will stop accepting it from the source. By closing boring video you may be doing everyone a favor.

What Limits My Transmission Rate?

Usually it's the bandwidth limit of your network. The default transmission cap, 80 kbps, is sensible unless you know that there is additional unused network capacity between the machines. The cap is automatically adjusted on the fly within the user-settable range on the basis of packet-loss reports returned by each CU-SeeMe client receiving your video stream. At some point, if you have a very "wide pipe" between machines, the processing power of your computer will become the limiting factor.

CU-SeeMe Sure Can Eat Bandwidth; How Can I Help Conserve It?

No discussion of CU-SeeMe bandwidth usage would be complete without considering what behavior is appropriate when bandwidth is limited. For example, is it good network behavior to broadcast the inside of an empty office? No, it's not good behavior to broadcast an empty office when bandwidth is limited, but it's also somewhat irrelevant since CU-SeeMe doesn't actually broadcast. The CU-SeeMe reflector only sends video to machines that want it, to clients who have that window open. A video source will stop transmission to the reflector if no one is watching.

Interestingly, the implication of this is that video receivers are just as responsible for bandwidth consumption as are video sources. A responsible bandwidth consumer closes uninteresting windows. A far greater sin than sending video of your office while you're at lunch is leaving CU-SeeMe running with several video windows when you're not there.

This point bears repition because CU-SeeMe behavior is contrary to that of broadcast television.

Does Changing the Bandwidth Limits in Preferences Limit Receiving Too?

No, the bandwidth limit applies only to your transmission. The only way you can reduce the incoming rate is by closing windows. The CU-SeeMe Development Team has indicated that eventually you'll be able to set a reception rate cap, and then allocate that bandwidth as you desire to the video resolution, window size, frame rate, and the number of windows displayed. In short, you'll have to manage the trade-off between watching several tiny windows at a slow frame rate or a single large window at a high frame rate.

What Kind of Bandwidth Is Required for Fluid Motion?

Because the answer depends upon a subjective evaluation of "fluid motion" and the subject matter being sent, this is a very tough question to answer. A "talking head"—a typical office shot—takes about 100 kbps. That's because there's not that much difference between frames. (This is a good number to remember when you're connecting to a reflector with a 14.4 kbps or 28.8 kbps modem.)

At the other extreme, consider some video stream where each frame is completely different from the preceeding frame. There are 75 kbits in an uncompressed 120 × 160 frame, which would translate to about 45 kbps with the lossless spatial compression. If you're willing to call 15 fps fluid motion, you'd need 675 kbps!

As Tim Dorcey said when dealing with these concerns, "since the software is free, the best thing to do is try it out on the sorts of video you have in mind."

Somebody Claimed 22 fps on a Modem Connection. Is That Possible?

Since CU-SeeMe only transmits the portions of a picture that have changed significantly from the preceding frame, it's entirely possible when the picture is not moving much. Of course, 22 fps is no more impressive than 1 fps when all the frames are the same.

How Does CU-SeeMe Compress Video?

Tim Dorcey of the CU-SeeMe Development Team explains:

> The first step in the CU-SeeMe video encoding is to represent the video image using 4 bits/pixel (16 shades of gray). The image is then subdivided into 8× 8 pixel squares, which are treated as independent units. When a new frame of video is acquired, a square is transmitted if it differs sufficiently from the version of that square that was most recently transmitted, that is, if it differs from what the recipients are currently displaying (assuming no packet loss). The index used to determine how different a square must be in order to trigger updating is roughly the sum of the absolute values of all 64 pixel differences in an 8× 8 square, with a multiplicative penalty for differences that occur near each other within the square. The cut-off value can be adjusted by the "Tolerance" control under "Compression" controls, and should be set as high as possible without corrupting the picture too much.

> Since CU-SeeMe uses an unreliable ("best-effort") transport mechanism (UDP), squares are sent on a periodic basis even if they haven't changed, insuring that a lost update won't corrupt the picture indefinitely. How often this forced update occurs is controlled by the "Refresh Rate" control, which specifies the number of frames that will be allowed to pass before a square is updated.

> Once the decision to transmit a square has been made, a locally developed lossless compression algorithm is applied to each individual square. The algorithm is designed to exploit spatial reduncancy in the vertical direction i.e., works well if each row in the square is not too different from the one above it. Based on informal observations, the algorithm averages around a 60% compression rate (compressed size is about 60% of the original).

Appendixes

The main objective in designing these algorithms was to be fast enough for operation on average Macintosh computers. This is achieved by operating on rows of 8 4-bit pixels as 32-bit words throughout the algorithms, achieving a degree of parallelism, in effect. Written down in mathematical terms with respect to individual pixels, the algorithms look rather goofy, but become appealing when represented in 680×0 assembly language.

As with any compression algorithm, your mileage will vary depending on the nature of the data to compress. In the case of CU-SeeMe, the most important factor is the amount of motion in the video.

Why Can't CU-SeeMe Resolve Host Names Using DNS?

Tim Dorcey of the CU-SeeMe Development Team explained: "DNS didn't seem particularly important as long as there was an ability to assign nicknames to IPs. And the nickname feature was essential since many desktop machines aren't registered for DNS. However, as it becomes increasingly common to advertise reflector addresses, it's clear that DNS would be useful. It's on the list of things to add."

Video in Particular

Why Does the Video Image I Send Vary So Much? Sometimes I Send a Sharp Image, at Other Times I See Lines, or the Image Is Muddy.

The way you illuminate the scene has a great impact on image quality. Flourescent light "flashes" at the frequency of the alternating current; if your camera's synchronization is close to that frequency, you'll see light and dark horizontal lines. (This is the reason you see "marching bands" when you point a camera at your display monitor, or when you see wagon-wheels going backwards on *Bonanza*; the signals are not synchronized. The next question goes in more detail.

Why Does My Frame Rate Drop When It Gets Dark Outside?

I've seen this happen when you're using a camera that doesn't automatically adjust to available light (such as the Connectix QuickCam). During the day you have a mix of daylight and office fluorescent light, in the evening you have only the latter. When the lights are out of sync with the camera, the camera sees drastic changes in the brightness of the scene (see previous item).

These oscillations annoy the viewer and completely defeat CU-SeeMe's image compression algorithm by causing the image to change completely each frame, causing huge amounts of data to be sent, and consequently dropping the frame rate.

Cameras that are able to automatically adjust to available light have their own set of problems. Minor changes in the scene can change the amount of light reaching the lens, causing it to open or close, and introducing spurious changes in parts of the image that have not changed at all. I've seen an autofocus mechanism do the same thing, again dropping the frame rate dramatically.

Is There Any Way To Reduce Flicker When You Point My Camera at a Computer or TV?

Short answer: What you're seeing isn't flickering from intensity variations in the displayed images, but rather the difference in the synchronization between the "top left" of the image being displayed and the "top left" of the camera that's watching. Professional videographers use dedicated hardware to synchronize the two.

Detailed answer: Video cameras scan the scene between 24 and 30 times per second (depending upon the video standard used); each of these "frames" are made up of two screen redraws which are interlaced to make up the whole picture. The flicker you see when recording a computer screen with a video camera is the mismatch of that scan rate to the redraw rate of the computer display (which varies considerably from one computer to the next). There are several things you can do to eliminate this flicker:

- Change the screen refresh rate of the computer's display to match that of the video camera. Not all monitors allow this.
- Use the variable sync adjustment on your video camera to match the display refresh rate of the monitor or TV you're filming. Not all video cameras have this ability. Sometimes changing the position of your lens (zooming in or out) helps.
- Do what the professionals do: use some combination of scan converter (convert between synchronizations), genlock (lock the synchronizations in step), and frame sync/timebase corrector.

Is there a reasonably-priced pan-and-tilt motor system with an RS-232 interface?

Canon's VC-C1 is an integrated camera/mic/pan/tilt unit with an RS-232 interface. You can get its specifications sheet from Canon's automated call-back fax server at +1.516.328.5960. (I don't know if it'll call overseas numbers.)

Audio

The questions and answers in this section deal specifically with the audio aspect of CU-SeeMe.

Why is sound choppy when using audio over a 14.4 kbps dial-up?

The short answer is that the encoding method takes more bandwidth than is available.

The best encoding scheme used by CU-SeeMe (and Maven), a scheme known as delta-mod, requires at least 16 kbps. There are other schemes, such as GSM (the standard in European cellular communications) and Intel DVI, but they're not available through CU-SeeMe. (You may want to check out NetPhone, or Philip Zimmermann's PGPfone, both of which work over 14.4 kbps modems.) There are better compression schemes on the horizon, but they require far greater CPU power; they may work over 14.4 kbps modems, but you'll require a PowerPC to use these audio encoding schemes.

According to one of the Apple software engineers who wrote MacTCP, PPP has a five percent overhead to handle multiple protocols. Switching to SLIP will theoretically give you extra five percent throughput—useful elsewhere but it won't help you getting audio in this case.

Macintosh

Video

Why do I get an "SPBOpenDevice Failed, err= -227" error when I start CU-SeeMe?

This error means "CU-SeeMe's attempt to open the Sound Parameter Block - how it initializes the Sound Manager, failed." These are some of the reasons you're seeing this error:

- An Apple GeoPort device attached.
- Terminal emulation or FAX software holding on to the serial port.
- Speech recognition is keeping the Sound Manager busy.
- The Express Modem Control Panel is turned on. You'll have to make sure it's turned off before you try to send CU-SeeMe audio.
- Some Macintosh models require the audio sampling be set to less than 22.1 khz.
- Some Macintosh models require you not use 16-bit stereo output.
- Your PowerMac AV is in a funny initial state; try playing an audio CD-ROM to reset it. Really.

Which Macintoshes work with CU-SeeMe?

All Macintoshes work with CU-SeeMe, the AV (audio-visual) series, the Quadras, PowerBooks, and the PowerPCs. You'll have to set the monitor to 256 colors (or less), use the correct video digitizer (vdig) component, power down to reset a VideoSpigot card, etc. (Read on for explanations of these requirements.)

Why is the broadcast image dark on my PowerMac AV?

The original AV Macintosh had a video digitizer (vdig) component that didn't allow for adjusting the brightness and contrast of the image. So CU-SeeMe modified the image "on the fly." The new PowerMac AVs allow control of the brightness and contrast through the vdig, but the current version of CU-SeeMe doesn't know about the new AV capabilities. It leaves the brightness and contrast set to their default values (which end up being low and muddy). The next release of CU-SeeMe should detect whether or not brightness and contrast are directly supported, and work correctly in either case.

Why do I get a "video component not found" error when I start CU-SeeMe?

This happens when your monitor is set to display more colors (or greys) than CU-SeeMe can handle. The Video RAM (VRAM) in your Macintosh limits the number of colors (or greys) that can be simultaneously shown. On a Macintosh 660AV, which has 1 MB of VRAM, you can display "thousands of colors"; when using CU-SeeMe, however, you'll have to use 256 colors (or greys).

Why do I see a big black border around some video windows?

Obscured CU-SeeMe usually updates the video images by drawing directly to the screen, which is the fastest method. When CU-SeeMe concludes that it must instead use the general Macintosh toolbox drawing method, CopyBits, a slower method, it draws the black border to warn you of this performance degradation (which may or may not be significant depending on how many windows you have open, how often they are being updated, how fast your machine is, and so on).

What causes CU-SeeMe to conclude it can't draw directly to the screen? Unobscured

- The video image is partially covered by another window.
- The display monitor is set to less than 16 colors (or greys).
- The video image spans two screens (for those of you with multiple display monitors).
- Something about your system configuration is confusing CU-SeeMe's decision-making process. Perhaps you're using some sort of Control Panel or Extention that's modified the Window Manager's behavior, which is incorrectly making CU-SeeMe think the video image is obscured.

Audio

Anything else I should know about Macintosh sound?

Yes. Pre-MacOS 7.5 users should get the Sound Manager 3.0 from ftp.support.apple.com. Without it you'll get annoying clicking during sound output, and your Macintosh will run very, very slowly while you're receiving audio. The Sound Manager is included in MacOS 7.5 and later.

Why do I get the "-23009" error when I try to speak?

This usually is an indication you're trying to push too much data through a modem connection. Setting your transmission rate to 40 or less (depending on the Mac you're using) should prevent this from happening.

Where are the Maven mavens?

(Cultural note: "maven" means "knowledgeable person" in Yiddish.) On the Maven discussion list. Subscribe by sending e-mail to listserv@cnidr.org with a message body that consists of

```
subscribe maven firstname lastname
```

Third-Party Hardware

Why does my Macintosh freeze when I try to use my SuperMac VideoSpigot's video digitizer version 1.5b18?

That's because versions over 1.0 don't work with CU-SeeMe. Sadly, the VideoSpigot has been discontinued in favor of more pricey models; the manufacturer has chosen not to support CU-SeeMe despite some rather energetic e-mail lobbying by the CU-SeeMe community.

I have both the QuickCam and the Apple TV Tuner on my Macintosh. Why do I get QuickCam when I try to use the TV Tuner card?

That's because Apple didn't implement the TV Tuner correctly. Rather than looking at all the video digitizers present, and selecting the appropriate one, it incorrectly uses the first one it finds.

The work-around is easy. Launch a program that uses the QuickCam, such as CU-SeeMe. This will keep the QuickCam drivers in use. Then launch a program that uses the TV Tuner card, such as VideoPlayer. It'll look for the next available video digitizer, which should be the TV Tuner vdig.

Can I use CU-SeeMe through the Apple TV Tuner card?

Not until an appropriate video digitizer is written.

Connectix QuickCam

How many frames per second will I get with QuickCam?

That depends upon a chain of variables, the weakest link of which determines the number of frames per second you'll get. The links in the chain are:

- How long the camera's sensing element, the CCD, is allowed to gather information for each frame. This is determined by the brightness setting.
- The available computer horsepower; how fast is your computer and how much of that power is available to CU-SeeMe, which requires processor time for compression of outgoing streams and decompression of incoming streams.
- The speed of your serial port (to which QuickCam is attached). Newer Macintoshes have faster serial ports than do older ones.
- The size of the image; a larger image has more points that need processing.

Connectix has said "QuickCam will produce about 15 fps on most Macs in a window size of 120× 160. FYI - Saturday morning cartoons are twelve frames per second. A few Macs will only achieve 10-12 fps. These include the SE/30, IIcx, IIvx, and PowerBook 165c. At smaller window sizes frame rates are higher (e.g., 30 fps at 80× 120), at larger window sizes frame rates are lower (e.g., about 4 fps at 320× 240)."

Remember that using QuickCam's built-in microphone will require that the audio data compete with the video data; the cable can carry only a fixed amount of data. For this reason it's recommended you use the Macintosh's built-in microphone for audio and QuickCam for video.

Where is QuickCam manufactured?

QuickCam is manufactured in the United States by an experienced manufacturing subcontractor to Connectix. (For trivia buffs: QuickCam is manufactured in the building that housed Apple's old Fremont factory, where many Macintosh innovations first saw the light of day).

Will QuickCam work with serial ports on a NuBus card?

No, QuickCam will only work plugged into a serial port on the Macintosh's motherboard.

Is there a limit to how long I can extend the serial cable from the CPU?

Yes. The cable should not extend beyond 12 feet. At longer lengths you will see black "snow" in the video image.

I plan on having multiple QuickCams plugged into Quadras via either an Axion switch or an AE Quadralink board, will this work?

With the current software, only one QuickCam will be recognized at a time. You may manually switch between multiple QuickCams with a serial switchbox, if the switchbox correctly switches all eight pins of the cable and the total cable length from the computer to the camera is no more than 12 feet.

Does QuickCam work on non-U.S. Macintoshes?

Yes, because QuickCam uses direct digital video instead of NTSC or PAL, QuickCam will work on all QuickTime-compatible Macintoshes. Since it draws its power from the computer, you do not need special power adapters.

What is meant by fixed focal point? Can I not focus the camera?

Fixed focal means that anything greater than a fixed distance is in focus. With QuickCam anything at a distance of greater than 18 inches is in focus. There's no need for you to focus.

How hard would it be to come up with a case enclosure so that I can mount QuickCam outside?

QuickCam has a tripod mount on the bottom and is spherical. It would be easy to build a case in which it fit (remember to leave room for the cable to escape). Mount the camera to the case via the tripod socket.

What temperatures can the QuickCam operate at?

The CCD is probably the most temperature-sensitive element and is rated by its manufacturer as being capable of working from -10 C to 40 C. In the course of Connectix's testing for various certifications, the camera was subjected to extended testing from 32 F to 90 F.

Can the CCD get an image "burned in" by leaving it pointed at the same subject for long periods of time?

No.

Will QuickCam work with a Commodore Amiga?

Connectix has had reports from users who have successfuly used QuickCam on an Amiga running the Emplant Mac Emulator, but has done no testing on Amigas.

I need access to the low-level stuff QuickCam's software is doing underneath QuickTime. Is there any documentation on this?

Under special cases we will release this information. You must sign a non-disclosure and special license agreement. Send your request to quickcam@connectix.com.

Could QuickCam be activated by sound, so when it hears a noise it records?

Yes, Connectix has implemented the VOX (voice activated recording) feature of the Apple's Macintosh Sound Manager.

Why does my hard drive spin down when I use QuickCam on a PowerBook?

You should use QuickCam's microphone, not the built-in microphone. Apple designed PowerBooks so that the hard drive is automatically spun down whenever the built-in microphone is activated.

My PowerBook 5xx doesn't display a picture, or freezes. Why?

Your PowerBook doesn't have enough power on the serial port to run the camera. Call Connectix's technical support to order a power adapter for your computer, available for a $9.95 shipping and handling charge.

Why doesn't my Quadra 605 (or Performa 475 or LC 475) display pictures correctly?

About one-third of the Quadra 605/475 motherboards cannot hold communications with QuickCam. We have a software patch available that corrects this problem. Call Connectix technical support to obtain a copy. This patch is included with all QuickCams starting with version 1.0.2.

Will there be a color version? Will I get stuck with my B&W version?

Connectix has announced that it is working on a color version of QuickCam and will offer an upgrade path to current QuickCam owners. Since color cameras will produce more data, your storage requirements for movies will at least double.

Will there be a Newton version?

Connectix is investigating the feasability of producing a Newton version. However, the Newton's current screen is incapable of displaying grayscale pictures, so it is probably impractical at this time.

Will there be a version of QuickCam for PCs?

By the time you read this book the Connectix QuickCam for PCs should be shipping.

Which Macintoshes can use QuickCam?

QuickCam will work with any Macintosh that has at least a Motorola 68020 processor, one available serial port on the motherboard, 4 MB of RAM available, hard disk space available for the QuickCam's supporting software (and resultant pictures and movies), and is running at least MacOS 7.0. QuickCam won't therefore work with:

- the Macintosh Portable
- the Macintosh 128 and 512

 Appendixes

- the Mac Plus and SE
- the Original Classic

Windows

Configuration

What does CU-SeeMe for Windows require to start operating?

CU-SeeMe for Windows requires three dynamically-linked libraries (DLLs):

1. msvideo.dll—Microsoft video capabilities - provided with the CU-SeeMe for Windows distribution.
2. ctl3d.dll—three-dimensional controls (buttons, etc.) - provided with the CU-SeeMe for Windows distribution.
3. winsock.dll—Windows sockets networking capabilities - provided with any Winsock package.

CU-SeeMe for Windows also looks for a cuseeme.ini, but doesn't require that it exists.

Why do I see the error "Task CUSEEME did not call WSACleanup"?

WSACleanup() is a function that Winsock networking applications call when they quit. If for some reason CU-SeeMe crashes, it won't clean up after itself. You'll have to restart Windows to clean up.

 **Note:** The CU-SeeMe Development Team moved WSACleanup() to the WM_DESTROY section of the hidden NETWORK procedure in the hopes that Windows will have a better chance to call WSACleanup() in case of a crash.

Why do I get the "No Response from [IP address]" when I try to connect to a CU-SeeMe reflector?

There are a variety of reasons that you aren't able to connect to a CU-SeeMe reflector, including:

- Your network setup is incorrect. Test other Winsock applications work to ensure that you've properly configured your system to provide basic network connectivity.

Troubleshooting Q&A

- The computer that's running the CU-SeeMe reflector is down for scheduled maintenance or caused by unscheduled catastrophe. Your Winsock package should allow you to "ping" a machine to determine whether it's responding to network traffic.
- The CU-SeeMe reflector software may not be running, by design or by mishap. Try several different CU-SeeMe reflectors; it's unlikely that they'll all be down at the same time.
- You're using some pseudo-IP network connection software, such as The Internet Adapter (TIA). TIA won't work with CU-SeeMe because it doesn't provide you with an IP address, which CU-SeeMe requires. You'll need a PPP or SLIP account where you're assigned a unique IP address each time you connect.
- There's a "firewall" between you and the CU-SeeMe reflector. A firewall is a security measure that prevents certain network traffic from flowing in and out of your network (or network of networks). A firewall may be configured to disallow a class of traffic, such as UDP, from passing through. If UDP is disallowed then ping, Network File System (NFS) connections, and CU-SeeMe won't work. A firewall may also be configured to allow only known types of connections (specified by "ports") through. Your network administrator will explain how your firewall is configured. In the Networking section of this chapter you'll find the information the firewall administrator will need to allow CU-SeeMe traffic in and out.
- Proxy services may be getting in the way. Another security measure, proxy services can cause your computer to tell CU-SeeMe an IP address of a proxy machine instead of its own. The proxy machine will forward traffic on to your computer. This doesn't work for CU-SeeMe. Ask your network administrator if your network uses proxy services.

Why do I see a *GetHostByName()* error when I try to start CU-SeeMe?

CU-SeeMe for Windows currently requires that your computer have a hostname.

- If your network provides Domain Name Services (DNS), then you'll need to ask your network administrator to assign you a hostname. Once done, each time your computer needs to know its hostname it'll ask the DNS computer.
- If your network doesn't provide DNS, you'll give your computer a hostname by adding an entry in your "hosts file," appropriately named hosts.

In your Windows Sockets (Winsock) directory, where winsock.dll resides, there should be a file named hosts. If there isn't, create one with your favorite text editor or the Notepad. If your assigned IP address is 204.182.15.100 and you want

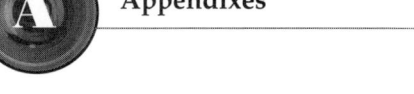

Appendixes

your computer to be named "guildenstern," then the hosts file would look like this:

```
204.182.15.100    guildenstern
```

(Don't use these values, these are from my hosts file.) When you restart Windows you're machine will have a hostname.

Verify that you've only got one hosts file by searching your entire hard drive with Windows File Manager. (Choose the File menu, select Search, start from c:\, check the "Search All Subdirectories" checkbox.) If you find other files named hosts, consider removing them.

If you're using Winsock Customization software to give your computer a hostname, ensure that you don't include your domain name in the hostname input area. For example, my computer's complete name is guildenstern.jungle.com; guildenstern is the hostname, jungle.com is the domain name.

If you're using FTP Software's PC/TCP software, ensure that you've provided your domain name in the Domain Completion input area.

Video Cards

What can I do about the reverse video image I get through the Reveal TV500 card?

Call Reveal at 1-800-4-REVEAL and say you're interested in having them fix this problem. They've said if enough interest were shown and it became clear to them that they were losing sales to competitors, Reveal would likely develop a fix for this problem.

What can I do about the reverse video image I get through the Media Vision ProMovStudio card?

Media Vision has said they'll "be unable to provide the additional support that has been requested." Send e-mail to Media Vision's technical support at techsupc@mediavis.com, and let them know that without a bug fix your next card won't be one of theirs.

What can I do about the reverse video image I get through the Nogatech Portable Digital Video PCMCIA card?

Steve Bernstein of Cisco Systems worked with the developers at Nogatech to fix this problem. You can obtain the appropriate DLL via the World-Wide Web, check http://www.jungle.com/CU-SeeMe/, or by sending Steve e-mail at sbernste@cisco.com.

What can I do about the upside-down image I get with the ProMovieStudio and Spectrum cards?

Turn the camera over.

Networking

How do I get CU-SeeMe to work through a firewall?

Your firewall doesn't know what CU-SeeMe traffic is, and is filtering it out. Your firewall administrator can remedy this by adding filtering rules that explain what CU-SeeMe traffic looks like (i.e. for which port it's destined). Following are sample filtering rules. Your firewall may use a slightly different syntax, but your firewall administrator will know what to do.

```
permit udp 0.0.0.0 255.255.255.255 xxx.xxx.xxx.xxx 0.0.0.0 eq 7648
permit udp 0.0.0.0 255.255.255.255 xxx.xxx.xxx.xxx 0.0.0.0 eq 7649
permit udp 0.0.0.0 255.255.255.255 xxx.xxx.xxx.xxx 0.0.0.0 eq 7650
permit udp 0.0.0.0 255.255.255.255 xxx.xxx.xxx.xxx 0.0.0.0 eq 7651
permit udp 0.0.0.0 255.255.255.255 xxx.xxx.xxx.xxx 0.0.0.0 eq 7652
```

Replacing the xxx.xxx.xxx.xxx with the address of your computer will allow CU-SeeMe traffic only to and from your computer, everyone else on your network will be unable to use CU-SeeMe. Replacing it with a broadcast address will allow everyone on your network to use CU-SeeMe. The safest arrangement allows CU-SeeMe traffic to a computer that's not connected to your remaining network, or one protected by a router that's properly-configured to provide very tight network security.

REFLECTORS AROUND THE WORLD

APPENDIX B

Since late 1993 I've maintained a list of public CU-SeeMe reflectors. This chapter is derived from the current version of that list. The reflectors listed here were in operation at the time I prepared this chapter. If a reflector seems to have gone off the air, please check the current list or ask the readers of the CU-SeeMe Discussion List.

If you're a reflector operator and wish me to include your site as a public reflector, send e-mail to reflectors@jungle.com.

USA Reflectors

ASU Geology Department

The Arizona State University, Department of Geology CU-SeeMe reflector, in Tempe, Arizona, USA, is open to the public. It will periodically be used for private conferences and for Mars Global Surveyor educational outreach programs.

The reflector is daffy.la.asu.edu (129.219.145.149). An accompanying web page is online at http://daisy.la.asu.edu/geopage.html. The reflector operator is Douglas A. Howard (d.howard@asu.edu).

Atlanta

The Atlanta CU-SeeMe reflector, in Atlanta, Georgia, USA, shows an around-the-clock view of 13th and Peachtree Streets.

The reflector is bwigw.bls.com (192.203.159.8). The reflector operator is Ken Evans (evans.ken@wgs-2.bwi.bls.com).

Classroom Connect

The Classroom Connect CU-SeeMe reflector, in Lancaster, Pennsylvania, USA, is operated in conjunction with the Classroom Connect newsletter.

The reflector is cyber.wentworth.com (198.51.81.112). An accompanying web page is online at http://www.wentworth.com/. The reflector operator is Tim McLain (tmc@wentworth.com).

CMU ARPA Speech

The Carnegie Mellon University, Advanced Research Project Agency Speech Group, School of Computer Science CU-SeeMe reflector, in Pittsburgh, Pennsylvania, USA, is available to the general public.

The reflector is cutter.speech.cs.cmu.edu (128.2.206.223). An accompanying page is online at http://www.cs.cmu.edu:8001/Web/SCS-HOME.html. The reflector operator is Eric H. Thayer (eht+@cs.cmu.edu).

CNIDR

The Clearinghouse for Networked Information Discovery and Retrieval CU-SeeMe reflector, in Research Triangle Park, North Carolina, USA, is a frequent site for CU-SeeMe events. The reflector operator requests that no still shots be sent here.

The reflector is hilda.ncsc.org (128.109.178.103). An accompanying web page is online at http://kudze.cnidr.org/. The reflector operator is Laura M. Craighead (lmc@cnidr.org).

Cornell University

The Cornell University Public Reflector CU-SeeMe reflector, in Ithaca, New York, USA, is the first stop for most CU-SeeMe surfers. Expect to see the dreaded "Too much CU-SeeMe traffic, try again later" message. Sending greater than 80 kbps will cause you to be booted from the reflector for ten minutes.

The reflector is pro60-test2.cit.cornell.edu (132.236.91.204). The reflector operators are Dick Cogger (r.cogger@cornell.edu) and John Lynn (jal7@cornell.edu).

Cream City

The Cream City CU-SeeMe reflector, is in Milwaukee, Wisconsin, USA.

The reflector is 129.89.70.27. An accompanying web page is online at http://129.89.70.27:1026/. The reflector operator is Matt Koster (matthewk@csd.uwm.edu).

CyberStudios

The CyberStudios Internet Radio CU-SeeMe reflector, in Ann Arbor, Michigan, USA, broadcasts audio in the Intel DVI 32 kbps format "around-the-clock since 4/1/95," according to the reflector operator. This is a receive-only reflector.

The reflector is (141.214.138.248). An accompanying web page is online at http://www.umich.edu/~johnlaue/. The reflector operator is John Lauer (cyber.studios@umich.edu).

Digital Jungle

The Digital Jungle CU-SeeMe reflector, in San Francisco, California, USA, is my very own. A rather experimental setup at the moment, I plan on providing an around-the-clock image of my neighborhood, the Haight-Ashbury, in the future. This reflector is open to the public. Please keep your transmission to less than 80 kbps.

The reflector is reflector.jungle.com (204.182.15.10). An accompanying web page is online at http://www.jungle.com/msattler/. The reflector operator is Michael Sattler (msattler@jungle.com).

Eden

The Eden CU-SeeMe reflector, in Austin, Texas, USA, has been the venue for a great variety of CU-SeeMe events.

The reflector is matrix.eden.com (199.171.21.8). An accompanying web page is online at http://www.eden.com/. The reflector operator is Jher (jher@eden.com).

Educational Computing Network

The Educational Computing Network CU-SeeMe reflector is in Chicago, Illinois, USA.

The reflector is uxb1.ecn.bgu.edu (143.43.32.61).

GTE-Albion

The General Telephone and Electric's Computer & Intelligent Systems Lab CU-SeeMe reflector, in Waltham, Massachusetts, USA, is a low-bandwidth (less than 30 kbps) public site.

The reflector is albion.gte.com (132.197.9.105). The reflector operator is John Nicol (nicol@gte.com).

GTE-Skyhawk

The General Telephone and Electric's Advanced Local Area Network Testbed CU-SeeMe reflector, in Waltham, Massachusetts, USA, is another low-bandwidth (less than 40 kbps) public site. Used for Fast Ethernet and ATM research, it's often unavailable to the public.

The reflector is skyhawk.gte.com (132.197.70.1). An accompanying web page is online at http://www-lanlab.gte.com/. The reflector operator is Alan Bugos (abugos@gte.com). Alan has published papers about research done at this site; ask him for a URL if you're interested in high-speed LAN research.

IITAP

The International Institute of Theoretical and Applied Physics CU-SeeMe reflector, in Ames, Iowa, USA, is a general-purpose public reflector.

The reflector is pv746d.vincent.iastate.edu (129.186.116.109). An accompanying web page is online at http://www.physics.iastate.edu/. The reflector operator is Douglas Fils (fils@iastate.edu).

Intelecom Data Systems

The Intelecom Data Systems (IDS) World Network Public CU-SeeMe reflector, in East Greenwich, Rhode Island, USA is a public site with a two-tiered usage system: the general public should adhere to customary bandwidth usage (no greater than 80 kbps) and IDS customers and IDS InterCable Net customers can "boost it up as high as they want."

The reflector is reflector.ids.net (155.212.1.12). An accompanying web page is online at http://www.ids.net/. The reflector operator is Andy Green (green@ids.net).

Indiana State University

The Indiana State University CU-SeeMe reflector, in Terre Haute, Indiana, USA, maintains a 24-hour-a-day signal of a greenhouse or of a laboratory.

The reflector is mama.indstate.edu (139.102.70.201). An accompanying web page is online at http://baby.indstate.edu/CU-SeeMe/. The reflector operator is Timothy Mulkey (lsmulky@scifac.indstate.edu).

Kent State University

The Kent State University CU-SeeMe reflector, in Kent, Ohio, USA, is a public reflector run by the College of Business Administration.

The reflector is business.kent.edu (131.123.5.2). An accompanying web page is online at http://business.kent.edu/. The reflector operator is Greg Madey (gmadey@synapse.kent.edu).

KJHK Radio

The KJHK 90.7 FM CU-SeeMe reflector, in Lawrence, Kansas, USA, broadcasts audio around the clock.

The reflector is 129.237.117.95. An accompanying web page is online at http://www.cc.ukans.edu/~burcham/index.html. The reflector operator is Rob Burcham (burchamr@falcon.cc.ukans.edu).

KVR-InterneTV

The KVR-InterneTV CU-SeeMe reflector, in Austin, Texas, USA is the "first broadcast station in cyberspace featuring "MuchMusic USA" most of the time. Austin MusicNetwork 1000-1400 CST (UCT-6) Sun-Thurs 'till 0400 CST; student/grassroots productions around the clock. They're willing to rebroadcast events over airwaves and cable (in Austin).

The reflector is huey.cc.utexas.edu (128.83.108.10). An accompanying web page is online at http://www.utexas.edu/depts/output/www/tstv.html. The reflector operator is Jay Ashcraft (ashcraft@uts.cc.utexas.edu).

LappDoggware

The LappDoggware Company CU-SeeMe reflector, located somewhere in cyberspace, is intermittently available to the general public.

The reflector is laird.ccds.cincinnati.oh.us (129.137.180.2). The reflector operator is John Lee (leejb@laird.ccds.cincinnati.oh.us).

laUNChpad EBBS

The laUNChpad Extended Bulletin Board Service CU-SeeMe reflector at the University of North Carolina, Chapel Hill, North Carolina, USA, is one service from a site that provides e-mail, Usenet, gopher, and other research services for free "to the world-at-large."

The reflector is lambada.oit.unc.edu (152.2.22.80). The reflector operator is Michael Williams (michael@lambada.oit.unc.edu).

Miami University (Ohio)

The University Libraries Systems Dept., King Library, Miami University CU-SeeMe reflector, in Oxford, Ohio, USA, is a general-purpose public reflector.

The reflector is old-holmes.lib.muohio.edu (134.53.24.5). The reflector operator is Peter Murray (MurrayPE@muohio.edu).

NASA TV at CMU GSIA

The Carnegie Mellon University, Graduate School of Industrial Administration CU-SeeMe reflector is part of a reflector chain that broadcasts NASA Select TV in receive-only mode. Please connect to the NASA Select TV outlet nearest to you.

The reflector is www.gsia.cmu.edu (128.2.230.10). An accompanying web page is online at http://netgopher.lerc.nasa.gov/NASA_TV/NASA_TV.html. The reflector operator is (jds@kudzu.cnidr.org).

NASA TV at IITAP

The International Institute of Theoretical and Applied Physics NASA Select TV CU-SeeMe reflector, in Ames, Iowa, USA, is part of a reflector chain that broadcasts NASA Select TV in receive-only mode. Please connect to the NASA Select TV outlet nearest to you.

The reflector is pv70f2.vincent.iastate.edu (129.186.112.242). An accompanying web page is online at http://www.physics.iastate.edu/ and http://netgopher.lerc.nasa.gov/NASA_TV/NASA_TV.html. The reflector operator is Douglas Fils (fils@iastate.edu).

NASA TV at Kent State

The Kent State University's NASA TV relay CU-SeeMe reflector, in Kent, Ohio, USA, is part of a reflector chain that broadcasts NASA Select TV in receive-only mode. Please connect to the NASA Select TV outlet nearest to you.

The reflector is axon.kent.edu (131.123.5.1). An accompanying web page is online at http://netgopher.lerc.nasa.gov/NASA_TV/NASA_TV.html. The reflector operator is Greg Madey (gmadey@synapse.kent.edu).

NASA Johnson Space Center

The NASA Johnson Space Center CU-SeeMe reflector is part of a reflector chain that broadcasts NASA Select TV in receive-only mode. Please connect to the NASA Select TV outlet nearest to you.

The reflector is 139.169.165.25. An accompanying web page is online at http://netgopher.lerc.nasa.gov/NASA_TV/NASA_TV.html.

NASA Lewis Research Center

The NASA Lewis Research Center CU-SeeMe reflector, in Lewis Research, Cleveland, USA, is part of a reflector chain that broadcasts NASA Select TV in receive-only mode. Please connect to the NASA Select TV outlet nearest to you.

The reflector is quark.lerc.nasa.gov (139.88.27.43). An accompanying web page is online at http://netgopher.lerc.nasa.gov/NASA_TV/NASA_TV.html. The reflector operator is Michael Baldizzi (mbaldizzi@lerc.nasa.gov).

NASA Marshall Space Flight Center

The NASA Marshall Space Flight Center CU-SeeMe reflector is part of a reflector chain that broadcasts NASA Select TV in receive-only mode. Please connect to the NASA Select TV outlet nearest to you.

The reflector is 128.158.1.154. An accompanying web page is online at http://netgopher.lerc.nasa.gov/NASA_TV/NASA_TV.html.

Network Solutions

The Network Solutions, Inc. CU-SeeMe reflector, in Herndon, Virgina, USA, is a high-bandwidth (up to 80 kbps) site configured to interoperate with NV and VAT. The reflector is nic.ops.netsol.com (198.41.0.200). An accompanying web page is online at http://www.netsol.com/.

The reflector operator is Stan (stanb@netsol.com).

North Carolina State University

The North Carolina State University Multimedia Lab CU-SeeMe reflector is in Raleigh, North Carolina, USA.

The reflector is magneto.csc.ncsu.edu (152.1.57.56). An accompanying web page is online at http://magneto.csc.ncsu.edu/. The reflector operator is Scott Callicutt (sfcallic@magneto.csc.ncsu.edu).

NYSERNet

The New York State Education and Research Network CU-SeeMe reflector, in Liverpool, New York, USA, is available for general use, provided that you don't send still shots. NYSERNet usually has a test image of a bird running at all times.

The reflector is nysernet.org (192.77.173.2). An accompanying web page is online at http://nysernet.org/. The reflector operators are Jean Armour Polly (jpolly@nysernet.org) and Don (don@nysernet.org).

Ohio State University

The Ohio State University CU-SeeMe reflector, run by the Academic Technology Services, is located in Columbus, Ohio, USA.

The reflector is davros.acs.ohio-state.edu (128.146.116.8). An accompanying web page is online at http://www.acs.ohio-state.edu/. The reflector operator is Harpal Chohan (chohan+@osu.edu).

Pacific Rim

The Pacific Rim Network CU-SeeMe reflector is in Bellingham, Washington, USA.

The reflector is olympic.pacificrim.net (204.96.68.1). An accompanying web page is online at http://pacificrim.net/. The reflector operator is Gavin Shearer, Promotions Director (gavin@pacificrim.net).

Penn State

The Pennsylvania State CU-SeeMe reflector, run by the Center for Academic Computing, is in University Park, Pennsylvania, USA.

The reflector is hornet.cac.psu.edu (128.118.58.54). An accompanying web page is online at http://www.psu.edu/. The reflector operator is John Kalbach (kalbach@cac.psu.edu).

Radio HK

The Radio HK - Hajjar/Kaufman CU-SeeMe reflector, in Info: Audio-only, receive-only. 24 hours a day, 7 days a week.

The reflector is 204.119.173.22. An accompanying web page is online at http://hkweb.com/radio/. The reflector operator is Norman Hajjar (norman_hajjar@hk.com).

Seattle Pacific University

The Seattle Pacific University CU-SeeMe reflector at the Archer Instructional Media Center in Seattle, Washington, USA is typically on from 8am–5pm Pacific Time, Monday–Friday.

The reflector is adam.spu.edu (192.190.33.9). The reflector operator is Tim Kennedy (tkennedy@spu.edu).

Sprintlink

The Sprintlink CU-SeeMe reflector, run by Sprint Telecommunications Corp., is in Herndon, Virginia, USA.

The reflector is tiny.sprintlink.net (199.0.55.90). An accompanying web page is online at http://www.sprintlink.net. The reflector operator is Richard Martin (rmartin@stealth.sprintlink.net).

Stanford University Medical Center

The Stanford University Medical Center CU-SeeMe reflector is in Stanford, California, USA.

The reflector is mednet2.stanford.edu (171.65.4.4). An accompanying web page is online at http://www-med.stanford.edu/MedCenter/reflect.html. The reflector operator is John Reuling (reuling@med.stanford.edu).

ThePoint

ThePoint's CU-SeeMe reflector is located just north of Louisville, Kentucky, USA. The reflector is cuseeme.thepoint.net (198.6.9.2). An accompanying web page is online at http://www.thepoint.net/.

The reflector operator is Michael Jung (mikej@thepoint.net).

University of Hawaii

The University of Hawaii Digital Media Lab CU-SeeMe reflector, at the Manoa Innovation Center in Hawaii, USA is currently the only reflector on that delightful island chain.

The reflector is makaha.mic.hawaii.edu (128.171.171.10). An accompanying web page is online at http://www.mic.hawaii.edu.

The reflector operator is Craig (webmaster@www.mic.hawaii.edu).

University of Kansas

The University of Kansas Special Education Videoconferencing CU-SeeMe reflector is chef.sped.ukans.edu (129.237.247.160).

University of Maine

The Administrative Information Systems CU-SeeMe reflector is located in Alumni Hall at the University of Maine, in Orono, Maine, USA.

The reflector is 130.111.120.13. An accompanying web page is online at http://www.umeais.maine.edu/. The reflector operator can be reached at (wheeler@cardinal.umeais.maine.edu).

University of Maryland

The University of Maryland CU-SeeMe reflector, in College Park, Maryland, USA, is an experimental site.

The reflector is haven.umd.edu (128.8.10.6). An accompanying web page is online at http://www.ni.umd.edu/. The reflector operator is Dan Magorian (magorian@ni.umd.edu).

University of Pennsylvania

The University of Pennsylvania Office of Data Communications and Computing Services CU-SeeMe reflector is in Philadelphia, Pennsylvania, USA.

The reflector is isis.dccs.upenn.edu (130.91.72.36). An accompanying web page is online at http://www.upenn.edu/. The reflector operator is (danu@dccs.upenn.edu).

University of Texas

The University of Texas CU-SeeMe reflector is in Austin, Texas, USA.

The reflector is 128.83.108.14. An accompanying web page is online at http://ccwf.cc.utexas.edu/~streak/. The reflector operator is Jason Williams (streak@ccwf.cc.utexas.edu).

Virginia Commonwealth University

The Virginia Commonwealth University CU-SeeMe reflector is in Richmond, Virginia, USA.

The reflector is 128.172.157.244. The reflector operator is Jeff Price (jprice@cabell.vcu.edu).

White Pine Software

The White Pine Software CU-SeeMe reflector, in Nashua, New Hampshire, USA, is run by the commercial entity that purchased the exclusive CU-SeeMe license. It's available to the general public. White Pine staff members are often online, ready to answer your questions.

The reflector is piney.wpine.com (192.80.72.4). An accompanying web page is online at http://www.wpine.com/. The reflector operator is Bill Ryan (bryan@wpine.com).

International Reflectors

Adelaide (Australia)

The Adelaide University CU-SeeMe reflector in Australia is another public reflector about which little is known other than its friendly regulars.

The reflector is reflect.adelaide.edu.au (129.127.12.42).

Geko (Australia)

The Geko CU-SeeMe reflector in Australia is yet another black hole of information.

The reflector is (203.2.239.3).

Murdoch University (Australia)

The Murdoch University CU-SeeMe reflector in Australia is a by-appointment reflector (even though I've noticed that sometimes it's left on for public use). Please transmit no more than 80 kpbs.

The reflector is cleo.murdoch.edu.au (134.115.224.60). An accompanying web page is online at http://134.115.224.48/. The reflector operator is Geoff Rehn (rehn@cleo.murdoch.edu.au).

Psy (Australia)

The Psy CU-SeeMe reflector at the University of Queensland in Australia is another reflector about which little is known. Sometimes the site of some eclectic ad-hoc get-togethers.

The reflector is psy.uq.oz.au (130.102.32.1).

RMIT (Australia)

The RMIT CU-SeeMe reflector in Australia is a virtual unknown.

The reflector is `reflector.rmit.edu.au` (131.170.9.1).

University of Melbourne (Australia)

The University of Melbourne CU-SeeMe reflector, in Melbourne, Australia, welcomes casual use as long as you send no more than 80 kbps. Use of this reflector for conferences is available by appointment.

The reflector is `reflector.unimelb.edu.au` (128.250.20.187). An accompanying web page is online at `http://www.unimelb.edu.au/`. The reflector operator is Martin Gleeson (`gleeson@unimelb.edu.au`).

University of Queensland (Australia)

The University of Queensland CU-SeeMe reflector in Australia is a public site.

The reflector is `clix.aarnet.edu.au` (130.102.128.59).

Vrije Univ AI-Lab (Belgium)

The AI-Lab Vrije Universiteit Brussel CU-SeeMe reflector, in Brussels, Belgium, is used for the transmission of seminars and live scientific experiments. It's available for the public, but please switch to receive-only mode when asked to by the staff.

The reflector is `arti.vub.ac.be` (134.184.26.10). An accompanying web page is online at `http://arti.vub.ac.be/welcome.html`.

The reflector operator is Peter Stuer (`peterst@arti.vub.ac.be`).

PUC-Rio (Brazil)

The Catholic University of Rio de Janeiro CU-SeeMe reflector, in Rio de Janeiro, Brazil, is available for those who transmit less than 80 kbps max. Hugo says "feel free to use anytime."

The reflector is `obaluae.inf.puc-rio.br` (139.82.17.17). An accompanying web page is online at `http://www.inf.puc-rio.br/`. The reflector operator is Hugo Fuks (`hugo@inf.puc-rio.br`).

University of Sao Paulo (Brazil)

The University of Sao Paulo CU-SeeMe reflector is in Sao Paulo, Brazil.

The reflector is suncisc.cisc.sc.usp.br (143.107.225.6).

Dalhousie University (Canada)

The Dalhousie University CU-SeeMe reflector, in Halifax, Nova Scotia, Canada, is available for those who broadcast less than 80 kbps.

The reflector is sparky.ucis.dal.ca (129.173.2.56). An accompanying web page is online at http://www.dal.ca/. The reflector operator is Vivien Hannon (Vivien.Hannon@Dal.CA).

University of Manitoba (Canada)

The University of Manitoba, Department of Electrical & Computer Engineering and Telecommunications Research Laboratories CU-SeeMe reflector is in Winnipeg, Manitoba, Canada.

The reflector is kinsner2.ee.umanitoba.ca (130.179.8.44). An accompanying web page is online at http://www.umanitoba.ca/. The reflector operator is W. Kinsner (kinsner@ee.umanitoba.ca).

University of Vaasa (Finland)

The Department of Communication Studies, Faculty of Humanities & Computer Center, University of Vaasa CU-SeeMe reflector is in Vaasa, Finland.

The reflector is zippo.uwasa.fi (193.166.120.3). An accompanying web page is online at http://www.uwasa.fi/. The reflector operator is Tuomas Eerola (te@uwasa.fi).

Telecomm Grande Ecole (France)

The Telecomm Grande Ecole CU-SeeMe reflector is in Brittany, France.

The reflector is 130.190.6.28.

Nijmegen University (Holland)

The Cognitive Science Department, Katholic University of Nijmegen (KUN) CU-SeeMe reflector, in Holland is a low-bandwidth public site.

The reflector is kunpu7.psych.kun.nl (131.174.200.28). An accompanying web page is online at http://kunpu7.psych.kun.nl/cogw/nici-cogsci.html. The reflector operator is De Haan (dehaan@nici.kun.nl), who has his own web page at http://dehaan1.psych.kun.nl/.

Rotterdam Management (Holland)

The Rotterdam School of Management CU-SeeMe reflector is in Rotterdam, Holland.

The reflector is reflector.fbk.eur.nl (130.115.150.2). The reflector operator is M.W. van Wetering (MWETERING@fac.fbk.eur.nl).

University of Ulster (Ireland)

The Interactive Systems Centre, Magee College, University of Ulster CU-SeeMe reflector in Northern Ireland is a low-bandwidth (less than 30 kbps) public site.

The reflector is claudia.iscm.ulst.ac.uk (193.63.68.162). An accompanying web page is online at http://www.iscm.ulst.ac.uk/. The reflector operator is Mike McCool (mike@iscm.ulst.ac.uk).

Weizmann Instistute (Israel)

The Weizmann Institute of Science's Computing Center CU-SeeMe reflector, in Rehovot, Israel has been up for a long time, but not many of the vital statistics are known about it.

The reflector is sunten.weizmann.ac.il (132.76.64.143).

Eurocube (Italy)

The Eurocube Internet CU-SeeMe reflector, in Italy, is a low-bandwidth (less than 30 kbps) public site.

The reflector is `reflector.eurocube.it` (194.20.44.111). An accompanying web page is online at `http://www.eurocube.it/video/`. The reflector operator is Guido Tripaldi Shamblin (`guido@eurocube.it`).

University of Calabria (Italy)

The Centro Interdipartimentale della Comunicazione - UniCal CU-SeeMe reflector is in Italy.

The reflector is `cedam.cubo20.unical.it` (160.97.8.200). The reflector operator is Giovanni Zicarelli (`giozic@cedam.cubo20.unical.it`).

University of Pisa (Italy)

The Tuscany Metropolitan Area Network CU-SeeMe reflector, in Pisa, Italy, is part of the Tuscany DQDB fiber optic network connecting Pisa, Firenze, and Siena. It's run in cooperation with SERRA (SERvizi Rete Ateneo network university services of Pisa).

The reflector is `indy.iet.unipi.it` (131.114.9.19). The reflector operators are Stefano Giordano (`stefano@iet.unipi.it`) and Giacomo Guarguaglini (`guargua@radar.iet.unipi.it`).

Eccosys (Japan)

The Eccosys, Ltd. CU-SeeMe reflector, in Tomigaya, Shibuya, Tokyo, Japan is the site of some very bizarre late-night conferences. They have a very cool logo.

The reflector is `neoteny.eccosys.com` (199.100.7.5). An accompanying web page is online at `http://www.eccosys.com/PEOPLE/JITO/joi.html`. The reflector operator is Joichi Ito (`jito@eccosys.com`).

Future Pirates (Japan)

The Future Pirates Broadcast CU-SeeMe reflector is in Japan.

The reflector is `bass.fpi.co.jp` (202.32.26.17). An accompanying web page is online at `http://www.fpi.jp/Welcome.html`.

Okazaki NRI (Japan)

The Department of Applied Molecular Science CU-SeeMe reflector at the Institute for Molecular Science, Okazaki National Research Institutes is in Myodaiji, Okazaki, Japan.

The reflector is solaris.ims.ac.jp (133.48.144.60). An accompanying web page is online at http://solaris.ims.ac.jp/videoconf.html. The reflector operator is Jiro Toyoda (toyoda@solaris.ims.ac.jp).

University of Tokyo (Japan)

The Research into Artifact Center for Engineering (RACE) CU-SeeMe reflector at the University of Tokyo is in Tokyo, Japan.

The reflector is race-server.race.u-tokyo.ac.jp (157.82.76.2). An accompanying web page is online at http://www.race.u-tokyo.ac.jp/. The reflector operator is Koji Ando (chutzpah@race.u-tokyo.ac.jp).

Ostfold/Fenris (Norway)

The Ostfold Regional College/Informatics Department Fenris CU-SeeMe reflector, in Halden, Norway, is a receive-only site.

The reflector is fenris.hiof.no (158.36.33.3). An accompanying web page is online at http://www.ludvigsen.hiof.no/webdoc/video.html. The reflector operators are Borre Ludvigsen (borrel@hiof.no) and Jon Kalnes (jonk@hiof.no).

Ostfold/Kark (Norway)

The Ostfold Regional College / Informatics Department Kark CU-SeeMe reflector, in Halden, Norway, is a receive-only site.

The reflector is 158.36.33.5. An accompanying web page is online at http://www.ludvigsen.hiof.no/webdoc/video.html. The reflector operators are Børre Ludvigsen (borrel@hiof.no) and Jon Kalnes (jonk@hiof.no).

University of Trondheim (Norway)

The University of Trondheim's Department of Informatics CU-SeeMe reflector, in Trondheim, Norway, is available to the general public during their daytime and evenings.

The reflector is `venus.ifi.unit.no` (129.241.161.225). An accompanying web page is online at `http://www.ifi.unit.no/`. The reflector operator is `eyvind.hope@ifi.unit.no`.

University of Lisbon (Portugal)

The University of Lisbon/Faculty of Sciences CU-SeeMe reflector, in Lisbon, Portugal, is maintained by the Department of Informatics as a public site.

The reflector is `master.di.fc.ul.pt` (192.67.76.40). An accompanying web page is online at `http://www.fc.ul.pt`. The reflector operators are `cap@di.fc.ul.pt` and `frazao@di.fc.ul.pt`.

University of Singapore (Singapore)

The National University of Singapore CU-SeeMe reflector is in Singapore.

The reflector is `biomed.nus.sg` (137.132.9.61). The reflector operators are K C Lun (`coflunkc@leonis.nus.sg`) and Tan Tin Wee (`bchtantw@leonis.nus.sg`).

Foeredrag i Lund/Fast (Sweden)

This CU-SeeMe reflector, located at Lund University, Lund, Sweden, broadcasts the Swedish show *Foeredrag i Lund* broadcast at 150 kbps. Persons with low-bandwidth connectivity should use the (Sweden) Foeredrag i Lund/Slow reflector.

The reflector is `ForLund-h.video.lu.se` (130.235.4.10). An accompanying web page is online at `http://www.lu.se/#Events`. The reflector operator is Jan Engvald (`Jan.Engvald@ldc.lu.se`).

Foeredrag i Lund/Slow (Sweden)

This CU-SeeMe reflector, located at Lund University, Lund, Sweden, broadcasts the Swedish show *Foeredrag i Lund* broadcast at 32 kbps. Persons with high-bandwidth connectivity should use the (Sweden) Foeredrag i Lund/Fast reflector.

The reflector is `ForLund-l.video.lu.se` (130.235.4.11). An accompanying web page is online at `http://www.lu.se/#Events`. The reflector operator is Jan Engvald (`Jan.Engvald@ldc.lu.se`).

NASA TV at Lund University (Sweden)

The Lund University Computing Center's CU-SeeMe reflector, in Lund, Sweden, is part of a reflector chain that broadcasts NASA Select TV in receive-only mode. Please connect to the NASA Select TV outlet nearest to you. This reflector is sometimes used for videoconferencing with and within Lund University.

The reflector is reflector.lu.se (130.235.128.100). Accompanying web pages are online at http://www.lu.se/ and http://netgopher.lerc.nasa.gov/NASA_TV/NASA_TV.html. The reflector operator is Jan Engvald (Jan.Engvald@ldc.lu.se).

Geneva University (Switzerland)

The Centre Universitaire d'Informatique CU-SeeMe reflector, in Geneva, Switzerland, is a small (ten participants at most) public site.

The reflector is cuisunf.unige.ch (129.194.12.26). An accompanying web page is online at http://cui_www.unige.ch/db-research/Members/mb/mb.html. The reflector operator is Michel Bonjour (bonjour@cui.unige.ch).

Swiss Telecom R&D (Switzerland)

The Swiss Telecom R&D experimental CU-SeeMe reflector, in Switzerland, is a medium-bandwidth (less than 60 kbps) public site. This reflector is available for conferences by appointment.

The reflector is manor.vptt.ch (193.5.232.55). An accompanying web page is online at http://www.vptt.ch/~cabano. The reflector operator is Claudio Cabano (cabano@vptt.ch).

Open University Computing Department (UK)

The Open University CU-SeeMe reflector, in the UK, is currently open to the public, but will be used for course tutorials from time to time.

The reflector is pepper.open.ac.uk (137.108.33.4). An accompanying web page is online at http://www-cs.open.ac.uk. The reflector operator is Blaine Price (B.A.Price@open.ac.uk).

Plymouth University (UK)

The Plymouth University CU-SeeMe reflector, in Plymouth, Devon, UK, is a high-bandwidth (70 kbps) public site.

Appendixes

The reflector is 141.163.100.8. An accompanying web page is online at http://tin.ssc.plym.ac.uk/. The reflector operator is Liz Thomson (lt@tin.ssc.plym.ac.uk). Her web site has many images of historic CU-SeeMe conferences.

Hallam (UK)

The Hallam Trial Reflector CU-SeeMe reflector is at the Sheffield Hallam University in the United Kingdom.

The reflector is kingfisher.cms.shu.ac.uk (143.52.51.15). An accompanying web page is online at http://pine.shu.ac.uk/. The reflector operator is Chuck Elliot (cmsce@teak.shu.ac.uk).

Glossary of Terms

APPENDIX C

I've created this glossary by looking through the questions asked by new CU-SeeMe users; the words and acronyms they asked about appear here. If you still can't find what you're looking for, look in the index, on my web pages, or ask the readers of the CU-SeeMe Discussion list.

ARPA—Advanced Research Projects Agency. Their machinations caused the ARPANET (cf) to be created.

analog—A method of transferring data by changes in signal strength. Frequency modulation (FM) and amplitude modulation (AM) are examples of analog information.

ARPANET—ARPA Network. An early collection of computers that evolved into the Internet.

audio—Sound. The portion of a conversation that is interpreted by the ears. The other portion is the video (cf).

Auxiliary Data Function Modules—Also known as AuxData. A programmatic interface that allows for the extension of CU-SeeMe's core capabilities developed by Aaron Giles. The Talk Window Function Module and the Slide Window Function Module are two examples of extentions to CU-SeeMe.

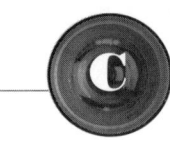

bandwidth—the carrying capacity of a particular connection medium, measured in bits per second (bps).

BRI—Basic Rate Interface. The standard configuration of home-based ISDN (cf), defined as two 64 kbps Bearer channels (cf) and one coordinating 16 kbps Data channel (cf), BRI is also known as a 2B+D connection.

baud rate—an obsolete term used for discussing bandwidth (cf). Refers specifically to the state changes in the modem (cf), not to the amount of data that could be transferred. The current term is bits per second, or bps.

Bearer channels—also known as B channels, these are the high-speed portion used in ISDN (cf). See also data channels.

BITNET—Because It's Time NETwork.

BOOTP—Boot Protocol. A system whereby a computer on a network gets its configuration information from a BOOTP server on the network. A predecessor to DHCP (cf), BOOTP is a great help to system/network administrators.

broadcast—the generic term for sharing an event via CU-SeeMe, NV (cf), or VAT (cf). The use of this term generates some controversy and worry in the CU-SeeMe community because there's great federal regulation of traditional broadcasters and no regulation over the contents of the Internet.

CCD—Charge-Coupled Device. Part of a camera that converts the (analog) light into (digital) signals sent to a computer, where scene-processing (and perhaps transmission) takes place.

CCITT—Consultive Committee for International Telephone and Telegraph. A standards-setting body, it's been renamed the Telecommunications Standards Bureau of the International Telecommunications Union, leading to the unwieldy acronym CCITT/ITU-TSB. (No, I'm not kidding.)

client—end-user software that interacts with a server (cf) elsewhere on the network. The CU-SeeMe client is the software run on Macintosh, Windows, or Amiga computers that allow one end-user to interact with others. The CU-SeeMe reflector software is the server end of the transaction; it coordinates the activities of the clients.

CIX—Commercial Internet Exchange. While the Internet disallowed commercial traffic (cf) the CIX was a for-profit alternative.

compression—the conversion of data into a smaller package. Compression is very important when bandwidth (cf) is low, because it's the only way to obtain enough data. Aggressive compression usually requires faster computers.

Cornell University—the home of CU-SeeMe. Located on the banks of the Finger Lakes, near the town of Ithaca, New York.

costware—software that is sold commercially. Contrast with shareware (cf) and freeware (cf).

Data channel—the low-bandwidth (cf) portion of ISDN (cf). Also known as the D channel, it's used to carry call set-up, coordination, synchronization, and signalling data; things we, the users, never see.

decoding—the complementary operation to encoding (cf).

decompression—the process used to extract data that was previously compressed (cf).

DHCP—Dynamic Host Configuration Protocol. A more advanced successor to BOOTP (cf), DHCP provides configuration information to computers on a network.

digital—information transmitted in discrete units, as opposed to analog (cf) methods. The best-known digital processors are personal computers.

digital switching system—The hardware in your telephone provider's central office that's used for servicing home-based ISDN (cf) connections.

digitizer—hardware that converts analog (cf) signals to digital (cf) signals. Most typically used allow consumer video cameras to provide data to personal computers.

domain—the collective name for a group of people on a network. Typical domain names include `jungle.com`, `acm.org`, `tlg.net`, `dockmaster.mil`, and `mit.edu`.

DNS—Domain Name System. A method for converting easy-to-read machine names (such as `guildenstern.jungle.com`) into the numeric network addresses used by computers (such as 204.182.15.100).

encoding—translation of a nontext file into a text format suitable for sending on the Internet.

error correction—the capability to detect and overcome errors in data transmission. The use of software error correction, such as TCP/IP, obviates the need for hardware error correction, such as is provided by some modems.

Ethernet—one of several types of physical wiring systems that result in a 10 mbps network.

FAQ—Frequently Asked Questions. A document, usually compiled by volunteers, that contains frequently asked questions about some topic and their answers.

freeware—software that is given away without the expectation of remuneration. Contrast with shareware (cf) and costware (cf).

FTP—File Transfer Protocol. A widely-available standard method for transferring files (text documents, images, sounds, movies, and the like) between computers.

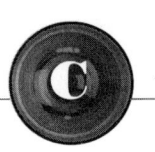 Appendixes

full-duplex—a communications connection that allows participants to send and receive simultaneously (like a telephone). All Macintoshes are full-duplex. Compare to half-duplex (cf).

gateway—the network device between your local network and the outside world. Often ignored in older communication schemes, the identity of the gateway is required by modern systems such as Apple's Open Transport.

grayscale—An method of representing an image in varying shades of gray.

GSN—Global SchoolNet.

half-duplex—a communications connection that requires the participants choose between sending and receiving (as in a walkie-talkie). Most standard Intel-based PCs are half-duplex. Compare to full-duplex (cf).

hardware handshaking—the use of a cable to toggle flow control on 14.4 kbps and faster modems. Slower modems typically use software flow control, also known as XON/XOFF.

HDTV—High-Definition television. Any one of several systems of new television hardware and changes in broadcast software that results in more detailed images.

host name—administrative name of a particular computer, required for identifying machines on a network.

Internet—a global network consisting of many national and regional networks.

IAB—Internet Architecture Board. The body that sets the communication standards for software and hardware systems that comprise the Internet.

IETF—Internet Engineering Task Force. A public forum dedicated to discussing and handling technical problems facing the Internet.

inverse multiplexing—The combining of one or more ISDN (cf) bearer channels (cf). Also known as bonding.

IP—Internet Protocol. One of the standard communications systems for computers connected to the Internet.

IP address—a unique numeric identifer of a network-connected computer.

IRTF—Internet Research Task Force. The body that handles issues that likely will affect the Internet in the next decade.

ISOC—Internet Society.

ISDN—Integrated Services Digital Network. A high-bandwidth (cf) network connection method, popular for connecting homes to the Internet or a corporate local area network. See also BRI, PRI, and inverse multiplexing.

KB—One kilobyte is 1024 bytes.

Local Area Networks—Two or more computers physically connected with short bits of wire.

manual addressing—the practice of assigning a fixed (or "static") IP address (cf) to a computer on a network. Compare to server-based addressing.

Maven—audioconferencing tool written by Charlie Kline. Before Maven was incorporated into CU-SeeMe to provide audio capability, it was used in tandem with CU-SeeMe. Charlie continues to upgrade Maven and has recently added even more audio encoding features.

MB—a megabyte is 1024 x 1024 bytes, or 1024 kilobytes.

MBone—The multicast backbone is a series of routers that forward incoming packets to other networks, configured so that streams never traverse any wire on the network twice. A very efficient broadcast system.

MOTD—Message of the Day. A greeting that informs users of current status, upcoming events, contact persons, and the like.

MTU/MRU—maximum transmit unit/maximum receive unit. Specifications for the largest packet of information that may be sent or received over a particular network connection. Typical numbers for MTU are 1006 (SLIP) and 296 (CSLIP); MRU is 1500 for PPP.

nameserver—one or more computers on a network that provide Domain Name Services (cf).

NASA—National Aeronautics and Space Administration.

NASA Select TV—around-the-clock broadcast of shuttle missions, press conferences, educational films, and other space-related programming.

NT1—Network Termination Device. Used in ISDN (cf) network connections, this device sits between the telephone company's digital switching service and your local ISDN network.

NNTP—Network News Transfer Protocol. A method for obtaining USENET newsgroups over TCP/IP networks.

NREN—National Research and Education Network.

NSF—National Science Foundation.

NTSC—National Television System Committee. A video transmission standard used in the USA.

PAL—Phase Alternation by Line. A video transmission standard used in much of Europe, Africa, the Middle East, and Far East. PAL uses color images at 625 horizontal lines of resolution (except in Brazil, where PAL-M is used and supports 30 FPS with 525 horizontal lines of resolution).

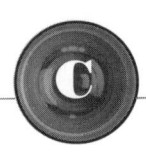 Appendixes

plug-ins—see Auxiliary Data Function Modules.

PPP—Point-to-Point Protocol. A popular connection method for modem-based Internet users.

PRI—Primary Rate Interface. A high-bandwidth (cf) network connection common in larger organizations (due to its greater capacity and cost). PRI configuration varies geographically. In the United States a PRI connection is defined as 23 64 kbps bearer channels (cf) and one coordinating 64 kbps data channel (cf). PRI is also known as a 23B+D connection. With a total carrying capacity of 1.544 mbps, a PRI is transmitted through a standard North American T-1 line (which may physically be nothing more than one twisted-pair copper wire).

reflector—software that allows CU-SeeMe users to hold multi-party conferences.

SECAM—Systeme Electronique Couleur Avec Memoire. A video transmission standard used throughout the world, in the former USSR, and in areas of French influence. SECAM uses color images of 625 lines of resolution at 25 frames per second.

server-based addressing—the practice of assigning an IP address (cf) from a pool of addresses when a computer makes itself known to the network. Also known as "dynamic" addressing (as opposed to fixed addressing).

shareware—software that's given away with the expectation that a user will pay a nominal fee once an evaluation period is over. Contrast with freeware (cf) and costware (cf).

SLIP—Serial Line Internet Protocol. A popular connection method for modem-based Internet users.

SMTP—Simple Mail Transport Protocol. A standardized method for sending electronic mail to a network.

sneakernet—tongue-in-cheek term for manually walking floppy diskettes between computers. What you use when the real network stops working.

spam—the indiscriminate flooding of USENET newsgroups, typically with commercial solicitations.

stream Talk Function Module TCP—Transmission Control Protocol.

traffic—data being sent over a network.

twisted-pair—simple two-strand copper wire used for local area networks and ISDN (cf).

U.S. Department of Defense (DOD)—See ARPA.

UNIX—very popular computer operating system developed at Bell Laboratories.

URL—Uniform Resource Locator. Method for describing the location of information on the Internet.

USENET—User's Network. A collection of discussion topics that are broadcast worldwide via the Internet.

WAN—Wide Area Network. Computers connected over a large area. Compare with LAN.

APPENDIX D

BIBLIOGRAPHY

My primary sources of information have been the CU-SeeMe Development Team and my fellow CU-SeeMe Discussion List members. In addition to the paper and web documents I've listed here, you'll find others in Chapter 8, "History, Culture, and Usage," and on my CU-SeeMe web page, `http://www.jungle.com/CU-SeeMe/`

> Apple Computer. Open Transport White Paper. 1995. Online at
> `ftp://seeding.apple.com/ess/public/opentransport/`
> Open Transport documentation for end-users and programmers. A bit thick on the goals and a bit thin on how it'll be delivered, but an all-around useful briefing about what Open Transport is and what it'll do for you.
>
> Allon. Timed Video Grabber for Macintosh. Online at
> `http://spiderweb.yoyodyne.com/allon/tvg.html`
> Timed Video Grabber captures an image from a camera attached to your Macintosh and converts it to a JPEG image suitable for viewing from a web browser.
>
> Arrowood, Adam. CU-SeeMe: Communications in an Emergent Technology. On-line at
> `http://bastille.oit.gatech.edu/adam/cuseeme/paper/CU-SeeMe.html`
> Another person's perspective on CU-SeeMe, complete with lots of screen-shots.

 Appendixes

Behr, Eric. MacTCP, online at
ftp://spider.math.ilstu.edu/pub/mac/mac-tcp.txt
This is the seminal online, step-by-step description on how to get MacTCP running (and how to debug it when you've done something ever so slightly wrong).

Brown, D. H. Getting CU-SeeMe to Interoperate with NV and VAT. On-line at
http://www.rspac.ivv.nasa.gov/~dhbrown/cucme_nv/cucme_nv.html
Yet another set of web pages to help folks use CU-SeeMe with NV and VAT.

Buckman School, The. CU-SeeMe and the Classroom. On-line at
http://buckman.pps.k12.or.us/
One of the schools that have jumped right in and used CU-SeeMe as part of their educational curriculum. They have pages devoted to CU-SeeMe use and their hardware setup.

Community of Mediterranean Universities. Computer Architecture and Computational Models and Their Implementations. On-line at
http://www.ege.edu.tr/MEDCAMP/
One of the summer school series of events organized by the Community of Mediterranean Universities in the framework of MedCampus Project 6 of the European Community, these web pages concentrate on distance learning and education via CU-SeeMe and other technologies.

Cornell University.
The CU-SeeMe Development Team is part of the Advanced Technologies and Planning Group (http://nr-atp.cit.cornell.edu) which in turn is part of the Network Resources division of Cornell Information Technologies (http://www.cit.cornell.edu).

Cornell University's Center for the Environment has used CU-SeeMe for well-known projects like Earth Day '95. Expect more interesting projects to grace their pages. Online at
http://www.cfe.cornell.edu/
Dr. Erde has been using CU-SeeMe for medical remote viewing. A student of his, Aaron Giles, was a pioneer in the development and use of the CU-SeeMe Auxiliary Data Function Modules. Online at
http://www.med.cornell.edu/oac/staff/staff.html#erde

Digital Vision, Inc. ComputerEyes video cameras. Online at
http://www.digvis.com/digvis/

Eden Matrix, The. Online at
http://www.eden.com/
The Eden Matrix was an early adopter of CU-SeeMe technology in broadcast performance art.

Engst, Adam. *Internet Starter Kit*. (Hayden)Voluminous tome that covers all aspects of connecting your Macintosh or Windows computer to the Internet. (There's a separate volume for each platform.) Well-researched, well-written, not a pocket book by any stretch of the imagination.

Engvald Jan, Lund University Computing Center. For Lund Swedish CU-SeeMe Reflector. Online at
http://www.lu.se/

Fortune, Daniel. Fortune's Web World. On-line at
http://www.best.com:80/~dfortune/
Daniel Fortune is one of a growing group of artists who use CU-SeeMe as both the message and the medium. This web page points to the works of like-minded artists.

Gibbs, Mark & Smith, Richard. *Navigating the Internet*, Sams.net (Macmillan), 1995, ISBN 0-672-30362-0.
My favorite book about the Internet, complete with useful cultural information like the Internet Hunt. Concentrates on how to use the Net, rather than how gosh-darn cool it all is.

Global Schoolhouse/Global SchoolNet Foundation. On-line at
http://www.aldea.com/
Yvonne Marie Andres has been a moving force in bringing CU-SeeMe to the educational community right from the beginning. Interesting uses of CU-SeeMe abound on these pages, as well as captivating input from GSN's Internet Student Ambassadors.

Hoffman, Paul E. *The Internet - Instant Reference* (2nd edition). Sybex.
Very terse coverage of the net and related hardware and software concerns. Really great for corporate MIS types who want a clue about the mutterings of the system and network administrators.

Izen, Joseph M. Connecting NV and VAT to a CU-SeeMe Reflector. On-line at
http://wwwpub.utdallas.edu/~joe/mbone_cuseeme.html
Targeting beginners, this discussion covers the basics of interoperating NV and VAT with CU-SeeMe reflectors.

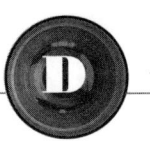

Izen, Joseph M. The Beijing Lepton Photon Conference. On-line at
`http://wwwpub.utdallas.edu/~joe/lp/`
Coverage of the Lepton Photon Conference that took place in Beijing.

JABRA Corporation. The EarPhone - hands-free, full-duplex communications hardware. Online at
`http://www.cts.com/browse/jabra/index.html`
An alternative to having everyone around you hearing the CU-SeeMe conference (and a way of preventing feedback between speakers and the built-in microphones).

Jet Propulsion Laboratory. Viewing an Eclipse via CU-SeeMe. Online at
`http://158.36.49.12/webdoc/eclipse/eclipse.html`
This web page shows screen-shots from a CU-SeeMe conference between scientists at the Jet Propulsion Laboratory and students. The images were taken from the GOES 8 weather satellite. Thumbnails are shown; 1200-by-600-pixel JPEG images are available as well.

Kac, Eduardo. CU-SeeMe and the arts. A short biography available on-line at
`ftp://service1.uky.edu/pub/artsource/kac/edubio.html`

> Eduardo Kac, an Assistant Professor of New Media at the University of Kentucky Department of Art, has long been a user of computer audio and video in his work. He publishes a NetPhone telephone number for reaching him at his studio, uses CU-SeeMe to discuss and share the arts with school children worldwide, and has created much computer-based art.
>
> Accident - Language is born and dies in this looped digital video. 1994. Online at
> `ftp://service1.uky.edu/pub/artsource/experimental.html`
>
> Aspects of the Aesthetics of Telecommunications (partial). Originally published in Siggraph Visual Proceedings '92, John Grimes and Gray Lorig, editors, ACM, New York, 1992, pp. 47-57. Online at
> `http://www.artcom.de:80/Videoweb/transconference/people/kac/kac.html`
>
> Brazilian technological art. (In progress). Online at
> `http://www-mitpress.mit.edu/Leonardo/home.html`
> (Directions: click on Members Forum, then choose Special Projects.)
>
> Dialogues, October 1994. On-line at
> `http://www-mitpress.mit.edu/LEA/bkissues/lea2-12.txt`

Bibliography

> Insect.Desperto - Verbal fireflies vanish between Portuguese and English. 1995. Online at
> `http://www.uky.edu/Artsource/whatsnew.html`
>
> Ornitorrinco in Eden, "realized on the Internet on" October 23, 1994. Online at
> `http://www.uky.edu/Artsource/kac/kac.html`
>
> Participation in Interface 3 Symposium, Hamburg, Germany. 1995. Online at
> `http://www.hfbk.uni-hamburg.de/interface3/participants/kac/kac.html`
>
> Storms - A hypertext piece based on the sefirotic tree of the Kabbalah. 1993. Online at
> `http://www-mitpress.mit.edu/LEA/gallery`

Kise, Halvor. Norwegian-language CU-SeeMe Pages. Online at
`http://www.hiof.no/smm/cusm/`
Halvor, in cooperation with B₀rre Ludvigson (cf), have championed the use of CU-SeeMe in Scandinavia.

Lauer, John. CU-SeeMe and the World Wide Web. Online at
`http://www.umich.edu/~johnlaue/cuseeme/`
John Lauer's goal is to integrate CU-SeeMe and the World Wide Web. To this end, he's created a CU-SeeMe phone book ("look up your friends and then call them on your CU-SeeMe videophone"), an events directory, and a reflector directory web page that controls CU-SeeMe for Windows.

Ludvigson, Børre and Eva. A Digital House-on-the-Net. On-line at
`http://www.ludvigsen.hiof.no/default.html`
Børre, a true renaissance man, student of the Middle East and digital carpenter, has wired his house with video cameras and remote-control motors. From these web pages one can see truly pioneering CU-SeeMe work, a humanizing force to high technology. There are many resources available here, both in English and Norwegian.

> Børre also has been developing things for Norwegian Broadcasting, including Radionettet, a Norwegian radio program for digital information culture. Børre says, "It is the first radio program I know of that is simultaneously being broacast on the air and on the net with accompanying content pages on the web (on-line at `http://nrk.hiof.no`). All the background stuff is in the pages. The broadcasts

 Appendixes

> are also digitized and retrievable from the server the day after transmission."

Meeks, Brock. Cyberwire Dispatch. On-line at
`http://cyberwerks.com/cyberwire`
Brock Meeks' reports highlight the pitfalls and problems in bringing computing to the masses. A must-read for folks who are dealing with the general public.

Molteno, Tim. Various Useful Macintosh Applications.

> Shutterbug is a shareware Macintosh application that takes repeated images from a Connectix QuickCam and writes them into a JPEG format file for broadcast via the World Wide Web. It provides automatic exposure, spot metering, and time-stamping. Online at
> `http://jurgen.physics.utoronto.ca/~tim/Cannibal.html`
>
> QuickPhoto is a replacement for Connectix's QuickPICT application. QuickPhoto saves files in JPEG format, provides automatic exposure and spot metering. Online at
> `http://newton.otago.ac.nz:808/timdocs/timpage.html`
>
> QuickCamTL creates time-lapse video; includes automatic exposure. Tim says it's "wonderful for filming flowers opening, clouds moving, etc." Online at
> `http://newton.otago.ac.nz:808/timdocs/timpage.html`

Pacific Bell. *ISDN: A User's Guide*. Publication number PB 2027-2 11/94, 1994. Online at
`http://www.PacBell.COM/Products/SDS-ISDN/Book/`
Pacific Bell's waiting room booklet that explains the basics of ISDN well, albeit in a rather business-centric way.

Roque, Francisco Luis. QuickCam and CU-SeeMe. Online at
`http://www.engin.umich.edu/~friscolr/QuickCamtm/readme.html`

Salus, Peter. *Casting the Net: From ARPANET to Internet & Beyond*. Addison-Wesley, 1995, ISBN 0-201-87674-4. An invaluable in-depth history of the growth of what we now call the Internet.

Bibliography

SUCCEED Campus Learning Effort. Investigations in Distance Learning. On-line at
http://fiddle.ee.vt.edu/succeed/videoconf.html
This web page presents investigations in distance learning, research collaboration, counselling/mentoring, and information dissemination.

Thomson, Liz. CU-SeeMe Images at Plymouth University (UK). Online at
http://tin.ssc.plym.ac.uk/pickies.html

> Liz has collected many screen-shots of CU-SeeMe sessions. These include the Electronic Cafe Interactive Forum at New Media Expo, the NHK HDTV Launch on Japanese TV with Arthur C. Clarke, an HDTV (High Definition TV) Plymouth-to-Tokyo conference, "Earth, Humans, and the Future," broadcast from Japan to Sri Lanka, the first BBC broadcast on the internet via CU-SeeMe, the CU-SeeMe House of Blues conference, the UK-LA demo (sans HRH Prince Charles), and much more.

Watson, David. CU-SeeMe in Australia. Online at
http://www.une.edu.au/~dwatson/
David and his wife are best described as travelling technologists based at the University of New England School of Health in Armidale, Australia. When they're not sharing experiences and educating others around the world, they're providing the native Aboriginal culture with another way of speaking their audience-based language across the Australian outback.

White Pine Software, Inc. On-line at
http://www.wpine.com/cuseeme.html
White Pine Software, purchasee of the exclusive CU-SeeMe commercial license, provides CU-SeeMe reflector software for a wide variety of platforms as well as commercial versions of CU-SeeMe.

INDEX

Symbols

4-bit video, 95
6th Joint European Networking Conference (JENC6), 184-185

A

A/UX (Apple UNIX), 129
AD Trace window, 114
Add/Remove Programs control panel, 89
addresses
    Internet connections
        computers, 42-43
        DNS (Domain Name System), 45-46
        networks, 43-45
    IP, 274
        nicknames, 100-101
addressing
    manual, 98-100, 275
    server-based, 276
Adelaide (Australia) reflector, 262
ADMIT reflector directive, 137
ADMIT-BCC-CLIENT reflector directive, 140
ADMIT-GENERAL-BCC reflector directive, 141
ADMIT-SENDER reflector directive, 143
Advanced Research Projects Agency Network (ARPANET), 30-33, 271
Aladdin's StuffIt Expander freeware, 94
ALLOW reflector directive, 137
analog, 271
    cameras (general-purpose), 57, 59-61
Andres, Yvonne Marie, 163
Antarctica, MacMurdo Station, 24
Apple TV Tuner card, 242
Arafat, Yasir, 22-23
archives, searchable, 121
Arizona State University reflector, 180
    Geology Department reflector, 251-252
ARPA (Advanced Research Projects Agency), 271
ARPANET (Advanced Research Projects Agency Network), 30-33, 271
Asynchronous Transfer Mode (ATM Cell Relay), 56-57
Atlanta (Georgia) reflector, 252

audio, 271
    future of technology, 231
    hardware, 62-64
    transmissions
        quality, 6-7
        stopping, 111
        troubleshooting, 239-240
            Macintosh, 242
Audio button (other users' windows), 102
Audio options, 107
Audio window, 103-104
audio-only reflector configuration, 127
Australia
    Adelaide reflector, 262
    Geko reflector, 262
    marsupials, 24
    Murdoch University reflector, 262
    Psy reflector, 262
    RMIT reflector, 263
    University of Melbourne reflector, 263
    University of Queensland reflector, 263
Austria, Salzburg, 25
Auxiliary Data Function Modules, 8, 113-117, 271
Avistar videoconferencing software, 202

B

bandwidth, 228-230, 272
    load reflector directives, 138-139
    troubleshooting, 236
Basic Rate Interface (BRI), 54, 272
baud rate, 272
Bearer channels, 272
Beijing Spectrometer experiment, 200
Being There videoconferencing software, 202-203

Belgium, Vrije Univ AI-Lab reflector, 263
Bell telephone systems
    online information sources, 48
    Pacific Bell ISDN plans, 56-57
BillVision (Dartmouth University), 191
birdcam (NYSERNet), 182
Bitfield Video Communication System (BVCS), 203
BITNET (Because It's Time NETwork), 36-37, 272
bonding, 53
BOOTP (Boot Protocol), 272
Brazil
    PUC-Rio reflector, 263
    University of Sao Paulo reflector, 264
BRI (Basic Rate Interface), 54, 272
broadcast (one-way) connections, 13, 17-26, 272
Buckman School, 196
built-in microphones, 62
Burnhanf, Terry, 166
Burning Man extravaganza, 18-19
buttons
    Flip Image (Local Video window), 105
    Freeze Video (Local Video window), 106
    Options Area toggle (Local Video window), 106-108
    Status Line toggle (Local Video window), 105-106
    windows of other CU-SeeMe users, 102-103
BVCS (Bitfield Video Communication System), 203

C

C-Phone videoconferencing software, 203-204
California Research and Education Network (CalREN), 56
call appearances, 52
Cambot add-on software, 225
Camel Personal Video System, 204
cameras (video), 57-63
Canada
    Dalhousie University reflector, 264
    University of Manitoba reflector, 264
cancer update for physicians via CU-SeeMe, 181
Canter & Siegel law firm (Green Card Debacle of 1994), 40-41
CAP reflector directive, 138
Cape Town, South Africa, 24
Carnegie Mellon University's ARPA Speech reflector, 252
CCITT (Consultive Committee for International Telephone and Telegraph), 42, 272
Chameleon software, 91
Charge-Coupled Device (CCD), 272
Charvoneau, Jill, 165
CIX (Commercial Internet Exchange), 38, 272
Clarke, Arthur C., 186
Classroom Connect reflector, 252
classroom instruction, 172-174
Clear command (Edit menu), 110

clients, 272
  CU-SeeMe reflector directives, 148
  video (UNIX) reflector directives, 145-148
Close Window command (File menu), 109
CNIDR reflector, 252
CNN via CU-SeeMe, 193
Cogger, Dick, 162
Collabarena Internet Festival, 187-188
college classroom instruction, 172-174
colors, Windows CU-SeeMe configuration, 96
commands
  Conference menu, 111-112
    Connect To, 15
    Connect..., 98-100
  Edit menu, 109-111
    Edit Nicknames, 100-101
    Preferences, 14
  File menu, 108-109
  Participants menu, 112
Commercial Internet Exchange (CIX), 38, 272
Communicator III videoconferencing software, 204-205
Communique! videoconferencing software, 205
compression, 272
  video, 237
Compression options, 107
computers, Internet connection addresses, 42-43
concerts, 172, 181-182
CONF-ID reflector directive, 136
CONF-MGR reflector directive, 136

Conference menu commands, 111-112
  Connect To, 15
  Connect..., 98-100
configuration
  CU-SeeMe, 96-98
  CU-SeeMe for Windows, 246-248
  modems, connection information, 66-67
  reflectors
    directives, 134-154
    types, 126-127
  SLIP, 88-89
  TCP/IP, 86-87
  TCP/IP software connection information, 66
    Macintosh, 68-80
  troubleshooting, 90-91
  Windows 3.1, 91-92
Connect 918 videoconferencing software, 206
Connect To command (Conference menu), 15, 111
Connect... command (Conference menu), 98-100, 111
connections, 13
  addresses
    computers, 42-43
    DNS (Domain Name System), 45-46
    networks, 43-45
  CU-SeeMe, 98-101
  Dial-Up Networking, creating, 87-88
  hardware, 49-57
  modems, information, 66-67
  one-to-many (reflector), 16-17
  one-way (broadcast), 17-26

  point-to-point, 14-15
  reflectors, 130-132
  TCP/IP software information, 66
    InterCon's InterSLIP, 80-81
    Merit's MacPPP, 85
Connectix's QuickCam videocamera, 58-59
Control Panel
  Add/Remove Programs, 89
  Monitors, 95
  Network, 86-87
  TCP/IP, 69-70
  Windows Setup, 95-96
Copy command (Edit menu), 110
Cornell University, 272
  CU-SeeMe Announcement List, 118
  CU-SeeMe Discussion List, 118
  reflector, 253
Cornerstone, 182
cost
  ISDN (Integrated Services Digital Network), 50-51
  modems, 49
  networks, 230-231
costware, 273
Cream City reflector, 253
CRL, 235
CU-SeeMe
  advantages, 8-10
  components, 4-8
  configuration, 96-98
  connections, 98-101
  history, 161-170
  installation, 93-96
  obtaining, 10-12
  online information sources, 117-121
  troubleshooting, 235-238
    Macintosh, 240-246
    Windows, 246-249

user reactions, 170-200
windows from other users, 102-104
CU-SeeMe Event Guide WWW page, 120
CU-SeeMe Events mailing list, 118-119
CU-SeeMe Reflector Operator's mailing list, 119
cultural changes, future developments in videoconferencing, 231-232
Curry, Adam, 19, 170, 177
Cut command (Edit menu), 110
CyberStudios reflector, 253

D

Dalhousie University (Canada) reflector, 264
Data channel, 273
Daughters at Work Day, 179
DEBUG reflector directive, 135
decoding, 273
decompression, 273
DECspin videoconferencing software, 206
dedicated digital cameras, 57-59
DEFAULT-INIT-RECV reflector directive, 151
DEFAULT-MAX-RECV reflector directive, 150-151
DEFAULT-MIN-RECV reflector directive, 150
DENY reflector directive, 137
DHCP (Dynamic Host Configuration Protocol), 273

dial-up connections, 49-57
Dial-Up Networking connections, creating, 87-88
dialog boxes
    Connect, 98-100
    Preferences, 96-98
digital, 273
    cameras (dedicated), 57-59
    switching systems, 273
Digital Jungle reflector, 253
digitizers, 273
direct connections, 49
DirectPC, 171
Disconnect command (Conference menu), 111
DNS (Domain Name System), 45-46, 273
domains, 273
Dorcey, Tim, 163
drop-in modules, 113-117
Duffy, Larry, 165
Dynamic Host Configuration Protocol (DHCP), 273

E

EarPhone Streamline (Jabra), 62
Earth Day 1995, 23-25, 196-199
Eccosys (Japan) reflector, 266
Eden reflector, 254
Edit menu commands, 109-111
    Edit Nicknames, 100-101
    Preferences, 14
Edit Nicknames command (Edit menu), 100-101, 110
Education First program (Pacific Bell), 56
Educational Computing Network reflector, 254
encoding, 273

Eris Personal Video Communications System, 206-207
error correction, 273
ethernet, 273
Eurocube (Italy) reflector, 265-266
event publicity, 158-159
external microphone, 62

F

Face 2 Face videoconferencing software, 207
FAQs (Frequently Asked Questions), 121, 273
feed reflector directives, 140-143
File menu commands, 108-109
files (log), reflectors, 153-154
Finland, University of Vaasa reflector, 264
firewalls, 249
Flip Image button (Local Video window), 105
flow control reflector directives, 149-151
Foeredrag i Lund/Fast (Sweden) reflector, 268
Foeredrag i Lund/Slow (Sweden) reflector, 268
Foo, Albert, 59-60
foreign language instruction, 183
Fortune, Daniel, 190
Frame Relay, 56
France, Telecomm Grande Ecole reflector, 264
FreeBSD, 128
freeware, 273
Freeze Video button (Local Video window), 106
FTP (File Transfer Protocol), 273

full-duplex, 274
    sound cards, 63-64
future developments of videoconferencing
    cultural changes, 231-232
    technology, 228-231
Future Pirates (Japan) reflector, 266

G

gateways, 274
Gay Pride Parade in New York City, 23
Geko (Australia) reflector, 262
general-purpose analog cameras, 57, 59-61
Geneva University (Switzerland) reflector, 269
Georgia, Atlanta reflector, 252
German, Greg, 165
Giles, Aaron, 113
Go CU-SeeMe Go Auto Web Launcher, 120
Goldin, Dan, 180
Goodall, Jane, 168
grayscale, 274
Green Card Debacle of 1994, 40-41
GSH (Global SchoolHouse), history of CU-SeeMe, 164-168
GSN (Global SchoolNet), 25-26, 163, 274
GTE-Albion reflector, 254
GTE-Skyhawk reflector, 254

H

half-duplex, 274
    sound cards, 63-64
Hallam (UK) reflector, 270
handshaking (hardware), 274
hardware
    audio, 62-64
    connectivity, 49-57
    online information sources, 47-48
    video, 57-61
Hartman, Ken, 168
Hawaii, University of Hawaii reflector, 260
HDTV (High-Definition TeleVision) standard, 6, 274
history
    CU-SeeMe, 161-170
    Internet, 29-37
    networking, 30
Holland, *see* The Netherlands
hostnames, 274

I

IAB (Internet Architecture Board), 274
IBM, 37
ICU Video Services videoconferencing software, 207
IETF (Internet Engineering Task Force), 39, 274
IITAP (International Institute of Theoretical and Applied Physics), 254
IITAP reflector, 254-255
Indiana State University reflector, 255
Infinity System's InterSLIP Strip Module, 80
InPerson videoconferencing software, 208
INRIA Videoconferencing System (IVS), 210
installation
    CU-SeeMe, 93-96
    InterSLIP (InterCon), 73-74
    MacPPP (Merit), 74
    MacTCP, 73
    Open Transport for Macintosh, 68-73
    SLIP, 88-89
    TCP/IP, 85-86
Integrated Services Digital Network (ISDN), 47-57, 274
Intelecom Data Systems reflector, 255
Interact videoconferencing software, 208-209
Internet, 28-29
    CIX (Commercial Internet Exchange), 38
    connections
        computer addresses, 42-43
        DNS (Domain Name System), 45-46
        network addresses, 43-45
    future, 38
    history, 29-37
    NREN (National Research and Education Network), 37-38
    NSFNET management companies, 37
    videoconferencing, 1-4
internet, 274
Internet Architecture Board (IAB), 274
Internet Engineering Task Force (IETF), 39, 274
Internet Research Task Force (IRTF), 274
InterneTV, 22
internetworks, 28
InterSLIP (InterCon)
    configuring, 77-80
    connections, 80-81
    installing, 73-74

INTERVu videoconferencing software, 209
inverse multiplexing, 53, 274
InVision videoconferencing software, 209
IP (Internet Protocol), 274
IP addresses, 274
    nicknames, 100-101
Ireland, University of Ulster reflector, 265
IRTF (Internet Research Task Force), 274
ISDN (Integrated Services Digital Network), 47-57, 274
ISOC (Internet Society), 274
Israel, Weizmann Institute reflector, 265
Italy
    Eurocube reflector, 265-266
    Lignano Sabbiadoro, 176
    University of Calabria reflector, 266
    University of Pisa reflector, 266
IVS (INRIA Videoconferencing System), 210

J

Jabra's EarPhone Streamline, 62
Japan
    Eccosys reflector, 266
    Future Pirates reflector, 266
    Japan-Stanford videobridge, 192-193
    NHK television, 185-187
    Okazaki NRI reflector, 267
    University of Tokyo reflector, 267

JENC6 (6th Joint European Networking Conference), 184-185
Jocya, Jocelyn, 170
Johnson Space Center reflector, 257

K

Kansas, University of Kansas reflector, 260
Kapor, Mitch, 25
KB (kilobyte), 275
Kent State University, 23
Kent State University reflector, 255
KJHK Radio reflector, 255
Kline, Charley, 7, 165
Knauer, Josh, 168
Knight, Peter, 166
Koop, C. Everett, 25
KVR-InterneTV reflector, 256

L

LANs (Local Area Networks), 28, 275
LappDoggware reflector, 256
laUNChpad EBBS reflector, 256
Lewis Research Center reflector, 257-258
Lignano Sabbiadoro, Italy, 176
linking reflectors, 154-159
Linux, 128
live concerts, 172
Local Video window, 105-108
log files, reflectors, 153-154
LOG reflector directive, 139
LOG-LIMIT reflector directive, 139

LTM-1 (model lunar rover), 177-178
Ludvigsen, Eva and Børre, 19

M

MachTen (Tenon), 129-130
Macintosh
    CU-SeeMe
        installation, 94-95
        nicknames for IP addresses, 101
        troubleshooting, 240-246
    reflectors, 129-130
    TCP/IP software, 68-80
Macintosh Monitors control panel, 95
MacMurdo Station, Antarctica, 24
MacPPP (Merit)
    configuring, 81-84
    connections, 85
    installing, 74
MacTCP, 68
    configuring, 74-76
    installing, 73
mailing lists
    CU-SeeMe online information sources, 118-119
    promoting events, 158-159
Maine, University of reflector, 261
manual addressing, 98-100, 275
many-to-many reflector configuration, 126
Mars journey simulation, 177
Marshall Space Flight Center reflector, 258
marsupials, 24

Maryland, University of Maryland reflector, 261
masks, 44-45
Maven program, 7, 275
MAX-LURKERS reflector directive, 139
MAX-MAX-RECV reflector directive, 150
MAX-MAX-SEND reflector directive, 149
MAX-MIN-RECV reflector directive, 149-150
MAX-MIN-SEND reflector directive, 149
MAX-PARTICIPANTS reflector directive, 138
MAX-SENDERS reflector directive, 139
maximum transmit unit/ maximum receive unit (MTU/MRU), 275
MB (megabytes), 275
MBone (Multicast Backbone) reflector configuration, 127, 156-157, 275
MC-GROUP reflector directive, 144-145
MC-IN reflector directive, 142
MC-OUT reflector directive, 142
MCI Telecommunications, 37
Mediafone/Fonewatch videoconferencing software, 210
Meeks, Brock, 181
Meet-Me videoconferencing software, 211
Merit Networks, 37
   MacPPP
      configuring, 81-84
      connections, 85
      installing, 74
Message of the Day (MOTD), 275

Miami University (Ohio) reflector, 256
Microphone button (other users' windows), 102
microphones, 62-63
MIN-MAC-VERSION reflector directive, 148
MIN-PC-VERSION reflector directive, 148
MINX videoconferencing software, 211
Mitchell, Don, 163
model lunar rover, 177-178
modems, 49
   connection information, 66-67
   Dial-Up Networking connections, creating, 87-88
   online information sources, 48
Monitors control panel, 95
Monkmobile, 18-19
Morgridge, John, 169
MOTD (Message of the Day), 275
MOTD reflector directive, 134-135
MTU/MRU (maximum transmit unit/maximum receive unit), 275
Multicast Backbone (MBone) reflector configuration, 127, 156-157, 275
multicast-to-unicast reflector configuration, 127
multiplexing, inverse, 274
Murdoch University (Australia) reflector, 262
Mystery Science Theater 3000, 20-21

N

names, hostnames, 274
nameservers, 275

NASA (National Aeronautics and Space Administration), 275
   Johnson Space Center reflector, 257
   Lewis Research Center reflector, 257-258
   Marshall Space Flight Center reflector, 258
NASA Select TV, 17-18, 275
   at CMU GSIA reflector, 256-257
   at IITAP reflector, 257
   at Kent State reflector, 257
   at Lund University (Sweden) reflector, 269
National Research and Education Network (NREN), 37-38, 275
National Science Foundation (NSF), 163-164, 275
National Science Foundation Network (NSFNET), 34, 37
National Television System Committee (NTSC), 275
The Netherlands
   Nijmegen University reflector, 265
   Rotterdam Management reflector, 265
Network control panel, 86-87
Network News Transfer Protocol (NNTP), 275
Network Solutions reflector, 258
Network Termination Device (NT1), 275
networking, 27, 30
networks
   ARPANET (Advanced Research Projects Agency Network), 30-33

networks

bandwidth, 228-230
BITNET (Because It's Time NETwork), 36-37
costs, 230-231
firewalls, 249
Internet connection addresses, 43-45
internetworks, 28
LANs (Local Area Networks), 28
NSFNET (National Science Foundation Network), 34
USENET (User's Network), 34-36
WANs (Wide Area Networks), 28
New York City, Gay Pride Parade, 23
newsgroups, 35-36
NHK (national broadcasting corporation of Japan), 185-187
nicknames for IP addresses, 100-101
Nijmegen University (Holland) reflector, 265
NNTP (Network News Transfer Protocol), 275
NO-LOCAL-SENDERS reflector directive, 143
North Carolina State University reflector, 258
Norway
    Ostfold/Fenris reflector, 267
    Ostfold/Kark reflector, 267
    University of Trondheim reflector, 267-268
NREN (National Research and Education Network), 37-38, 275
NSF (National Science Foundation), 163-164, 275

NSFNET (National Science Foundation Network), 34, 37
NT1 (Network Termination Device), 275
NTSC (National Television System Committee), 5, 275
Ntv videoconferencing software, 212
nv (Network Video) videoconferencing software, 212
NV-MC-IN reflector directive, 146
NV-MC-OUT reflector directive, 146
NV-MC-PORT reflector directive, 146
NV-STREAMS reflector directive, 146-147
NV-UC-PORT reflector directive, 145
NYSERNet birdcam, 182
NYSERNet reflector, 258

O

OBTAIN-BCC reflector directive, 140
OBTAIN-GENERAL-BCC reflector directive, 141
Ohio
    Kent State University, 23
    Kent State University reflector, 255
    Miami University reflector, 256
    Ohio State University reflector, 259
Okazaki NRI (Japan) reflector, 267
Oklahoma City bombing (live news feed), 194
OLD-RATE-ADAPT reflector directive, 151

one-to-many (reflector) connections, 13, 16-17, 126-127
one-way (broadcast) connections, 13, 17-26
Open Slide Window command (Conference menu), 112
Open Transport for Macintosh, 68-73
Open University Computing Department (UK) reflector, 269
operating systems, reflector requirements, 128-130
Options Area toggle button (Local Video window), 106-108
Ostfold/Fenris (Norway) reflector, 267
Ostfold/Kark (Norway) reflector, 267

P

Pacific Bell's ISDN plans, 56-57
Pacific Rim reflector, 259
packet-switched call set-up and signalling connections, 53-54
PAL (Phase Alternation by Line), 5, 275
PAP (Password Authentication Protocol), 83-84
Paradise Software Video Conferencing (PSVC), 217
Participants menu commands, 112
Party Girl, 187
Paste command (Edit menu), 110
Pennsylvania
    Penn State reflector, 259
    University of Pennsylvania reflector, 261

People Pages (WWW), 120
Person to Person videoconferencing software, 213
Personal Viewpoint videoconferencing software, 213
Ph.D. defense via CU-SeeMe, 175
Phase Alternation by Line (PAL), 5, 275
PICFON videoconferencing software, 214
Picture options, 106
PictureTel Live PCS 100 videoconferencing software, 214
PictureTel Live PCS 50 videoconferencing software, 214-215
PictureTel LiveLAN videoconferencing software, 215
PictureWindow videoconferencing software, 215-216
PKZIP freeware, 95
PlainTalk microphone, 62
Plan 10 from Outer Space, 19-20
plug-in modules, 113-117
Plymouth University (UK) reflector, 269-270
point-to-point connections, 13-15
Point-to-Point Protocol (PPP), 276
Polly, Jean Armour, 161
Portugal, University Lisbon reflector, 268
postings, 35
PPP (Point-to-Point Protocol), 276
Preferences command (Edit menu), 14, 110-111
Preferences dialog box, 96-98
PRI (Primary Rate Interface), 54, 276
Prince Charles, 169
Project BillVision (Dartmouth University), 191
promoting events, 158-159
ProShare Video System 150 videoconferencing software, 216
ProShare Video System 200 videoconferencing software, 216-217
protocols
    BOOTP (Boot Protocol), 272
    DHCP (Dynamic Host Configuration Protocol), 273
    FTP (File Transfer Protocol), 273
    IP (Internet Protocol), 274
    NNTP (Network News Transfer Protocol), 275
    PAP (Password Authentication Protocol), 83-84
    PPP (Point-to-Point Protocol), 276
    SLIP (Serial Line Internet Protocol), 88-89, 276
    SMTP (Simple Mail Transport Protocol), 276
    TCP/IP (Transmission Control Protocol/Internet Protocol), 29
PSVC (Paradise Software Video Conferencing), 217
Psy (Australia) reflector, 262
PUC-Rio (Brazil) reflector, 263

Q-R

QuickCam videocamera (Connectix), 58-59, 242-246
Quit command (File menu), 109
Rabin, Ytizhak, 22-23
Radio HK reflector, 259
RATE-ADAPT reflector directive, 151
reflector (one-to-many) connections, 13, 16-17, 126-127
reflectors, 276
    Adelaide (Australia), 262
    Arizona State University, 180
        Geology Department, 251-252
    Atlanta (Georgia), 252
    Classroom Connect, 252
    CMU ARPA Speech, 252
    CNIDR, 252
    configurations
        directives, 134-154
        types, 126-127
    connections, 130-132
    Cornell University, 253
    Cream City, 253
    CyberStudios, 253
    Dalhousie University (Canada), 264
    Digital Jungle, 253
    Eccosys (Japan), 266
    Eden, 254
    Educational Computing Network, 254
    Eurocube (Italy), 265-266
    Foeredrag i Lund/Fast (Sweden), 268
    Foeredrag i Lund/Slow (Sweden), 268
    Future Pirates (Japan), 266

reflectors

Geko (Australia), 262
Geneva University (Switzerland), 269
GTE-Albion, 254
GTE-Skyhawk, 254
Hallam (UK), 270
IITAP, 254-255
Indiana State University, 255
Intelecom Data Systems, 255
Kent State University, 255
KJHK Radio, 255
KVR-InterneTV, 256
LappDoggware, 256
laUNChpad EBBS, 256
linking, 154-159
list of, 120
Miami University (Ohio), 256
Murdoch University (Australia), 262
NASA Johnson Space Center, 257
NASA Lewis Research Center, 257-258
NASA Marshall Space Flight Center, 258
NASA TV at CMU GSIA, 256-257
NASA TV at IITAP, 257
NASA TV at Kent State, 257
NASA TV at Lund University (Sweden), 269
Network Solutions, 258
Nijmegen University (Holland), 265
North Carolina State University, 258
NYSERNet, 258
Ohio State University, 259
Okazaki NRI (Japan), 267

Open University Computing Department (UK), 269
operating system requirements, 128-130
Ostfold/Fenris (Norway), 267
Ostfold/Kark (Norway), 267
Pacific Rim, 259
Penn State, 259
Plymouth University (UK), 269-270
Psy (Australia), 262
PUC-Rio (Brazil), 263
purpose, 125
Radio HK, 259
RMIT (Australia), 263
Rotterdam Management (Holland), 265
running, 133
Seattle Pacific University, 259
software, 132-133
Sprintlink, 260
Stanford University Medical Center, 260
Swiss Telecom R&D (Switzerland), 269
Telecomm Grande Ecole (France), 264
ThePoint, 260
University of Calabria (Italy), 266
University of Hawaii, 260
University of Kansas, 260
University of Lisbon (Portugal), 268
University of Maine, 261
University of Manitoba (Canada), 264
University of Maryland, 261
University of Melbourne (Australia), 263

University of Pennsylvania, 261
University of Pisa (Italy), 266
University of Queensland (Australia), 263
University of Sao Paulo (Brazil), 264
University of Singapore (Singapore), 268
University of Texas, 261
University of Tokyo (Japan), 267
University of Trondheim (Norway), 267-268
University of Ulster (Ireland), 265
University of Vaasa (Finland), 264
UNIX, 125-126
up and running quickly, 124-125
Virginia Commonweath University, 261
Vrije Univ AI-Lab (Belgium), 263
Weizmann Institute (Israel), 265
White Pine Software, 262
Refmon (Reflector Monitor), 152-153
REFMON reflector directive, 138
resolution, 5
resources
    CU-SeeMe online information sources, 117-121
    hardware online information sources, 47-48
    promoting events, 158-159

RMIT (Australia) reflector, 263
Rotterdam Management (Holland) reflector, 265

S

Salzburg, Austria, 25
Sarajevo peace conference, 176
satellite videoconferencing, 170-171
Save Window Positions command (File menu), 108-109
searchable archives, 121
Seattle Pacific University reflector, 259
SECAM (Systeme Electronique Couleur Avec Memoire), 6, 276
security
  networks, 249
  reflector directives, 136-138
Select All command (Edit menu), 110
SELF-REFLECT reflector directive, 135-136
Serial Line Internet Protocol (SLIP), 276
server-based addressing, 276
Setup control panel, 95-96
sexually explicit digital images, 232
ShareVision Mac 3000 videoconferencing software, 217-218
ShareVision PC videoconferencing software, 218
shareware, 276
ShowMe videoconferencing software, 218-219
ShutterBug add-on software, 226

Simple Mail Transport Protocol (SMTP), 276
simulated space shuttle mission, 179-180
simulcast interviewing, 190
Singapore
  Singapore National Day Parade, 178
  University of Singapore reflector, 268
Slide Window (Auxiliary Data Function Module), 115-117
SLIP (Serial Line Internet Protocol), 88-89, 276
SMDS (Switched Multi-megabit Data Service), 56
SMTP (Simple Mail Transport Protocol), 276
sneakernet, 30, 276
societal problems, Internet future, 40-41
software
  Aladdin's StuffIt Expander freeware, 94
  Avistar, 202
  Being There, 202-203
  Bitfield Video Communication System (BVCS), 203
  C-Phone, 203-204
  Cambot, 225
  Cameo Personal Video System, 204
  Communicator III, 204-205
  Communique!, 205
  Connect 918, 206
  costware, 273
  DECspin, 206
  Eris Personal Video Communications System, 206-207
  Face 2 Face, 207
  freeware, 273
  ICU Video Services, 207
  InPerson, 208

INRIA Videoconferencing System (IVS), 210
Interact, 208-209
INTERVu, 209
InVision, 209
Mediafone/Fonewatch, 210
Meet-Me, 211
MINX, 211
Ntv, 212
nv (Network Video), 212
Paradise Software Video Conferencing (PSVC), 217
Person to Person, 213
Personal Viewpoint, 213
PICFON, 214
PictureTel Live PCS 100, 214
PictureTel Live PCS 50, 214-215
PictureTel LiveLAN, 215
PictureWindow, 215-216
PKZIP freeware, 95
ProShare Video System 150, 216
ProShare Video System 200, 216-217
reflectors, 132-133
Refmon (Reflector Monitor), 152-153
ShareVision Mac 3000, 217-218
ShareVision PC, 218
shareware, 276
ShowMe, 218-219
ShutterBug, 226
TCP/IP
  connection information, 66
  Macintosh, 68-80
TelePro with VisionTime, 219
TeleView 1000C, 220
Trumpet Winsock shareware, 91-92

VC8000, 220
VicPhone, 220-221
VidCall, 221
VideoVu, 221-222
VISIT, 222
Vistium 1200, 223
Vistium 1300, 223
Vivo 320, 224
VS1000, 224
sound, *see* audio
sound cards, 48, 63-64
South Africa, Cape Town, 24
spamming, 40, 276
Springsteen, Bruce, 22
Sprintlink reflector, 260
standards for video signals, 5-6
Stanford University Medical Center reflector, 260
Stanford-Japan videobridge, 192-193
starting Refmon, 152
Status Line toggle button (Local Video window), 105-106
Stone, Carl, 21, 182
Stop Receiving command (Conference menu), 112
Stop Sending command (Conference menu), 111
StuffIt Expander freeware (Aladdin), 94
subnetting, 44
SuperMac VideoSpigot's video digitizer, troubleshooting, 242
surveilance systems (uses of CU-SeeMe), 194-195
Sweden
    Foeredrag i Lund/Fast reflector, 268
    Foeredrag i Lund/Slow reflector, 268
Switzerland
    Geneva University reflector, 269

Swiss Telecom R&D reflector, 269
Switched Multimegabit Data Service (SMDS), 56
synchronization reflector directives, 143-145
Systeme Electronique Couleur Avec Memoire (SECAM), 6, 276

T

Talk (Auxiliary Data Function Module), 114-115
TCP/IP (Transmission Control Protocol/Internet Protocol), 29
    configuration, 86-87
    Dial-Up Networking connections, creating, 87-88
    installation, 85-86
    software
        connection information, 66
        Macintosh, 68-80
TCP/IP control panel, 69-70
technology
    future developments in videoconferencing, 228-231
    problems, Internet future, 39-40
Telecomm Grande Ecole (France) reflector, 264
telephones, Regional Bells online information sources, 48
Pacific Bell ISDN plans, 56-57
TelePro with VisionTime videoconferencing software, 219

TeleView 1000C videoconferencing software, 220
television
    HDTV (High-Definition TeleVision), 274
    NHK (national broadcasting corporation of Japan), 185-187
Tenon MachTen, 129-130
Texas, University of Texas reflector, 261
Text in the Video Window command (Conference menu), 112
ThePoint reflector, 260
third-party microphones, 62
Timed Video Grabber (TVG), 184
Toad the Wet Sprocket, 22
Trace (Auxiliary Data Function Module), 113-114
traffic, 276
Transmission options, 106-107
Transmission Statistics button (other users' windows), 102-103
troubleshooting
    audio, 239-240, 242
    configuration, 90-91
    CU-SeeMe, 235-238
        installation, 93-94
        Macintosh, 240-246
        Windows, 246-249
    QuickCam, 243-246
    video, 238-239
        Macintosh, 240-241
        Windows, 248-249
Trumpet Winsock shareware utility, 91-92
TV Tuner card, 242
TVG (Timed Video Grabber), 184
twisted-pair cable, 276

U

Undo command (Edit menu), 109
UNICAST-REF reflector directive, 143-144
unicast-to-multicast reflector configuration, 127
unicasting, 154-156
United Kingdom (UK)
    Hallam reflector, 270
    Open University Computing Department reflector, 269
    Plymouth University reflector, 269-270
    Prince Charles, 169
University Lisbon (Portugal) reflector, 268
University of Calabria (Italy) reflector, 266
University of Hawaii reflector, 260
University of Kansas reflector, 260
University of Maine reflector, 261
University of Manitoba (Canada) reflector, 264
University of Maryland reflector, 261
University of Melbourne (Australia) reflector, 263
University of Pennsylvania reflector, 261
University of Pisa (Italy) reflector, 266
University of Queensland (Australia) reflector, 263
University of Sao Paulo (Brazil) reflector, 264
University of Singapore (Singapore) reflector, 268
University of Song, 170
University of Texas reflector, 261
University of Tokyo (Japan) reflector, 267
University of Trondheim (Norway) reflector, 267-268
University of Ulster (Ireland) reflector, 265
University of Vaasa (Finland) reflector, 264
UNIX, 276
    reflectors, 125-126
    video client reflector directives, 145-148
URLs (Uniform Resource Locators), 277
USENET (User's Network), 34-36, 277
users
    reactions to CU-SeeMe, 170-200
    windows from other users, 102-104

V

VAT-CONF-ID reflector directive, 148
VAT-MC-IN reflector directive, 147
VAT-MC-OUT reflector directive, 147-148
VAT-MC-PORT reflector directive, 147
VAT-UC-PORT reflector directive, 147
VC8000 videoconferencing software, 220
Version/IP button (other users' windows), 103
VicPhone videoconferencing software, 220-221
VidCall videoconferencing software, 221
video
    4-bit, 95
    capture boards, 59-61
    clients (UNIX), reflector directives, 145-148
    compression, 237
    future of technology, 231
    hardware, 57-61
    online information sources, 48
    signal standards, 5-6
    stopping receiving, 112
    stopping transmissions, 111
    troubleshooting, 238-239
        Macintosh, 240-241
        Windows, 248-249
Video options, 107-108
Video State button (other users' windows), 102
videoconferencing, 1-4
    college classroom instruction, 172-174
    future developments
        cultural changes, 231-232
        technology, 228-231
    via satellite, 170-171
videoconferencing software
    Avistar, 202
    Being There, 202-203
    Bitfield Video Communication System (BVCS), 203
    C-Phone, 203-204
    Cameo Personal Video System, 204
    Communicator III, 204-205
    Communique!, 205
    Connect 918, 206
    DECspin, 206
    Eris Personal Video Communications System, 206-207
    Face 2 Face, 207
    ICU Video Services, 207
    InPerson, 208

videoconferencing shareware

INRIA Videoconferencing System (IVS), 210
Interact, 208-209
INTERVu, 209
InVision, 209
Mediafone/Fonewatch, 210
Meet-Me, 211
MINX, 211
Ntv, 212
nv (Network Video), 212
Paradise Software Video Conferencing (PSVC), 217
Person to Person, 213
Personal Viewpoint, 213
PICFON, 214
PictureTel Live PCS 100, 214
PictureTel Live PCS 50, 214-215
PictureTel LiveLAN, 215
PictureWindow, 215-216
ProShare Video System 150, 216
ProShare Video System 200, 216-217
ShareVision Mac 3000, 217-218
ShareVision PC, 218
ShowMe, 218-219
TelePro with VisionTime, 219
TeleView 1000C, 220
VC8000, 220
VicPhone, 220-221
VidCall, 221
VideoVu, 221-222
VISIT, 222
Vistium 1200, 223
Vistium 1300, 223
Vivo 320, 224
VS1000, 224
VideoSpigot, troubleshooting, 242

VideoVu videoconferencing software, 221-222
Virginia Commonwealth University reflector, 261
Virtual Human Body, 188-189
VISIT videoconferencing software, 222
Vistium 1200 videoconferencing software, 223
Vistium 1300 videoconferencing software, 223
Vivo 320 videoconferencing software, 224
Voices for Diversity, 187-188
Vrije Univ AI-Lab (Belgium) reflector, 263
VS1000 videoconferencing software, 224

W

WANs (Wide Area Networks), 28, 277
"Web Belly: The Art of Belly Dancing on the Web", 176
Weizmann Institute (Israel) reflector, 265
White Pine Software, 120
White Pine Software reflector, 262
Windows
    audio support, 63-64
    CU-SeeMe
        installation, 95-96
        nicknames for IP addresses, 101
        troubleshooting, 246-249
    version 3.1, configuration for Internet, 91-92
windows
    AD Trace, 114
    Audio, 103-104

closing, 109
Connection, 15
CU-SeeMe, from other users, 102-104
Local Video, 105-108
Preferences, 14
saving positions, 108-109
Slide, 115-117
Talk, 114-115
Windows NT reflectors, 129
Windows Setup control panel, 95-96
Woods, Jacqueline F., 195
World Party Tour, 189
World Wide Web
    CU-SeeMe online information sources, 120-121

X-Z

Xiao-Fen, Min, 21
Yoshide, Otomo, 21, 182
Yugoslavia, Sarajevo peace conference, 176

GET CONNECTED
to the ultimate source of computer information!

The MCP Forum on CompuServe

Go online with the world's leading computer book publisher! Macmillan Computer Publishing offers everything you need for computer success!

Find the books that are right for you!
A complete online catalog, plus sample chapters and tables of contents give you an in-depth look at all our books. The best way to shop or browse!

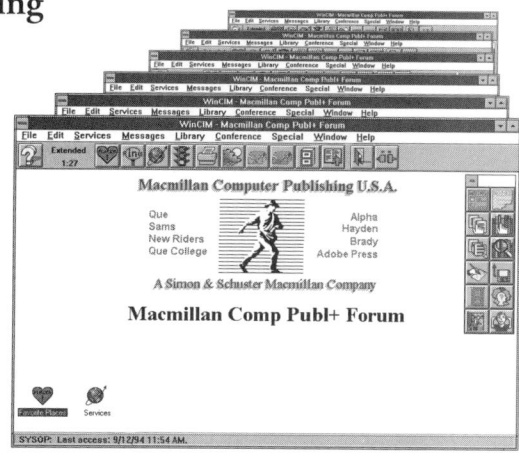

- ➤ Get fast answers and technical support for MCP books and software
- ➤ Join discussion groups on major computer subjects
- ➤ Interact with our expert authors via e-mail and conferences
- ➤ Download software from our immense library:
  - ▷ Source code from books
  - ▷ Demos of hot software
  - ▷ The best shareware and freeware
  - ▷ Graphics files

Join now and get a free CompuServe Starter Kit!

To receive your free CompuServe Introductory Membership, call **1-800-848-8199** and ask for representative #597.

The Starter Kit includes:
- ➤ Personal ID number and password
- ➤ $15 credit on the system
- ➤ Subscription to *CompuServe Magazine*

Once on the CompuServe System, type:

GO MACMILLAN

for the most computer information anywhere!

PLUG YOURSELF INTO...

The Macmillan Information SuperLibrary™

Free information and vast computer resources from the world's leading computer book publisher—online!

FIND THE BOOKS THAT ARE RIGHT FOR YOU!

A complete online catalog, plus sample chapters and tables of contents give you an in-depth look at *all* of our books, including hard-to-find titles. It's the best way to find the books you need!

- **STAY INFORMED** with the latest computer industry news through our online newsletter, press releases, and customized Information SuperLibrary Reports.
- **GET FAST ANSWERS** to your questions about MCP books and software.
- **VISIT** our online bookstore for the latest information and editions!
- **COMMUNICATE** with our expert authors through e-mail and conferences.
- **DOWNLOAD SOFTWARE** from the immense MCP library:
    - Source code and files from MCP books
    - The best shareware, freeware, and demos
- **DISCOVER HOT SPOTS** on other parts of the Internet.
- **WIN BOOKS** in ongoing contests and giveaways!

TO PLUG INTO MCP:

GOPHER: gopher.mcp.com
FTP: ftp.mcp.com

WORLD WIDE WEB: http://www.mcp.com

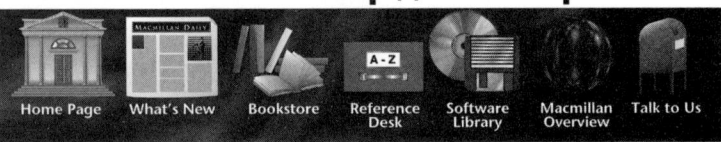

Add to Your Sams.net Library Today
with the Best Books for Internet Technologies

ISBN	Quantity	Description of Item	Unit Cost	Total Cost
0-672-30737-5		The World Wide Web Unleashed, 1996	$49.99	
0-672-30714-6		The Internet Unleashed, 1996	$49.99	
0-672-30667-0		Teach Yourself Web Publishing with HTML in a Week	$25.00	
1-57521-005-3		Teach Yourself More Web Publishing with HTML in a Week	$29.99	
0-672-30764-2		Teach Yourself Web Publishing with Microsoft Word in a Week	$29.99	
1-57521-039-8		Presenting Java	$25.00	
0-672-30735-9		Teach Yourself the Internet in a Week, Second Edition	$25.00	
1-57521-004-5		The Internet Business Guide, Second Edition	$25.00	
0-672-30595-X		Education on the Internet	$25.00	
0-672-30718-9		Navigating the Internet, Third Edition	$25.00	
0-672-30669-7		Plug-n-Play Internet for Windows	$35.00	
1-57521-010-X		Plug-n-Play Netscape for Windows	$29.99	
0-672-30723-5		Secrets of the MUD Wizards	$25.00	
		Shipping and Handling: See information below.		
		TOTAL		

Shipping and Handling: $4.00 for the first book, and $1.75 for each additional book. If you need to have it NOW, we can ship product to you in 24 hours for an additional charge of approximately $18.00, and you will receive your item overnight or in two days. Overseas shipping and handling adds $2.00. Prices subject to change. Call between 9:00 a.m. and 5:00 p.m. EST for availability and pricing information on latest editions.

201 W. 103rd Street, Indianapolis, Indiana 46290

1-800-428-5331 — Orders   1-800-835-3202 — FAX   1-800-858-7674 — Customer Service

Book ISBN 1-57521-006-1